To California
by Sea

William N. Still, Jr., Series Editor

Studies in Maritime History

Classics in Maritime History

To California by Sea

A Maritime History of the California Gold Rush

James P. Delgado

University of South Carolina Press

Copyright © University of South Carolina 1990

Published in Columbia, South Carolina, by the
University of South Carolina Press

Manufactured in the United States of America

Library of Congress Cataloging-in-Publication Data

Delgado, James P.
  To California by sea : a maritime history of the California gold
rush / James P. Delgado.
    p.   cm. — (Studies in maritime history)
  Includes bibliographical references.
  ISBN 0-87249-673-2
  1. Navigation—California—History—19th century.   2. Shipping-
-California—History—19th century.   3. California—Gold
discoveries.   I. Title.   II. Series.
VK24.C2D45   1990
387.5′09794—dc20   89-39117
                                                      CIP

To
Doug Nadeau
and
Ted Hinckley

CONTENTS

ILLUSTRATIONS

PREFACE

I have attempted to relate the story of the transportation of people and goods by water to and from California especially during the gold rush of 1848–1856. Isolated by 14,000 miles of sea routes from the rest of the United States, California depended on ships for the link to people back home as well as to manufactured goods and commodities not yet available on the frontier. And yet because of the regular maritime traffic between coasts, California was never actually a frontier in the true sense of the word. The tremendous buying power of California gold and the daily arrival of dozens of vessels at the Golden Gate meant that the most up-to-date items—and the most fashionable—were available in San Francisco and the inland satellite ports not long after they hit the streets of New York, Boston, London, or Paris.

Popular concepts of the California Gold Rush portray hardy immigrants working their way westward on foot, trudging behind wagons, or crouching waist deep in an icy Sierra stream as they panned for gold. Little consideration has been granted the image of a doughty merchantman battling the gales off Cape Horn—the hold packed full of fortune-seekers—or of a ship, shorn of masts, housed over in the mud of San Francisco harbor and transformed into a warehouse. The general impression depicts a nation's trend westward by the Oregon Trail. It is important, however, to remember that the California Gold Rush was first and foremost a maritime event.

The first rush for gold was by sea from the seafaring New England states. Far more emigrants, particularly Europeans, came by sea than overland. Historian David Lavender, assessing for the National Park Service in 1980 the impact of overland migration, estimated that 23,000 people came across the continent to California in 1849 and that approximately 45,000 poured across the Sierras the following year. Working from available government records, James Parker, who compiled statistics for San Francisco's 1852 City Directory, found that between April 1849 and April 1850 approximately 62,000 persons had arrived at San Francisco on a variety of vessels. Of these 39,888 had arrived in the first eight months! The number of gold-seeking passengers arriving in ships was bolstered by the Panama Route, crossed in 1848–1851 by at least 36,097 people on their way to San Francisco. The importance of Panama is perhaps best reflected in the thousands who made their way home via the Isthmus; as J. S. Holliday noted, few people who came via the Horn or overland returned the same way—they went home on Panama or Nicaragua steamers.

The true significance of the maritime aspects of the Gold Rush is not to be found in arrivals and departures of passengers but in the vessels that carried them. Without ships, goods to keep the mines going would not have arrived. San Francisco was the heart, the rivers were the arteries, and the small schooners, scows, and steamers on those rivers were the lifeblood of the Gold Rush. Not only San Francisco but Stockton, Sacramento, and Marysville became prominent ports. In addition, the first manifestation of federal power in California was maritime—the United States Navy and the United States Revenue Marine (today's Coast Guard) were powerful entities in California during the Gold Rush, surpassing the desertion-weakened and dispersed Army.

The importance of ships and shipping to the Gold Rush encompassed more than freight. The first industries in California were maritime-related: the depot and shops of the Pacific Mail Steamship Company and smaller foundries and shipbuilding firms in San Francisco. Many pioneer buildings in the major cities were ships converted into floating warehouses, offices, jails, restaurants, boarding houses, even a church. Ships kept open the lines of communication with the rest of the world. Before the Pony Express, and long before the telegraph, news arrived in the form of newspapers and mail in the holds of Pacific Mail steamers. Even the news that California had been admitted to the Union was brought by the Pacific Mail steamer *Oregon,* which steamed into the harbor flying a specially made pennant, "California a State!"

A wealth of historical studies documents the maritime saga of California's rush for gold. Excellent histories exist of the Panama and Nicaragua routes, the Cape Horn passage, the clipper ships, riverboats and steamers, the Navy's Pacific Squadron, and tales of San Francisco and Sacramento. Most notable are the works of John Haskell Kemble and Oscar Lewis. Many published primary accounts of California Gold Rush voyages and diaries detail the experiences and perceptions of argonauts sojourning or settling in the Golden State. New manuscripts found in archives and maritime museums add little to these published accounts. This book is intended to demonstrate that maritime history is the pervasive thread in the fabric of Gold Rush history and to offer a comprehensive look at the Gold Rush from a mariner's perspective. If this book succeeds in furthering the story, it is only because it was written standing on the shoulders of giants. The book is not—nor would I ever construe it to be, despite the title—the final word on the maritime history of the California Gold Rush. The story is so vast and all-encompassing that a great many facts and fascinating stories could only be alluded to. I hope therefore that this book serves as a starting point for new, more detailed histories that focus on the maritime aspects of the Gold Rush.

ACKNOWLEDGMENTS

There are many friends and colleagues who have helped in the years of research and the writing of this book. My wife, Mary, and our two children, John and Beth, are the first to thank for their patience and support through the many lost weekends when I stayed put writing. After my family, the considerable advice and support of John Haskell Kemble is foremost in my gratitude, as is the always superlative editing and writer's advice I get from Joy Waldron Murphy, whom I recommend to anyone, even those writing nonmaritime works, as the best in the business. Her partner, Larry Murphy, a close friend, and another good friend, Dan Lenihan, helped me to apply my university-learned anthropology to the maritime world, particularly through shipwreck research. I "met" my first two Gold Rush ships buried in landfill and the next two underwater. Ray Aker of Palo Alto took me under his wing and, with the late Harry Dring, Karl Kortum, John B. Goodman III, and Harlan Soeten, taught me much of what I know about ships. Another close friend, Kevin Foster, generously loaned books, offered advice, and endured late-night phone calls to hear parts of chapters. Tom Layton graciously shared his *Frolic* research for which I am grateful, and my friend Allen Pastron of Archeo-tec provided the means for much of this research as we worked together excavating the buried remains of Gold Rush San Francisco. I also am grateful for the counsel and continual support of Dr. William N. Still, for whom some of these passages first took form as my thesis.

To those many friends and colleagues who helped but who are not mentioned by name, I offer my heartfelt thanks and gratitude. The entire manuscript was read by Joy Murphy, Bill Still, J. S. Holliday, and Bill Dudley. Their insightful criticisms and suggestions were essential tools in forging this manuscript into a book. Any errors and omissions, however, remain my sole responsibility.

The staff at the following institutions were of tremendous assistance and are here gratefully acknowledged: Baker Library, Harvard University; Bancroft Library, University of California, Berkeley; The Book Club of California; California Historical Society; California Room of the San Jose Public Library, California; California State Library; City of Benicia, Office of the City Clerk; Columbia University Library, New York; The Essex Institute; Federal Archives and Records Center, San Bruno, California; Georgia Historical Society; Holt-Atherton Center for Pacific Studies, University of the Pacific, Stockton, California; The Henry E. Huntington Library; Marin County Historical Society; The Mariner's Museum; Massachusetts Historical Society; The National Archives, Judicial, Fiscal and Social, Diplomatic, and Old Army and Navy Branches; National Maritime Museum, San Francisco; Mystic Seaport Museum; New-York Historical Society; New York Public Library, North Carolina State Library; The Peabody Museum of Salem; Sacramento History Center; San Francisco History Room and Archives, San Francisco Public Library; Society of California Pioneers; Solano County Office of the Recorder and County Clerk; The Sutro Library, San Francisco; Tennessee State Library; United States District Court, Northern District of California, San Francisco; Naval Historical Center, Washington, D.C.; Webb Institute of Naval Architecture; and Wells Fargo Bank History Department.

To California
by Sea

PROLOGUE
Maritime Trade and California Prior to 1848

Robert Greenhalgh Albion once observed that maritime trade with California was "of slight concern to any one except a few Boston merchants" until the California gold discovery.[1] In fact, it was those Boston traders who provided many Americans with an image of a desirable, far-off province. The maritime activity of those Boston traders also was the impetus for interest in California. Without the China trade and the hide-and-tallow trade, California would not have been a prize worth conquering during the Mexican War.

The early history of California is preeminently maritime. First sighted by Spanish explorer Juan Rodriguez Cabrillo in 1542, the land was intermittently explored by Spanish mariners through the early seventeenth century. Yet Spain made no move to settle California until the eighteenth century. Fearing the growing presence of other European powers on the Pacific, Spain sponsored an effort by land and sea that established a settlement at San Diego in 1769. By 1800, a chain of religious, military, and civil settlements tenuously linked isolated pockets of Spanish colonial ambition as far north as San Francisco Bay. The coast always remained the primary area of Spanish and, after 1821, Mexican hegemony.

The system of colonization depended on the successful congregation of the region's indigenous peoples and conversion to Catholic, Spanish-speaking colonists on their own land. Presidios, military outposts constructed to defend the province, also supported the missions, while three civil settlements, or pueblos, grew crops to support the presidios. Apart from soapmaking, leather-working, weaving, viniculture, and blacksmithing, there was no industrial base. The agrarian society of California depended upon shipments of manufac-

1

tured goods by sea from Mexico, but trade with foreigners was forbidden as a result of Spanish mercantile policy.

Several factors opened California to the outside world. At times the vessels supplying the Californias failed to bring needed goods and supplies—or to arrive at all. This, as well as the isolation of California from the central government, instilled an incipient independence and nationalism in the inhabitants, who styled themselves "Californios," not Spaniards. These isolated citizens were increasingly drawn into illicit trade and the smuggling of "contraband."

Mexico's revolution in 1821 severed California from Spain and made it part of the new Mexican empire (later republic) in 1822. Under Mexico, prohibitions against foreign vessels calling at California were abolished, but prohibitively high customs duties continued to inspire smuggling. At the same time, regulations governing land grants to private citizens relaxed, giving rise to a new institution. By the 1830s, privately owned "ranchos" supporting huge herds of longhorn cattle occupied the former mission lands along the coast. The principal business was ranching, and hides and tallow from cattle provided California not only with an economic base but also with a raw commodity worthy of trade.

Initial contact with the United States, however, resulted from the China trade, not ranching. By the first decade of the nineteenth century the young United States of America had established a toehold, by sea, into the Pacific. In the aftermath of the American Revolution, Yankee merchants eager to trade with the Orient sailed from New York, Philadelphia, and Boston to commence the American China trade. At the same time, American and European trade with the Pacific coast provided furs for trade with the Chinese. Captain James Cook obtained numerous furs on the Pacific Northwest coast during his third voyage in 1778 and inspired other mariners to follow suit when he sold them at substantial prices in China. Anxious to obtain an item that could be readily converted into lucrative China trade cargoes of tea, silk, porcelain, and other commodities, vessels from various countries, notably Great Britain, began to call on the Pacific Northwest coast. Interests in the United States were quick to follow. In 1787, the American ship *Columbia* sailed from Boston. Reconnoitering the coastal area and entering the river that bears her name, *Columbia* returned to the United States by way of Hawaii and China, marking America's first major incursion into maritime endeavors on the Pacific coast.

Vessels, most from Boston mercantile houses, began actively trading for furs along the Pacific Northwest coast. Their activities, often overlooked as opposed to the better-known and romanticized fur-trading drives of the mountain men, mark one of the most significant maritime activities of the young United States. Between 1785 and 1795, 10 American vessels worked the fur trade as contrasted with 35 British vessels. This role reversed between 1795 and 1805, as 68 American vessels—and only 10 British—participated in the trade.[2] Individual British traders, handicapped by restrictive trade regulations and the virtual monopolies of the East India and Hudson's Bay companies, had little incentive to continue.

American mariners soon realized that large numbers of sea otters could be harvested off the California coast. Sea otter pelts were much in demand, and the first visit by a Yankee ship came in 1796 when the appropriately named *Otter* of Boston arrived at Santa Cruz. A number of American vessels followed to hunt and illicitly trade for pelts off California and Oregon. Russian endeavor also extended into California in search of the otter, as the Russian-American Co., established agricultural and otter-hunting colonies in California, including an outpost on the Farallone islands, twenty-six miles west of the Golden Gate.[3] Spanish California, hitherto *terra incognita* for Americans, was slowly forced open by the necessities of this trade.

The rise of maritime fur trade inspired a new China trade route. Vessels laden with goods now sailed for California and the northwest coast to acquire furs and otter skins. Bartering and selling the furs and skins in China, the ships, packed with Chinese trade goods, returned to the United States and Great Britain, where the goods were sold at tremendous profit. California was increasingly brought into contact with the outside world as Pacific trade routes developed; the Hawaiian Islands commenced trade, taking otter pelts, cow hides, and other commodities for exchange in the new China trade. The circular route that linked California, Hawaii, and China blossomed as trade between the newly independent South American nations and California also began, all part of a great sailing ship rush occasioned by fur.

The number of vessels calling at California ports for otter pelts increased dramatically after 1820. Under Mexican rule, California's formerly restrictive trade regulations were gradually relaxed, allowing legitimate commercial intercourse with foreign vessels. Meanwhile, American vessels slowly began to shift from the northwest coast to California because of diplomatic tensions between the United States, Russia, and Great Britain.

The increasing Americanization of the Pacific coast alarmed many nations with designs on the territory, notably the British, who actively employed the Hudson's Bay Company to thwart Yankee expansion.

Commencing in 1827, the company began to establish a coastal trading fleet to oppose the incursions of the "Boston men." At first it employed its own supply ships while building a fleet of small coasting schooners at the Company's shipyard on the banks of the Columbia River at Fort Vancouver. British settlers occupied the Oregon Territory, overwhelming by sheer numbers the few Americans residing there. The strenuous efforts of the Hudson's Bay Company to occupy the Oregon Territory in the 1820s and 1830s, coupled with other factors, such as the decline of sea otters off Oregon due to over-fishing, focused American maritime attention on California. By 1837 most Americans had withdrawn from maritime commerce on the northwest coast.[4]

Beginning in 1823, American trade with California had boomed as sea-otter pelts and cattle hides were purchased from the Californios. Hides and tallow gradually surpassed fur. Although the sea otter trade continued through the 1840s, the conditions of the China trade changed. Chinese demand for pelts had already begun a decline in the 1820s. At the same time the greatly overfished California otter herds also began to yield smaller returns. Meanwhile, the rise of ranchos in Mexican California led to supremacy of a cattle economy. The voyage of the Boston vessel *Sachem* first illustrated the change. Departing Boston in January 1822, *Sachem* sailed to California. Loading hides, she returned to Boston in 1824 with a cargo sold at considerable profit to the Massachusetts shoe factories at Brockton. The voyage marked the first time a Boston vessel had sailed for the Pacific and returned directly without stopping at Hawaii or China. It was a harbinger of things to come.

California's economy changed from fur to the rawhide. A lack of cash but a plethora of cattle meant that a barter economy, largely based on the most common products—now hides and tallow—fueled the Californio ambition to acquire manufactured and luxury items (largely Chinese) from the foreign vessels. Now the vessels, rather than loading California otter pelts for trade with China, brought Chinese goods to California to exchange for hides. The hide-and-tallow trade was good business; one American in California, remarking in 1847 that hides valued at $1.50 to $2.00 a piece had been exported to the United States, continued: "More than one hundred thousand, on an average, have been exported from this country [California] yearly, for many years past. . . ."[5]

Before the first shots were fired in the Mexican War, California had already fallen by sea to Boston trade ships. William Garner summed up the relationship between California and the United States as evidenced by the hide-and-tallow trade in 1846:

> Notwithstanding that ox-hides are sold here for a dollar and fifty cents each for cash, you cannot buy, one-half the time . . . a pair of shoes. . . . Still, ox-hides can be taken from California to America . . . tanned and dressed, and made into shoes, and then brought around Cape Horn, and an importation duty paid. . . . and after all this trouble and expense, they are sold here at the same price as those manufactured in the country [California], and very frequently, from twenty to fifty percent less.[6]

The lack of industrial facilities meant that the production of finished goods was expensive in California. Thus, despite the overhead, Boston merchants made tremendous profits in California by importing those goods, which early American settler Josiah Belden described as "dry goods, articles of clothing, groceries, wines and liquors, hardware, and most of the common necessaries of life."[7] The facility of purchasing goods cheap from the Boston ships, and the absence of competitive, locally manufactured items, kept a mutually beneficial trade alive. Between 1800 and 1847, an estimated 200 vessels carried 5,000,000 hides from California.[8]

California hides and tallow culled from Mission herds were traded prior to 1828 to the British firm of McCulloch, Hartnell and Company. In 1828, however, the firm's monopoly ended when large numbers of Yankee ships lay off the coast, calling for otter pelts. New firms, in particular the Boston houses of Bryant, Sturgis and Company, William Appleton and Company, and Joseph B. Eaton and Company, moved into the gap. Each year found an increasing number of Boston ships moving from port to port, loading hides and trading. Vessels sailed up and down the California coast, calling at the ports of San Diego, San Pedro, Santa Barbara, Santa Cruz, San Francisco, and occasionally at small coves to reach isolated coastal ranchos. Various ships from the eastern seaboard of the United States at times remained on the coast for months while vessels calling from South America or the Hawaiian Islands made frequent and shorter voyages.

Vessels sailing from the Hawaiian Islands were regular arrivals. American merchants in Hawaii were eager to continue as handsomely rewarded intermediaries in the circular trade route between Boston, California, and China. Many of the Hawaiian traders were smaller vessels, usually brigs or schooners. The most famous Hawaiian trader, the 137-ton brig *Euphemia,* frequently lay at anchor off California ports through the late 1840s. Purchased from the China trade firm of

Henry Skinner and Company by E. and H. Grimes of Honolulu and William Heath Davis of Yerba Buena, *Euphemia* sailed along the California coast in February 1846. Returning in November, she remained through March 1847. In California again in July 1847, *Euphemia* stayed two months. Finally, sailing to California from Hawaii in 1848, she never returned, caught up in the gold excitement.[9]

South American ports also regularly sent vessels up the coast to California. The best known of these craft, the small brig *Ayacucho*, was glowingly described by Richard Henry Dana as "a long, sharp brig of about three hundred tons, with raking masts and very square yards. . . . We afterwards learned she was built at Guyaquil . . . and was now owned by a Scotchman named Wilson, who commanded her, and was engaged in the trade between Callao and other ports in South America and California."[10] *Ayacucho* made annual voyages to California from 1831 to 1841 under three different owners, finally ending her career on October 27, 1841, when the brig ran aground and was lost on Limantour Spit in Drakes Bay.

In addition to the foreign vessels engaged in the trade, a large number of Mexican-registered vessels on the coast sailed from Mazatlán, Acapulco, and other ports to California. Among the frequent traders was the 206-ton brig *Dolphin*, later renamed *Leonidas*, which continually sailed along the coast from 1833 to 1837, and the 160-ton brig *Catalina*, which operated on the coast and between Callao and California for the nine-year period between 1831 and 1840. These vessels were regular traders, but as a general rule did not command the trade because they did not bring the variety of goods that the foreign ships did.

The American presence in California commenced by the fur and hide-and-tallow trades was expanded by whaling; endeavors in the Atlantic decimated the cetacean population. In search of richer grounds, the British whaler *Emelia* rounded Cape Horn and commenced whaling in the Pacific in 1787. *Emelia* was quickly followed by Yankee vessels, and in 1791 seven American whalers operated off Chile. By the early nineteenth century, more than a dozen American whalers regularly cruised the South Pacific.[11] In the aftermath of the War of 1812, as Boston traders renewed their push into the Pacific to resume the maritime fur trade, whalers began fishing the same waters with success. By the 1820s, American whalers operated off Chile, Japan, the Hawaiian Islands, the South Pacific Islands, and in the Indian Ocean. The whaling trade was becoming more important; by 1845, whalers composed twenty-one percent of the nation's merchant marine fleet.[12] While most Americans learned of California through

Dana's hide-and-tallow trade novel, the desire to take California was whetted by the significance of the province as a port of call for whalers.

Whaling voyages were prolonged affairs of three or four, and at times, five years' duration. Pacific ports where the whalers could provision, refit, and recruit sailors were essential for the trade's survival. Whaling ports of call ranged from Talcahuanao, Chile; Payta, Peru; the Galapagos Islands; a number of South Seas islands, including the Solomons and Marquesas; and most important, Hawaii. The Hawaiian ports of Honolulu, Lahaina, and Hilo were popular due to their protected anchorages, numerous sailors "on the beach" who were available to fill out a crew, and the commercial opportunities afforded by the islands' involvement in the California and China trades. As the major transshipment point in the Pacific, the Hawaiian islands profited from whalers reprovisioning and sending their catches back on homeward-bound vessels.

The development of the Sea of Japan whaling grounds in the 1820s and 1830s first brought whalers to California at a time when restrictions on foreign vessels relaxed due to the change in governments. The first whaling vessel to arrive in San Francisco Bay was the British *Orion* in 1822, followed weeks later by five American whalers. A favorable reception, good anchorage, readily available fresh water, firewood, and opportunities for some trade on the side brought more whalers to California in the following years. The number of whaling vessels on the coast declined in the 1830s due to Mexican trade restrictions aimed at curbing trade abuses, but a major influx of whalers in the Pacific following the discovery of rich new grounds off the Northwest Coast instituted a new boom in the 1840s. William Heath Davis noted large numbers of whaling vessels visited San Francisco Bay in 1843, 1844 and 1845: "As many as thirty or forty whalers were in the bay at one time during each of those years. They generally had on board a few thousand dollars' worth of goods for trading, and were allowed by the customhouse authorities to exchange goods for supplies for their own use, at any point they touched along the coast, to the extent of $400, but were not allowed to sell goods for cash."[13]

The whalers were encouraged by Anglo merchants located in California. In August 1839 Thomas Oliver Larkin of Monterey advertised in the newspaper of America's whaling capital, New Bedford, that he had "sufficient buildings for storage and being well acquainted in the interior of the country has every facility of supplying whalers with refreshment immediately on arrival."[14] Another whaler's friend, William Antonio Richardson, grantee of the Rancho Sausalito on San Francisco Bay, was an ex-whaler himself. The small bay off

Richardson's home was a temporary anchorage for more than a dozen whalers a year who called for water and firewood; it earned the name of "el puerto de los balleneros," or "the port of the whalers."[15]

Increasing numbers of whalers arrived after 1844. At the end of the year Consul Larkin noted in his official despatches: "The increase of our Whale Ships on the N.W. Coast is rapidly improving and in two or three years there will in all probability be over six hundred vessels, having on board a complement of some twenty thousand men, engaged in whaling, within twelve or fifteen days sail of this port."[16] California would boom as its ports offered "many inducements to them [whalers] to visit us in the months of September, October, November & December. In these months they are in general sure to find vegetables here, and can find no better port in the Pacific as far as regards health."[17]

The port that fared best was San Francisco Bay. Despite Larkin's blandishments, the port of Monterey was too close to government scrutiny for whalers who wished to engage in illicit smuggling of trade goods, a frequent occurrence. Hawaiian Consul William Hooper noted in his despatches "the disposition on the part of the whalers to frequent the port of St. Francisco" in the summer of 1845.[18] This increased in 1846, 1847, and 1848 following the American conquest of California, and a "friendlier" commercial climate, and lasted until the Gold Rush disrupted the patterns of maritime trade.

YERBA BUENA

A former whaler who boosted San Francisco Bay's fortunes was British-born William Richardson. Arriving at San Francisco in 1822 on the whaler *Orion*, Richardson became a naturalized Mexican citizen, wed the daughter of the comandante of the Presidio, and applied his skills as a mariner to various tasks, including boat-building and piloting vessels entering San Francisco Bay.

Richardson also served as mate and master on various vessels on the coast, ranging from Sitka, Alaska all the way south to Callao. In 1835 he applied for a grant to the lands opposite the Golden Gate. He operated a launch to gather hides and other produce from the various ranchos onshore. With the closure of the Presidio in 1835, he built a home on the Rancho Sausalito and encouraged vessels to call at a shallow cove tucked into the northeast corner of the peninsula. Richardson was in a perfect position to do so; he was appointed captain of the Port of San Francisco that same year by Governor José Figueroa. The site of Richardson's new endeavor, Yerba Buena Cove, took its name from the nearby fragrant herbs. The new anchorage attracted both whalers and hide-and-tallow trade vessels.

By 1844 Richardson's small settlement had grown into a town of about twenty houses, including a trading outpost of the Hudson's Bay Company, two other trader's shops, several grocery stores, two grog shops, three carpenter's shops, and a blacksmithy. Josiah Belden described Yerba Buena in 1841:

> It . . . was simply a landing place where vessels came in to lie and ship hides and deliver goods. There were some fifteen or twenty houses of all kinds in the place, mostly small shanties. The people were perhaps half Californian, half foreigners. There were probably . . . about 150 [persons]. Occasionally a vessel came. . . . there were one or two trading between here and the Sandwich Islands. . . . There was one vessel from Callao and Valparaiso. . . . and the Boston ships. . . . I carried on trade here for about a year, sold goods on credit, collected hides and tallow round the bay, sending out launches for this purpose.[19]

The number of vessels calling at Yerba Buena increased dramatically through the 1840s. In 1844, in an effort to better regulate, or perhaps to merely get a cut of the trade, a Mexican customs house was belatedly established on the plaza of Yerba Buena.

The Hudson's Bay Company departed Yerba Buena in 1845 because of the declining fur trade business and the suicide of its agent, William Glen Rae, but others stepped in to continue the trade, albeit for whalers and hide droghers. On the eve of the American conquest in 1846, Yerba Buena was decidedly a maritime mercantile town. "There is no doubt that San Francisco will be the great commercial point of California, on account of its great internal resources, and the extent and security (after once entered) of its harbor."[20] The town was not designed as an easily defended citadel, but rather was an open city built on a grid, ready for trade and commercial intercourse, centered on the shallow waters of Yerba Buena Cove. The coming of war and the arrival of Mormon settlers boosted the town's fortunes, but the natural advantages of San Francisco Bay (termed a "miniature Mediterranean" in 1847 by the Philadelphia *North American*) and the town's role as a maritime center of trade, served it best. In 1848, renamed San Francisco, it blossomed into the principal American port on the Pacific.

AMERICAN DESIRES FOR A PACIFIC PORT

Long before Dana published *Two Years Before the Mast*, American politicians had already learned of California—in particular they had heard of the commercial and strategically important bay of San Francisco and had even offered to buy it. As early as 1835, the year that hide-and-tallow enterprise and whalers in the Pacific induced Richardson to found Yerba Buena, President Andrew Jackson instructed his charge' d'affaires in Mexico to commence negotiations "with the great object of securing the bay of San Francisco" through the purchase of Northern California.[21]

Jackson's desire to acquire San Francisco Bay came to naught. It also was not a novel idea. The advantages of the harbor for trade and commerce had been evident since its discovery and first charting. Fray Juan Crespi, a member of the expedition that had discovered the bay, wrote a few months later: "This port of San Francisco . . . is very large, and without doubt the port . . . could [contain] not only all the armadas of our Catholic Monarch but also all of those of Europe."[22] Foreign appreciation of the harbor ensued just a few decades later, when British explorer George Vancouver sailed through the Golden Gate in 1792. Others followed Vancouver; the most significant (to the future of San Francisco Bay) arrival was the 1826 visit of HMS *Blossom* under the command of Captain Frederick William Beechey. Anchoring off the Presidio in November for supplies, Beechey and his men freely navigated the bay, charting and mapping its waters. Beechey's painstakingly rendered chart, published by the British Hydrographic Office in 1833, gave the world its first accurate and detailed view of the port. His remarks on the territory, published in 1831, served notice of Anglo intentions toward the province and port:

> Possessing all these advantages, an industrious population alone seems requisite to withdraw it from the obscurity in which it has so long slept under the indolence of the people and the jealous policy of the Spanish government. . . . this indifference cannot continue; for either it must disappear under the present authorities, or the country will fall into other hands, as from its situation with regard to other powers. . . . and to . . . commerce. . . . It is of too much importance to be permitted to remain longer in its present neglected state.[23]

Other portentous visits included those of Captain Edward Belcher in 1837–1839. Belcher charted the Sacramento River to what he considered the head of navigation.

French interests were first represented in the 1837 voyage of Abel Dupetit-Thours, who stopped at Monterey, and later by the 1839 voyage to San Francisco of Cyrille Pierre Theodore Laplace. During 1841–1842, when French diplomat Eugene Duflot de Mofras to investigated his nation's possible acquisition of the region, the French position was confirmed.[24]

The United States, represented in California from the last decade of the eighteenth century solely by merchant vessels, finally sent a naval vessel in 1836. The sloop of war *Peacock* sailed from Oahu to

Monterey in October of that year, at the request of Hawaiian merchants. The gesture was designed to insure the protection of American and Hawaiian maritime commerce in California in the aftermath of the seizure of the American brig *Loriot* after her 1833 arrival in at San Francisco and the arrest of her supercargo, Alpheus B. Thompson, for smuggling. Thompson complained it was "the most outrageous thing ever inflicted on an American in these seas."[25]

The next American naval visit was in 1840. The United States man-of-war *St. Louis* arrived at Monterey following Governor Juan B. Alvarado's arrest and deportation of numerous foreigners, including several Americans, whom the governor believed were plotting to overthrow his government. The U.S. Secretary of the Navy had ordered the ship to cruise to California. The commander of *St. Louis*, French Forrest, asked for and received an explanation from Governor Alvarado. In late 1841, another man-of-war, *Yorktown*, also called at Monterey. Increased visits demonstrated a new American policy calling for a stronger naval presence in the Pacific. In December 1841, the Secretary of the Navy requested that the Pacific Squadron be doubled to better protect American interests, notably those in California.[26] A major exploration of the Pacific, undertaken under the auspices of the United States Navy also touched at California in 1841. The United States Exploring Expedition, commanded by Lieutenant Charles Wilkes, visited Monterey and San Francisco. The expedition navigated the Sacramento River, charted the bay, and made numerous observations about the country.[27]

In the United States, the desire for acquisition of California increased each year. Difficulties with Mexican authorities in California over American smuggling exacerbated the desire, inflaming Yankee pride as politicians, editors, and commercially minded entrepreneurs focused on the supposed Mexican failure to make something of California. Given the troubles with Mexico, and the ardent attentions paid to the province by Great Britain and France, the United States was by far the most eager foreign power waiting for the right moment to take it. The conquest of California was "inevitable, given the unbridled energy of a young nation. . . . A lust for land, a quest for independence beyond the frontier, trade and profit, fear of foreign deterrence."[28] Sir George Simpson of Great Britain wrote of his strong belief that, whatever "may be the fate of Monterey and the more southerly ports, San Francisco will, to a moral certainty, sooner or later fall into the possession of Americans."[29] California's ports were the key to dominating the Pacific Basin. As such, the prize was worth whatever it took to win it.

Events tipped the American hand in 1842 when Commodore Thomas Ap Catesby Jones, commanding the Pacific Squadron, heard of rumors of war between the United States and Mexico. Fearing that the recently departed French and British Pacific squadrons intended to take California, Jones left his regular anchorage at Callao and proceeded with two warships to Monterey. Anchoring off the town, he demanded the surrender of the province. Landing with sailors and marines the next day on October 20, Jones seized Monterey and raised the flag, but quickly learned there was no conflict with Mexico. After a thirty-hour tenure as American territory, Monterey was returned apologetically by Jones.[30]

In the aftermath of Commodore Jones's "conquest," the question was not if, but when, the United States would come to possess California and the all-important port of San Francisco. A large American naval force remained at station in California until early 1843, and five warships visited between 1844 and 1845. In 1845 the new commodore of the Pacific Squadron, John Drake Sloat, was explicitly ordered, in the event of war, to "possess yourself of the port of San Francisco, and blockade or occupy such other ports as your force may permit."[31]

Diplomatic disputes with Mexico—over the annexation of Texas, the boundary of the United States and Mexico, and American designs upon California—led to increasing tension from 1843 through the early months of 1846. In April 1846, two opposing armies met near the Rio Grande near Texas, each demonstrating their determination to protect national honor and defend soil believed to be theirs. On April 25 Mexican troops attacked the Americans. President James K. Polk sent a war message to Congress, which obliged him by declaring war on May 11. An eighteen-month conflict began, the first successful offensive war for young America. In an unbroken string of victories, American troops fought their way to the Mexican capitol, occupied the Mexican provinces of New Mexico and California, and forced the capitulation of Mexico by the end of 1847. While the army fought its way through Mexico's heartland, the U.S. Navy swept up the Pacific coast, conquering California.

The formidable U.S. Pacific Squadron was eight vessels strong at the outbreak of war. The flagship USS *Savannah*, a 54-gun first-class frigate, was accompanied by another first-class frigate, *Congress* (54 guns), the sloops-of-war *Portsmouth* (22 guns), *Warren* (24 guns), *Levant* (22 guns), and *Cyane* (20 guns), the schooner *Shark* (12 guns), and the storeship *Erie* (4 guns). One vessel, *Portsmouth*, lay at anchor at Monterey when the first shots were fired on April 25, 1846. As rumors of war reached the Pacific, *Portsmouth* sailed north to San

Francisco Bay, reaching Yerba Buena on June 2. USS *Savannah*, *Cyane*, and *Levant* reached Monterey in early July, confirming the news. A landing party from the three ships seized Monterey on July 7. Two days later *Portsmouth* took the Yerba Buena in bloodless conquest. Naval forces landed and occupied the port of Santa Barbara on August 4, taking San Pedro on August 6. The conquest of California, first and foremost a naval affair, remained so even with the arrival of U.S. Army troops. The impressive force of naval vessels, which held the principal ports and cruised the coast, and the use of sailors and marines from those vessels as foot soldiers, secured and held California for the United States.[32]

Observers viewed the American acquisition of California as the beginning of a new era of commercial greatness. Larkin, writing to former Vice-Consul William A. Leidesdorff of Yerba Buena in the fall of 1846, said, "We both may now consider ourselfs out of office and Government employ. Still we have not lost but gained. Commerce will revive. In fact, all and every one may now flourish in California."[33] Larkin would ultimately be proved correct, though in a fashion he would not have thought possible.

The immediate result of the Mexican War in California was a loss of trade. The Mexican coastal trade, which brought a variety of vessels to California's shores, halted when the U.S. Navy blockaded Mexico's west coast in 1846. Warships cruising the coast captured twenty-nine vessels from 1846 to 1848, including one off California and two others actively involved in the California trade.[34] Some of the prize vessels were sailed to California and auctioned off. Among these were the English schooner *William* and the Mexican brig *Malek Adhel*. The schooner *Julia*, was reported at Yerba Buena in November 1846, where her cargo was sold at auction and she was refitted for coastal trade in California under the Hawaiian flag.[35] The hide-and-tallow trade, disrupted by falling prices and the war, offered little inducement to merchants. The principal maritime business in California during 1846–1848 was the supply of the troops and the navy, who were cut off from their regular means of supply. Other flourishing maritime traders were the whalers: twenty-three whaling vessels called at Yerba Buena in 1846.[36]

The Mexican War boosted the fortunes of Yerba Buena. The tiny town, occupied by the conquering United States, benefitted from several strokes of fate; as the largest settlement on San Francisco Bay, it had hosted the Mexican customhouse for the bay since 1844 and lay close to the Presidio of San Francisco, which although abandoned by the Mexican government in 1835, was reactivated by U.S. troops.

During the war years, Yerba Buena became the headquarters for the army, and the site of the U.S. Army Quartermaster's store. Its adobe customhouse was designated as an American institution. The town's population doubled when the ship *Brooklyn* of New York, filled with Mormon emigrants, arrived on July 31, 1846.

By November of 1846, one observer wrote that in Yerba Buena "commerce seems to be increasing, and the launches and small crafts of the Bay are constantly employed in bringing the crops to market."[37] The growing population and commerce of the town gave rise to competition. In 1846 Robert Semple, Larkin, and others founded a small community on the straits of Carquinez as a rival to burgeoning Yerba Buena. Named Francisca, the new town was enough of a threat to induce action from Yerba Buena Mayor Lieutenant Washington Bartlett. On January 30, 1847, Bartlett decreed that the town's name be changed from Yerba Buena to San Francisco. The change linked the world-recognized port to the town:

> Whereas, the local name of Yerba Buena, as applied to the settlement or town of San Francisco, is unknown beyond the district; and has been applied from the local name of the cove on which the town is built; Therefore, to prevent confusion and mistakes in public documents, and that the town may have the advantage of the name given on the public map. It is hereby ordained that the name of San Francisco shall hereafter be used in all official communications and public documents or records appertaining to the town.[38]

The other town immediately changed its name from Francisca to Benicia. San Francisco's new name was followed later in the year by the town's first elections. An alcalde and six councilmen were elected in September 1847 in response to an edict from Colonel Richard Barnes Mason, U.S. Army, military governor of California, who had told George Hyde, Bartlett's replacement, "There may soon be expected a large number of whalers in your Bay, and a large increase in population. . . . it is therefore necessary that you should, at an early day, have an efficient town police, proper town laws, town officials, &c. for the enforcement of the laws for the preservation of order."[39]

San Francisco received another boost in March of 1847 as three military transports, bearing volunteers recruited to "conquer and colonize" the new territory, arrived at San Francisco. *Susan Drew, Thomas H. Perkins*, and *Loo Choo* brought 599 new souls to the bay town. Most of the volunteers dispersed to Santa Barbara and Monterey, but three companies remained to man the Presidio of San Francisco, swelling the population of the town.[40] By the end of 1848, San Francisco's population stood near 1,000, a rise seven times higher than five years earlier.

Given the maritime nature of the town, not surprisingly the first ordinances sought to stem desertions from naval and commercial vessels. The new regulations licensed merchants and took steps to obtain sufficient revenue for public improvements—the first to be a municipal wharf for loading and discharging vessels. The means for raising funds, in addition to licenses and fees, was the sale of submerged real estate in Yerba Buena Cove that had been granted to the town in 1847. The sales of these "water lots" commenced in the summer of 1847, paving the way for the ultimate expansion of the town into the cove during the Gold Rush. Although San Francisco hosted a mere eight or nine vessels in 1848—the exact number is still disputed—"The site of the town of San Francisco is known to all navigators and mercantile men acquainted with the subject to be the most commanding commercial position on the entire eastern coast of the Pacific ocean, and the town itself is . . . destined to become the commercial emporium of the western side of the American continent."[41] Thus San Francisco possessed the advantage of being the only port in California capable of greeting a large fleet of gold-seeking vessels rushing in response to the California gold discovery.

THE GOLD RUSH BEGINS

The discovery of gold on the banks of the American River was kept secret at first, but within a matter of months the story leaked out. From California, the news spread by ship to the two areas that carried on regular trade with the territory—Hawaii and various South American ports. In late 1848, reports reaching the eastern seaboard of the United States told of scarcely believable gold discoveries in recently acquired California. Letters, including correspondence from military officers stationed in the West, and newspaper reports added to the growing excitement. "Your streams have minnows and ours are paved with gold," wrote Monterey alcalde Walter Colton to a Philadelphia newspaper.[42] California had responded with great enthusiasm to the news of gold: "The whole country . . . resounds with the sordid cry of "gold! Gold!! GOLD!!!," while the field is left half planted, the house half built, and everything neglected but the manufacture of shovels and pickaxes."[43]

Interest in California's gold quickly spread beyond its borders, and by the end of 1848 reached a fever pitch. The President's annual message to Congress, delivered on December 5, 1848, discussed the California news. Standing before Congress with fresh dispatches from

California in hand, President Polk announced, "The accounts of the abundance of gold in that territory are of such an extraordinary character as would scarcely command belief were they not corroborated by the authentic reports of officers in the public service and derived from the facts which they detail from personal observation."[44] Two days after Polk's speech, Lieutenant Lucien Loeser arrived in Washington, D.C., with additional reports from Colonel Richard Barnes Mason, California's military governor. Mason dispatched proof of California's mineral wealth. Loeser carried a leather tea caddy packèd with 230 ounces of near-pure gold. The presidential verification of the California tales and the public display of the "golden tea caddy" were the catalysts of the Gold Rush.

By mid-December, newspapers throughout the United States carried editorials about the gold discovery. Everywhere preparations were being made to go to California. The Hartford, Connecticut *Daily Courant* commented on the rush in its December 6, 1848, issue: "The California gold fever is approaching its crisis. We are told that the new region that has just become a part of our possessions, is El Dorado after all. Thither is now setting a tide that will not cease its flow until either untold wealth is amassed, or extended beggary is secured."

The lure of an easy fortune from the California gold fields brought the "argonauts of '49," as many fancied themselves, from every walk of life in every section of the country:

> The spirit of emigration which is carrying off thousands to California so far from dying away increases and expands every day. All classes of our citizens seem to be under the influence of this extraordinary mania. . . . Poets, philosophers, lawyers, brokers, bankers, merchants, farmers, clergymen—all are feeling the impulse and are preparing to go and dig for gold and swell the number of adventurers to the new El Dorado.[45]

In the winter of 1848–1849, the traditional route of migration to the Pacific—the great plains—was impassable due to rain-swollen rivers and mud. Mountain passes were blocked by snow and ice. The only way to go to California was by sea.

To a nation still feeling some of the effects of the great Panic of 1837–1844, particularly in New England ports where vessels lay idle at anchor, the rush to outfit vessels for the Cape Horn passage harkened a booming maritime economy. The American merchant marine was then lucratively engaged in whaling, deep-water trading voyages with Africa, China, and the Mediterranean, transatlantic passenger and cargo trade with Great Britain and the continent in packet ships, a domestic coasting trade with links to the Caribbean and the Gulf of Mexico, and fishing.[46] The merchant marine had also been affected by two developments of the era: (1) a search for speed under sail, particularly for China traders, culminating in the development of sleek "clippers" and clipperlike craft; and (2) an increasing reliance on steam power extending from the nation's Western rivers to coastal and transatlantic transportation. The after-effects of the panic, and the changes in the types of vessels employed, resulted in the laying up of some craft and a diminishing need for certain kinds of vessels. The "dead wood" clogging America's ports and harbors would be swept up and away into the gold rush traffic, clearing the way for shipyards to turn out newer style vessels. The California trade provided an extra boost to the clipper ships, and created a sea-based economy bolstered by California's need for supplies and goods. Boston had been the major link with the Pacific coast until the Mexican War, but after the discovery of gold in the newly conquered territory, New York and the rest of the maritime world came in large numbers to California.

Chapter One
BY WAY OF CAPE HORN

As news of the California gold discovery swept the United States and Europe, fortune-seekers made hasty preparations to go as soon as possible. Many, particularly from the seafaring New England states, chose to sail into the Pacific around the tip of South America. All cargoes bound for California also came by way of Cape Horn, with the exception of high-duty freight via Panama. The Cape Horn passage, although difficult, was the traditional means of reaching the Pacific, and China traders, whalers, and California-bound, Boston men in the hide-and-tallow trade had charted the way. The time it took to navigate Cape Horn, sometimes weeks because of fierce storms and strong currents, had shortened, thanks to the current-charting work of Lieutenant Matthew Fontaine Maury, who provided a "road-map" for masters less experienced in the nuances of Cape Horn. Journals, diaries, letters, and logbooks kept by the Gold Rush fleet record a 13,328-mile route that was followed with little variation. After a vessel departed from one of the eastern seaboard ports, it would follow the coast into the Gulf Stream. Striking out into the Atlantic, many vessels sighted African shores or the Cape Verde Islands to get the trade wind. Some of their spars were even dusted by a scirocco wind from the Sahara.

Running back across the Atlantic, most vessels put in at Rio de Janeiro, where sea-weary passengers toured the city and stocked up on liquor and fresh fruit while their ships replenished stores. Leaving Rio, the ships chose to go by either the Cape or the narrow Straits of

Magellan. Battling Antarctic gales, many vessels struggled for westing, at times spying the rocks of Diego Ramirez or Cape Horn before being driven back into the Atlantic. Finally reaching the Pacific, the battered vessels stopped at Chilean or Peruvian ports, usually Talcahuano or Callao, some pausing at Juan Fernandez, Robinson Crusoe's island. From the South American coast, the vessels made their way well into the Pacific, where they were at times becalmed, before tacking east for the California coast. Making landfall on the coast, they felt their way, sometimes in heavy fog, to the Golden Gate. There they dropped their anchors in the soft mud of the bay off San Francisco.

The number of vessels journeying into the Pacific was phenomenal; between December 1848 and December 1849, historian John B. Goodman has accounted for at least 762 vessels that cleared North American ports for California.[1] As early as October 31, 1849, the Boston shipping list noted that 573 vessels had departed for California, with 101 vessels advertised to sail from various ports in the immediate future.[2] Goodman, who has measured interest in the Gold Rush by tracking vessels advertised to sail from New York, Boston, and the New England states, charts a dramatic rise at the beginning of 1849, which begins to taper off in February and March, plummeting in the summer and rising again in the fall. In January 1850, the editors of the San Francisco Daily Alta California recounted the flood tide of emigration by way of the Horn by citing the harbormaster's records: 39,888 persons had arrived in San Francisco on 805 vessels between April 1849, and January 1850.[3] In October 1850, the Sacramento Transcript noted from eastern newspaper accounts that 1,031 American vessels had cleared for California (presumably from the beginning of 1849 through August 1850), but "foreign vessels are not taken into the . . . account, and when they are considered, it shows a pretty tall commerce for the little settlement on the Pacific side."[4] In all, as many as 1,400, perhaps more, vessels sailed to California by way of Cape Horn in 1849 and 1850.

The greatest initial response came from New York. Already the busiest American port, New York was the most active in the Gold Rush; the majority of vessels sailed from there—some 214 clearing for California in 1849 alone. Boston, the next busiest port, had 151 clearances, followed by the whaling port of New Bedford, which sent 42 vessels, many of them whalers disrupted in the trade; Baltimore had 38 clearances; New Orleans, 32 vessels; and Philadelphia, 31. These figures add up to only 508 vessels of the 762-vessel total, "showing that virtually every seaport town had its sailings."[5]

The shipping advertisements in the New York newspapers illustrate initial maritime response to the Gold Rush. In New York, vessels were advertised for California even as the Mexican War drew to a close in early 1848. In January of that year, James Bishop and Company, announced its vessel *Undine* was available to carry freight to California if sufficient cargo could be booked. No other vessel for California or the Oregon territory was advertised until March. The pace increased with two vessels, *Seramphore* and *Chile,* in August 1848, the latter bound for California's capital, Monterey. In September another vessel announced it would sail for "ports in the North Pacific Ocean."[6]

The first vessel for San Francisco direct was *John W. Cater.* Built at Killingsworth, Connecticut, the seventeen-year-old *Cater* was a sturdy 217-ton vessel originally used in both the transatlantic and coastal packet trades, for a time as one of Charles Morgan's Charleston packets.[7] Laden with $70,000 worth of tools, fabric, building materials, crockery, tobacco, clothing, hardware, and notions, *John W. Cater* sailed for San Francisco on October 19, 1848. On March 12, 1849, the editors of the *Daily Alta California* called the arriving *Cater* "the first ship that left New York after the receipt of the intelligence of the gold discovery."[8] The first multiple listings appeared in the November editions of the New York papers. Four vessels advertised for San Francisco—*Brooklyn, Sylvie de Grasse, Whiton,* and *Henry Nesmith:* six vessels for the Pacific coast on December 1, 1848, a figure that jumped to twenty-seven on December 12, as President Polk's message spread.[9]

In Boston, few vessels advertised for California in 1848; although one, sailing for Honolulu in September, was said to be "as good an opportunity for passengers to California or Oregon" as could be found. The first ship to actually clear Massachusetts's shores direct for California departed from Salem.[10] *Mary and Ellen* cleared Salem on October 8, 1848. By December 5, 1848, the bark *Maria,* advertised direct from Boston to San Francisco, "provided sufficient inducement . . ."[11] The inducement came with the President's message to Congress delivered on the same day. By the end of December, the Boston advertisements, although not as numerous as New York's, did indicate that the Gold Rush influenced that port, with nineteen ships advertised to sail. The next year Boston sent 151 vessels to California.

The whaling port of New Bedford was second to Boston in sending ships from Massachusetts to California. Some forty-two vessels cleared New Bedford for San Francisco. The whaler *Aurora* was the first vessel to depart New Bedford, clearing on January 2, 1849. The next day the town's newspaper, the *Mercury,* reported the ship sailed with a cargo of prefabricated buildings, lumber, naval stores, provisions, and sperm candles (a commodity a whaling port had no scarcity of). The passengers were described as "young men . . . mostly mechanics [who] go out to California in search of a less crowded field of industry, with the hope, too, of being able to gather their share of the golden harvest."[12] No other vessels cleared New Bedford or Nantucket, the next active port, until the end of the month, "not from lack of interest but lack of ships. The shipyards . . . were busy converting whaling vessels and fishing schooners into vessels fit for a California voyage."[13] By January 22, 1849, some were nearly ready, and the Nantucket paper reported eleven vessels posted to sail. Additional vessels followed at a slower pace in the spring and fall.

In January of 1850, Jethro C. Brock of Nantucket published a list of "persons from Nantucket, now in California or on their way there." He listed twenty-one New Bedford and Nantucket vessels, many of them old whalers, including the previously mentioned *Aurora*.[14] Other New England ports sent a fair number of vessels as well, helping that region provide the greatest number of aggregate sailings per month by the end of 1849. These ports other than Boston, Philadelphia, Nantucket, and New Bedford included Beverly, Edgartown, Fairhaven, Mattapoiset, Fall River, Newburyport, Holmes Hole [Woods Hole], Plymouth, and Salem, Massachusetts; Providence, Warren, Newport and Bristol, Rhode Island; and New London, Mystic and New Haven, Connecticut. Salem, a busy port active in the spice trade, had declined as the trade dwindled. The gold discovery "provided a new incentive to shipping merchants and bolstered the sagging economy of Essex County."[15] By October 1849, Salem had already sent eleven vessels to California.[16]

Other ports sending large numbers of vessels to California were the major shipping centers of Baltimore, New Orleans, and Philadelphia. In addition to the large sailings from those principal ports, many seaports sent a few vessels to California. In North Carolina, an active coastal trade in naval stores was scarcely disrupted by news of the gold discovery. However, in December 1848 following the President's message, a Wilmington, North Carolina merchant, George Harriss, advertised that the 138-ton schooner *General Morgan* would sail for California "if a suitable amount of freight and passengers should offer" when the schooner touched at Wilmington on her way south from New York.[17] *General Morgan's* owners apparently did not receive enough offers and the schooner did not stop at Wilmington following departure from New York on February 23, 1849, with twenty-five passengers. Merchant Harriss tried again the same month, announcing in the Wilmington *Weekly Commercial* a proposal to form a cooperative company with the subscribers paying a "sum to be in proportion to the number of passengers or adventurers" to purchase "a good and substantial vessel."[18] Another unsuccessful sailing was that of the coastal packet *Lowell*. Disrupted from the New York–Savannah run, the 219-ton brig advertised plans for sailing from Wilmington on November 20, 1849, for "San Francisco, Bernecia [sic] and Sacramento City."[19] Without much apparent interest, the vessel sailed instead for New York, clearing on February 19, 1850, with fifteen passengers. Gold-seekers from North Carolina seemingly followed the same pattern, taking one of the coastal packets to New York and sailing in one of the constantly departing vessels for San Francisco.

Only two vessels sailed from North Carolina for California in 1849. On August 30, 1849, the schooner *John Storey* (also described as a brig) cleared Wilmington for San Francisco with a cargo of lumber and three passengers.[20] One other vessel cleared North Carolina's shores in 1849, but never reached California. Wilmington packet agent George W. Davis advertised the new bark *John A. Taylor* would sail "For San Francisco California Direct!" after completion in April 1849.[21] In early May, *John A. Taylor* arrived at Wilmington. As the ship's cabin was fitted up, the editors of the *Weekly Commercial* called "the attention of those in this section who may contemplate going to the "Gold Region," to the propriety of engaging passage on board of her."[22] *John A. Taylor* sailed from Wilmington on December 8, 1849, with one passenger. After unsuccessfully being able to round Cape Horn, she put into Rio de Janeiro where she remained for at least another year, well into 1851. The record did not improve in the first months of 1850, when only two vessels sailed from North Carolina. The brig *Bordeaux* cleared Wilmington in early February 1850. At the same time, the 394-ton bark *Louisa Bliss,* a former New Orleans packet, sailed from Beaufort, North Carolina on February 4 with seven passengers and lumber cargo.[23]

The southern ports of Mobile, Savannah, Norfolk, and Richmond also cleared vessels for San Francisco in 1849. Baltimore and New Orleans were the most active southern ports participating in the Gold Rush. New Orleans's thirty-two clearances indicate steamers on the Panama route and several sailing vessels, including the clipper ship *Architect*. The process of advertising, fitting out, booking passengers, and departure were no different from those in New England, save in numbers. The South was not a major maritime participant in the Gold Rush probably because New England and New York dominated maritime trade and commerce in the United States; the population of the northern states were swelled by European emigrants, a likely source of gold seekers; and most of the vessels that sailed to and from southern ports in the cotton and general carrying trades cleared from their home ports of New York or Boston for San Francisco.

One small state, Maine, invested substantially in maritime trade and commerce during the Gold Rush. Ports in Maine provided nearly nine percent, or sixty-seven vessels, of the total number that sailed to California in 1849. The first departing vessel, the bark *Suliot*, cleared Belfast, Maine on January 30, 1849, with fifty passengers and assorted cargo composed largely of lumber, prefabricated houses, and sundries that fetched a considerable profit when *Suliot* arrived at San Francisco on July 18, 1849.[24] Ironically, only four vessels that sailed from Maine in 1849 arrived the same year, the majority clearing later in the year, arriving at San Francisco in 1850. Those included the ship *Eudorus* of Bangor, clearing February 15 and arriving on September 15, 1849; *Golconda* of Bangor, arriving on November 22, 1849; *Montano* of Bangor, arriving on November 27, 1849; and *Suliot*. In early 1850 vessels arrived from many other Maine ports.[25]

The number of ships sailing from other nations was rather small in 1849; only thirty-six vessels cleared various foreign ports between January 1 and October 9 of that year.[26] The numbers increased in the late fall as vessels cleared not only Europe but also Australia, New Zealand, and other South Seas ports. Europe responded with greater numbers of sailings in 1850, when vessels hailing from Great Britain, France, the Scandinavian countries, South American ports, the German states, and Mediterranean nations embarked for San Francisco. In the first nine months of 1850, 93 ships left British ports, followed by 10 French ships, 10 vessels from the various British provinces, and 62 vessels (29 ships, 19 barks, six brigs, two schooners, and six steamers) from "other foreign ports."[27] The number of British gold-seekers sailing to California was probably greater, as emigrants stepping off the Liverpool packets in New York could just as easily board the San Francisco-bound ship moored alongside. One Liverpool emigrant to do so in 1850, Prussian-born Adolph Sutro, later gained fame and fortune in his Pacific coast career as a mining engineer, entrepreneur, and mayor of San Francisco. Typical ports of departure included Antwerp, London, Bremen, Le Havre, Hong Kong, Liverpool, Bordeaux, Hamburg, Amsterdam, Manila, Genoa, Halifax, Honolulu, Lahaina, Glasgow, and Stockholm.

Initial French response to the Gold Rush was slow, inhibited by political disorder and mistrust of the news of the discovery. Sailings began in late 1849 and picked up considerably in 1850, increasing in the following years. As was the case in America, companies were formed in some instances; in others lotteries were held for tickets to California.[28] The circumstances of most voyages were similar to other vessels in the "California fleet." In July 1850, for example, the Saint-Malo *La Verite* announced the sailing of the new ship *Le Montalembert* for California in an advertisement nearly identical to those posted by Yankee shipowners in American ports.[29] The advertisement promised regular service between Le Havre and San Francisco, an early admission of the importance of the new California trade to Europeans. British shipowners in particular were eager to participate because vessels could now sail on a lucrative, circular route that linked Great Britain, the United States, California, and China.

The nature of the Gold Rush fleet traditionally has been described as a motley collection of ships, barks, brigs, schooners, and steamers that included older vessels languishing for lack of trade, or worn-out vessels and even some laid up hulks responding to the gold discovery. One historian noted that "most of the ships . . . were . . . whalers, cargo boats hastily fitted with bunks. . . . Condemned hulks were pressed into service and lake boats, built for sheltered waters, were sent forth to battle Antarctic gales. The bark of three hundred tons was a respectable vessel, and a thousand ton ship was considered colossal."[30]

Vessels of various sizes, rigs, and registries sailed to California, the majority less than full-rigged. Historian John Lyman, tabulating the numbers of vessels sailing to California from North American ports in 1849 noted that 242 ships, 218 barks, 170 brigs, 132 schooners, and 12 steamers "cleared for San Francisco" in 1849.[31] John B. Goodman, basing his comments on research into each of these vessel's careers, notes that most "were stout vessels, a few less than stout," and while "a few had lost the bloom of youth," the majority of vessels that sailed to California in 1849 had been built between 1844 and 1849 "with several sailing on their maiden voyages."[32]

All of the principal maritime trades were represented in the "California fleet:" transatlantic packets, Mediterranean, Caribbean, general "tramps" and coastal traders, whalers, and passenger and freight-carrying steamers. The packet trade, which had boomed in the aftermath of the War of 1812, contributed a large number of former packets to the Gold Rush. "Many of the old packets gathered for a last round-up during the California gold rush in '49. . . . the veteran *York*, 25 years old with considerable whaling to her credit, was bought for $8,050. The *John Jay,* her junior by three years, was also purchased at New Bedford, and at least a dozen other ex-packets joined the mongrel flotilla that ventured to . . . San Francisco."[33] More than a dozen packets sailed to California in 1849, among them some famous craft, such as *James Monroe,* which in 1818 had inaugurated service on the celebrated "Black Ball Line." Other less famous packets included *Henry Allen, Louis Philippe, Sutton, Sylvie de Grasse, Arkansas, Apollo, Rhone* and *Montano.*

A large number of Gold Rush vessels were general and coastal traders, including many that had plied the cotton trade between New York and various southern ports. Some were older vessels but a large number were relatively new, indicating the disruptive effect of the Gold Rush on established patterns of maritime trade. One such vessel was the 288-ton bark *John G. Colley* of Norfolk, Virginia, built in late 1847. *Colley* served for only a year as a New Orleans packet on the Dispatch Line before the owners withdrew the bark and sent it to California in March 1849 with twenty-nine passengers.[34]

The Gold Rush fleet reportedly topped all others except the entire fleet of American-registry whalers, and a large number of the California vessels were whalers diverted from their trade. Goodman noted that one in ten whalers "defected to join the Gold Rush . . ." indicating that the majority of Gold Rush vessels were either general and coastal traders, or whalers.[35] The whalers included some already in the Pacific, like *Niantic* of Sag Harbor and *Norman* of Nantucket. *Niantic's* captain, Henry Cleaveland, learned of the gold discovery while provisioning at Paita, Peru, and he immediately cleared for Panama. There in May 1849 he loaded 249 passengers for San Francisco, arriving at the Golden Gate on July 5, 1849. Another whaler, *Zoroaster,* had a more common Gold Rush career. Built at Thomaston, Maine, in 1836, the 159-ton brig commenced whaling out of New Bedford in 1839, *Zoroaster* made five whaling voyages before being withdrawn from service in 1846. In the fall of 1849 the vessel was advertised to sail from New Bedford to San Francisco, departing on October 10 with eleven passengers. After an uneventful passage, *Zoroaster* arrived at San Francisco on April 7, 1850.[36]

The various steamers clearing for San Francisco by way of the straits carried passengers as did any sailing vessel, but unlike many of the sailing ships, they actually had an assured career upon arrival, whether on the Isthmus of Panama or on California's rivers. Those vessels included the pioneer steamers of the Pacific Mail line via Panama—*California, Oregon* and *Panama*—that cleared just as the news of gold was breaking, and were followed by additional steamers for the Pacific Mail, including the Cunarder *Unicorn* and a few interrupted coastal steam packets such as the former New York to Savannah steamer *Tennessee.* Other steamers included a few small vessels built for more sheltered waters: among the more famous the riverboat *New*

World, launched in 1850 for service on New York's Hudson River. Attached for debts, *New World,* although neither designed nor built to withstand ocean storms, was stolen by its master, Captain Ned Wakeman, who in a daring display of piracy and seamanship piloted *New World* to California through the Straits of Magellan.[37]

A few smaller steamers also made the voyage, but not on their own power—they traveled disassembled on other ships by way of the Horn. Among these was the tiny 60- by 22-foot steamer *Commodore Jones,* which came to California with the Salem and California Mining and Trading Company in the bark *LaGrange* in 1849. Discharged at Benicia, the vessel was rebuilt by members of the company and launched in the waters of the Straits of Carquinez to triumphantly steam upriver to Sacramento.[38]

The Cape Horn voyages of a heterogeneous collection of vessels and tens of thousands of passengers was a short-lived phenomenon, lasting only through 1850. The number of arrivals did not drop off, but cargo began to replace passengers as the Panama Route became the easier way of traveling to and from the Pacific. The arrival of large numbers of passengers by way of the Horn had become rare enough in San Francisco by July of 1852 to occasion comment. When the ship *Governor Morton* arrived, 124 days out of New York with 108 passengers, the *Daily Alta California* proclaimed: "This is the largest number of passengers that has arrived in one ship by way of Cape Horn, in many months. It recalls the days of early emigration to California, when a Cape Horn passage was the most comfortable trip to the gold mines."[39] Even three years after the "days of '49," an aura of romance had begun to pervade the saga of sailing to California via Cape Horn, as editors recalled the good old days of booming gold rush trade.

THE COMMON EXPERIENCE

The story has been told many times of the ships, passengers, and crew who journeyed around Cape Horn to California. More than a hundred published accounts detail Gold Rush voyages, and contemporary newspapers contain numerous published letters or portions of journals sent in from correspondents. Hundreds of unpublished manuscript diaries and letters repose in archives around the country. Historian Oscar Lewis, writing in his classic *Sea Routes to the Gold Fields,* noted a "marked similarity" in the Cape Horn journals. Most, he said, were the result of the diarists making a "barren record of the day's run, the state of the weather, and a catalogue of the meals served, ships sighted, and fishes caught."[40] Although there are many "barren" journals, there are also many others that, if not containing "the gift of bringing to life the feel and flavor of these long coast-to-coast passages" that Lewis described, chronicle fascinating common experiences and perceptions. Among these elements relate the problems of provisioning and getting ready to sail, the first week at sea, learning about "life on the ocean wave," disgust over the food, and contact with strange foreign lands as ships touched at South American ports.

The Gold Rush journals of the Cape Horn voyages document the relationships of the shipboard community, a closed society only periodically opened with each stop at a different port.[41] Many entries address the stress of continual personal contact in a cramped, filthy ship, the problems of self-sufficiency and survival, and the increased self-imposed familiarity with the formerly alien technology and manufactured environment of a ship. Accounts of drunkenness indicate that many passengers found a comforting outlet for the stress of shipboard life and the move to a strange land. Quarrels, fights, and sexual promiscuity were features of some stress-filled voyages. Other comforts included reassuring patriotic celebrations, complete with speeches and amateur theatrical presentations, "whaling" for porpoises and sharks, fishing in the wind for albatrosses off Cape Horn, practical jokes, and various other amusements, all common to the experience of a Cape Horn voyage to California in 1849 and 1850. Perhaps the most common experience of all was the striking clash between expectations and reality. For the first time in American history, a large proportion of the nation's population went to sea with no prior understanding of life in a ship. Like Richard Henry Dana, they found more than they had bargained for.

COOPERATIVE COMPANIES

Most of the initial sailings for California in response to the news of the gold discovery were vessels owned or chartered by cooperative or joint-stock companies. A common means of arranging passage was by joining a cooperative company, usually formed by would-be argonauts who pooled their resources and businessmen and speculators who did not go but chose to finance others in their stead for a cut of the profits. These companies were quickly created in late December of 1848 and the early months of 1849. Many companies started up when one "hundred persons of enterprize advance $300 each, which enables the party to purchase a substantial vessel, and fit her out with cargo and provisions, the ship being used, when in California, as a home for her owners."[42] Shipping merchants and companies formed others.

One such firm, Hamden and Company of New York, in the midst of organizing several cooperative companies, wrote to prospective investor Henry L. Dodge, a New York lawyer, on December 23, 1848. Apologizing for a late response to his inquiry, Hamden and Company wrote that "the numerous letters received upon this subject has made it impossible to give an earlier reply." Three means of investing were available. The first, termed the "most desirable," was to pay $500 for passage, the company chartering the ship "at the lowest price she can be had for" and providing provisions for a round trip. The $500 share would also be used to purchase a speculative cargo, the profits to be split among the shareholders "less our remission as mutually agreed." The second plan called for an investment of $250, but "on arrival out the expedition terminates, each man, after taking his own share of the cargo, goes on his own hook." The final deal involved a $200 investment:

> This enables any gentleman not wishing to go to buy a share . . . for any man as a miner, he may wish to send. The first gold the man gets is to refund the $200 and interest. After that, one-third goes to the miner, and the other two-thirds to the shareholder, for one year—after which the agreement ceases—to the paid over in California to our agents there, ten percent to us out of what may be paid to the shareholder.

The company promised to engage "first rate sailing ships with experienced commanders" for a Cape Horn voyage averaging five months.[43]

Various individuals, usually neighbors or associates from a given town or village, formed other companies. As many as 102 of these joint-stock companies, with an aggregate membership of 4,200 souls, were incorporated in Massachusetts alone in 1849.[44] The names reflect the down-home flavor: Bristol County Mining and Trading Association, Cape Ann Pioneers, Cotuit Port Association, Gloucester Fishing, Mining and Trading Company, Hyannis Gold Company, Nantucket Mining Company, and the Old Harvard Company of Cambridge are but a few. The basic premise of each company was "that all could work in harmony together . . . all standing on the basis of perfect equality in the division of the combined product."[45] George Webster, chronicler of the voyage of the ship *Henry Lee* of the Hartford Union Mining and Trading Company said, "There were to be no bloated stockholders—all should share equal in interest and profits; one share to each man and no more. We were a *commune*—a socialistic order—who believed in the old Spartan division of all spoils. The sick, and the weak, were to be on one common level with the strong and well."[46]

Each company as a formally incorporated body elected officers and voted on bylaws. Directors were to stay in the town of incorporation, while elected managers were to sail with the ship. The number of members and the capitol stock were limited. Members of the Salem and California Mining and Trading Company required a two-thirds vote for admission, and applicants were to be of "good moral character" and pay their $250 share.[47] Specific rules and regulations were enacted for orderly and safe life on board. The Hartford Union Mining Trading Company's rules, for example, stated that lights were to be extinguished by ten P.M., no guns were to be fired on board without permission, smoking between decks was not allowed, powder was to be kept in a magazine, it was "the duty of the members" to keep the "between" decks clean, and members would be divided into messes of twelve.[48] On board the bark *LaGrange*, the Salem and California Mining and Trading Company disallowed work on the Sabbath, and gambling, drinking, or trading for personal benefit. Fines were assessed for violations. On the other hand, all profits were to be equally shared. Members too sick or injured to work would continue to receive their share of the profits, and return passage home would be financed by the company. A nearly identical set of bylaws can be found in the papers of the Essex County and California Mining and Trading Company of Beverly, Massachusetts.[49] The bylaws of most cooperatives companies reflect idealistic and moralistic codes of conduct, and the concept of a socialistic brotherhood.

Despite the regulations, however, codes of conduct dissipated on many long voyages to California. Failure to observe the Sabbath, drunkenness and gambling prevailed on many vessels, particularly as California drew nigh. Disagreement sowed discord as idealism fell prey to reality when the monotonous life at sea gave way to intermittent sprees ashore. The ultimate disillusionment came in California. Every company disbanded immediately upon arrival or soon thereafter. The San Francisco *Daily Alta California*, as early as March 1849 indicated that the fault lay in the failure to invest sufficient funds for "their support far from home. The sum of $300 [per member] is scarcely sufficient for so long a voyage."[50] A member of the Boston and California Mining and Trading Joint Stock Company summed up the experience he and his peers shared as "delusive."[51] The cooperative companies worked best in organizing and bringing parties to the gold fields primarily by way of Cape Horn, "through a combination of capital and effort to secure an economical method of reaching California."[52]

FITTING OUT THE SHIP
The majority of vessels used for transporting passengers via Cape Horn to California had carried few passengers previous to the Gold

Rush. Many were older craft and required repairs, and in some cases, "cosmetic surgery" before they booked passengers and sailed. According to historian John B. Goodman, the ships were "generally, unless new, given a slight reconditioning with a few being recoppered. The ship's furniture, masts, rigging, sails, tackles, stores . . . were overhauled or replaced for the hard usage they would be compelled to withstand."[53]

Captain George Coffin, a packet-trade veteran, who arrived at New Orleans in 1849, and was placed in charge of the ship *Alhambra* "with *carte blanche* to put her in condition for the voyage, and to fit her for two hundred passengers," did just that.[54] Coffin's preparations indicate a responsible outfitting. Costs were high: $10,000 to refit *Alhambra*, including drydocking and recoppering. Coffin left a detailed account of refitting the ship's berth deck to accommodate the passengers. Thirty-eight double staterooms lined the port and starboard sides of the deck, opening onto a deck cleared of all obstructions except the masts. The staterooms, illuminated with sidelights, were well-ventilated: a "large draft hole was cut in each bow." A double row of open berths was built midships between the fore and mainmasts, with four large tables and benches straddling either side and running aft of the mainmast. At the luff of the bows lay rooms and berths for the cooks and stewards. Open cabins at the stern served as the surgeon's quarters and the pantry. Across the stern, rows of shelves held dishes, and six windows opened from the transom to assist in ventilation. A row of washbasins lined the bow. A proud Captain Coffin later noted that "every stateroom was furnished with new mattresses, linen and blankets, and an abundance of spare bedding filled a large clothes-chest, fitted up near the pumproom. Everything was done and furnished that I could think of to make passengers comfortable."[55]

Others had it worse. Edwin Ayer, a passenger on board the bark *Anna Reynolds,* stated in a reminiscent account that "we had a house built on deck which was as near to being the Black Hole of Calcutta as anything I ever knew of. . . . Its dimensions were 14 by 20 feet, with 18 double berths for thirty-six men to sleep and live in. The rest stowed in the cabin, about 20, and 6 sailors in the forecastle."[56] Although cabins built on the decks of other vessels were more spacious, many vessels were crowded. Every bit of space not absolutely mandatory for sailing the ship was packed with cargo or housed over for passengers. Samuel Upham, on board the brig *Osceola* in January 1849, complained that the brig's owners had removed the table and benches for feeding the steerage passengers from the tween deck, and the space was "stowed with cases, chests and trunks . . . consequently the steerage passengers have been compelled to mess on chicken-coops, pig-pens, water-casks, and trunks. . . . The brig has been a perfect Hades since she sailed . . ."[57]

Since the tween decks of many vessels offered little space, ships were outfitted often with new cabins on deck. When the bark *James W. Paige* was readied to sail to California in 1852, the hold was "made into a cabin with fourteen double berths on either side," and three houses were built on deck, one aft with fourteen berths, and one midships with six berths, with the galley placed between the two. "These houses did not occupy the whole width of the deck, but a narrow space was left for a walk around them. There was also a small open space between the cook's galley and the after house, and at the ends of the houses."[58] The quarters built to accommodate passengers were for the most part better than those of the crew in the forecastle, although only a select few on board former passenger ships or vessels like *Alhambra* enjoyed the luxury of a well-appointed stateroom.

Fitting a vessel up with the necessary provisions was also an expensive and laborious task. Although ship chandlers sold the requisite supplies, food, and gear for a ship and her crew, the necessity of feeding several dozen people taxed supplies. In December 1848 and January 1849, Captain Charles Coffin of the ship *Apollo* scoured New York for provisions. His frequent advertisements in the New York *Sun* give evidence of the quantities needed. The good captain asked for 600 barrels of salt pork and beef, 50 barrels of flour, 50 barrels of dried white beans, 25 tierces of rice, 30 hogsheads of molasses, 50 bags of coffee, 20 hogsheads of sugar, "a quantity of rum puncheons suitable for putting up ship bread . . . " and "large water casks or rum puncheons, suitable for carrying water on a voyage to California."[59] Ingenuity marked the efforts of some shipmasters to prepare the food; when his regular whaling voyage was interrupted in order to sail to San Francisco from Panama in 1849, Captain Henry Cleaveland of the whaling ship *Niantic* took his huge cast-iron trypots and converted them into soup kitchens, a unique claim for *Niantic* as a Gold Rush "greasy spoon."

Throughout 1849 and 1850, advertisements of vessels sailing for California stated either that the ship was a new, preferably white oak-built and copper-fastened craft or, like the ship *Sacramento*, was being "rigged, coppered, and fitted up for the comfort and accommodation of passengers."[60] Readied for the passengers and laden with cargo, these ships were then loaded and cleared for California.

DEPARTURE AND THE FIRST WEEK AT SEA

The departure of most Gold Rush ships brought large crowds of family, friends, well-wishers and curious onlookers. When the ship *Xylon* sailed from Baltimore on February 3, 1849, "on the wharves were assembled a dense crowd, principally men, waiting to take their leave of the handful of adventurers who were about to quit their homes."[61] The sailing of the bark *LaGrange* from Salem, Massachusetts, a month later was witnessed by a large crowd; "I should think the whole of Salem was on the wharves to bid us good bye and Godspeed."[62]

The day a vessel left the wharf was not necessarily the day of its final clearance for California. Many were towed through the harbor to the open sea, where pilots were delivered to their stations and favorable winds were sought. In some cases the interval between departure and clearance was prolonged; the bark *Anna Reynolds*, ready to sail on March 12, 1849, was detained at New Haven, Connecticut by stormy weather for five days. Other intervals were short: the ship *Apollo* was towed clear of the ice on January 16, 1849. Moving downriver to Sandy Hook, the following morning *Apollo* sailed south for California.[63]

The vast majority of Gold Rush passengers had never been upon the waters of a lake or a river, let alone the ocean, so often the first week at sea was a time of sickness, despair, soul-searching, and gradual accommodation as reality began to clash with expectations. On board the ship *Apollo* of New York, supercargo Joseph Perkins Beach recorded in his pocket diary a "great deal of grumbling by the passengers [and] if a vote could have been taken & the majority afforded to rule, we should have put back, leaving the 'gold diggins' to persons of greater stability & hardihood" after only three days at sea.[64] The first common experience shared by passengers was seasickness. Two days out of Philadelphia, only three passengers out of sixty-five on board the brig *Osceola* had not succumbed; "the lee-rail is lined with demoralized passengers who are paying their tribute to Old Neptune. Those who are not able to pay their respects to the deity of the great deep over the rail, are casting up their accounts in buckets, wash-basins, and spitoons."[65]

Many voyages, particularly in the beginning months, commenced with violent winter storms at sea. Inevitably trunks, bags, and other effects had been improperly stowed by passengers, causing later problems. Edwin Franklin Morse, on board the ship *Cheshire* of Boston in December 1849, observed "The first night out was very rough and as none of our chests were lashed down they slid and bumped about in all directions, making it as much as a man's life was worth to attempt to get out of his bunk."[66] Joseph Lamson, on board the ship *James W. Paige,* wrote that "The trunks in our cabin were dashing from side to side, breaking chairs and stools and whatever else came their way. The earthenware in the lockers was . . . crashing up in a style that threatened its speedy demolition. All was noise and confusion."[67]

The passengers soon learned about staying put on ship. Some souls, seeking escape from the confines of tween decks that must have rivaled that of the ship *Apollo* (described in January 1849 as "the damp and dirty 'between decks', the 'oniony' smell of which is enough to vomit a horse") ventured on deck during the early storms.[68] Alexander McFarlan, on board the ship *California Packet,* described the scene in March 1850 during the first storm his vessel encountered. Even as the sailors were pitched about in the rigging, and a crewman nearly washed overboard, a group of passengers remained on deck. Then "a heavy sea struck the weather side and gave about 20 of the passengers a complete washing. I was in my bunk when the sea struck . . . when I reached the deck some was picking up their hats and others laying hardly able to rise with the shock. . . . Some wished themselves back with their Mama."[69] On board the ship *Henry Lee* in February 1849, George Webster wrote of a similar if less threatening experience. Holding fast to the bulwarks, "not yet having learned to walk the deck at a very acute angle," and watching the sea, "in a moment we found ourselves under water. . . . we had not been washed often enough in this way to lose our good nature—though we did lose sundry letters and papers which became water-soaked."[70] Sea-legs and sea-smarts came after the first week.

While they became accustomed to their new surroundings in a constantly pitching, confined world, the passengers sized up their fellows as well as captain and crew. Some travelers, immediately disliking the master and his officers, hated shipboard discipline and the imposition of an absolute rule in their lives. Others adapted by striving to be sailorlike, noting the ship's position in their daily journals and acquiring nautical jargon. Close contact with people from every walk of life invariably provided trouble as well as amusement. Joseph Perkins Beach, writing about the passengers assembled on the ship *Apollo* of New York, noticed that they seemed to consist of four "castes—1st of a few gentlemen 2d—half genteel and mighty nice boys—3d—a choice lot of regular New York 'Be Jesus and Holy Krister' boys—4th—The piggish, swinish loafers, and a private party of Philadelphia Killers."[71] Cyrus W. Pease, on *Walter Scott* in June 1849, noted that "for all the *romance* of our situation as treasure-seekers and all that . . . from the associations and associates with which we are surrounded, good Lord deliver us."[72]

FOOD

Lacking refrigeration, shipowners and masters stocked up for a long voyage by purchasing nearly imperishable—and sometimes inedible—salted meats, densely baked biscuits known as "hardtack," beans, rice, molasses, vinegar and, occasionally for the officer's tables—tinned meats, preserves, and condensed milk. The menu on a ship was monotony itself, drawing upon the four staples of salted meat, hardtack, rice, and beans. Twice a week the ship's cook prepared duff, a pudding baked with suet, dried fruit, and flour. Occasionally the cook prepared lobscouse, a hash made from boiling potatoes, onions, salt meat, and hardtack. Lobscouse was a favorite diversion in the menu, its absence prompting a near-mutiny on at least one California-bound Gold Rush vessel. In 1849, as *Apollo* of New York stood off the Peruvian coast, a passenger demanded that the cook serve lobscouse every morning for the passengers' mess. "The Capt. told him it could not be allowed, whereupon Mr. Stokes said the passengers *would have it by force.* Some conversation held on deck, then a meeting was called below—a committee appointed to *argufy* & after waiting upon the Capt. found themselves no better off than before."[73]

Undoctored salt meat was horrible. Unscrupulous contractors who provided the meat counted on the salted barrels being stowed away and unopened for months—usually thousands of miles out to sea. Poorly selected cuts, hastily butchered pieces, weight and mass achieved mostly by bone, fat and salt were common. Salted meat had to be steeped in water for at least twenty-four hours to be edible. On some ships the meat was placed in a metal cage and towed astern to wash the salt out before the still-tough flesh was boiled into a meal.

Sailors constantly grumbled over their provisions; the forty-niners were even more vociferous in their condemnation of the fare. John N. Stone, on board the ship *Robert Bowne* in 1849, said, "Heretofore divers complaints had been made to Captain Cameron by word of mouth and by different passengers of the most intolerable privations of proper food. . . . The beef, bread and pork that was good or eatable were stowed beyond reach; the passengers compelled to eat what was familiarly called 'old horse,' [beef as dry and tasteless as a piece of oak wood], pork frequently yellow and tainted—sometimes even very offensive to the smell; and old navy bread, that was both mouldy and wormy."[74] Another man complained that he was sick of the salt beef served because every time he ate he thought of the sailor's ditty that the mate obligingly sang for the passengers at meal time:

Old Horse! Old Horse! what brought you here?
From Sacarap' to Portland pier
I've carted stone this many a year;
Till, killed by blows and sore abuse,
They salted me down for sailors' use.
The sailors they do me despise;
They turn me over and damn my eyes;
Cut off my meat and pick my bones,
And pitch the rest to Davy Jones.[75]

Other passengers were more subdued. Richard L. Hale, a passenger on the brig *General Worth* in 1849, commented,

It is impossible to appreciate the value of fresh food on shipboard. The usual fare is hard baked biscuit, called by the sailors 'hard-tack,' baked very hard to prevent moulding, and beef as salty as salt itself, to keep it from spoiling, named in sea language 'salt-junk,' and 'salt-horse' with 'duff' or boiled pudding, served once a week, and a hash when they are fortunate enough to have potatoes, while an occasional dish of beans, together with tea and coffee constitute the sea-going bill of fare.[76]

Yet passengers adapted to the food. "Our friends would have difficulty in recognizing us as the same persons that sailed from New York last January. We have become reconciled to the privations of physical comforts; we drink our bitter coffee, without milk, with relish; we never grumble at the salt beef and pork while we have soft bread and vinegar, for we have 'duff' or pie for dessert."[77] Howard Gardiner recorded the same phenomenon: "We had not been out long before every man on board had found his place and become in a measure reconciled to his surroundings. . . . though the quality of the food was far below what we had been accustomed to, good appetites gave it a relish and we always came up hungry at meal time."[78]

ADJUSTING TO A STRANGE NEW WORLD

Most passengers quickly identified with the world of the mariner. Thrust into a new environment where the captain was absolute master in name and deed, the majority strove for acceptance by consorting with officers and crew, at times helping to work the ship. Many passengers adopted the language and characteristics of maritime subculture, their journals increasingly containing the jargon of a seafaring life—"up" and "down" being replaced by "aloft" and "below"—and emulating logs kept by the officers, replete with notations of latitude and longitude, the number of nautical miles sailed, the handling of sails, and weather and sea conditions. A number of vessels had passengers participate in "crossing the line" ceremonies.

During some voyages only new members of the crew were inaugurated by Father Neptune, but on others, passengers also participated. On board the ship *London* of Liverpool in November 1849, Thomas Kerr described a two-day celebration by passengers and crew wherein all passengers escaped the traditional initiation of a dunking and a shave by paying Neptune a gallon of grog. Everyone got wet, however, because the steerage passengers threw buckets of water, and the sailors unleashed torrents of water from casks and buckets lashed to the rigging.[79] One passenger on *Alhambra* refused to pay Neptune's fee. Blindfolded, lathered with a paintbrush full of grease, and shaved with a rusty hoop of iron, he was baptized in a tub of seawater in the best sailor fashion.[80]

On *Apollo,* passenger Joseph Perkins Beach discussed how acclimated he had become: "[We] went through the business of hair cutting—2nd Steward *the barber* a ten-gallon keg *the chair,* a coil of rope to brace the feet, and a round pocket shaving glass, *the mirror,* truly a life on the ocean wave."[81] A regular day on board *Henry Lee* was described by George Webster in 1849. "To give our friends a more lifelike view of the mode of passing our time at sea," he detailed everyone and everything he saw on deck the afternoon of August 1. A number of passengers were engaged in sitting and reading or holding discussions. Some were playing chess, backgammon, and checkers, and a heated game of cards was transpiring in the mizzentop. Others were slumbering; "one at his side is sleeping soundly; two are on their backs, and three on their faces. A group of passengers sat in a cluster, "guessing ages," while another man sat polishing his knife, and another carved a ship model. As the evening falls, the passengers "assemble on deck, standing in groups along the waist and are either discussing the prospects awaiting them, or some other subject . . . or listening to the songs of someone near them." Late at night, in the tropics, a regular pillow fight breaks out over sleeping space on the hurricane deck. "Our mothers at home would scold if they could see how the mattresses, blankets, and pillows fly."[82]

But these events became commonplace, even boring, as Garrett Low on the ship *Washington Irving* lamented in May 1851. "Every day hears the same stories told, the same book read. Old games have been worn out, new ones invented, and they are gone, and we have nothing left but to walk or climb the rigging."[83] Still, diversions in the routine served as comforts in the alien world of the ship. Among the diversions that continually appear in Cape Horn journals, diaries, and letters are practical jokes, "whaling" for porpoises and fishing for sharks, musical and theatrical entertainment, debates and discussions, patriotic celebrations, drinking sprees, and fighting with the skipper.

Both passengers and crew indulged in practical jokes. The passengers on board the ship *Sutton* were particularly clever. When Thomas Whaley set his seawater-soaked mattress on deck to dry, several passengers, aided by the crew, tied a line to it, hauled it to the mizzentop, and raised a cry that it had blown overboard. The distraught Whaley begged the skipper to lower a boat to save it, offering him five dollars to do so, all the while "lamenting the loss of the bed." The skipper, searching from the stern with his glass, was let in on the joke, and as Whaley went below, the line was cut, allowing the bed to plunge through the open hatch into the tween deck, where it landed before a thoroughly flabbergasted Whaley.[84]

Several jokes were played out on board the ship *James W. Paige* in 1852. A "simple, honest, credulous" passenger was told that a passing brig was a pirate vessel. Later that night, several other passengers threw empty barrels overboard, yelled that the pirates had sent boats to board them, and opened fire with pistols and rifles. "Then came a man tumbling and rolling about with terrible groans and yells, pretending to be wounded, and a moment after a cry went through the ship that the pirates were boarding us." The passenger for whose benefit the scene was being enacted rushed on deck, armed and prepared to defend the ship with his life, only to be met with considerable merriment.[85] On another occasion, some wags replaced the heels of the chief steward's boots with hardtack. The angry steward complained to the mate, who suggested he not complain since the hardtack might last longer than leather.[86] On another occasion, a passenger who could successfully imitate the captain's voice dressed in the skipper's coat and hat late at night, put the mate on watch through the paces, and was discovered only when he gave an order "not in a nautical style. . . . the mate hesitated, someone in [on] the secret laughed and betrayed the joke."[87]

Many passengers put themselves in a jollier humor by drinking. One of the more sodden voyages happened on the ship *Apollo* in 1849. Three weeks out of New York, a group of passengers "brought out brandy, wine, liquors &c and made a huge pail of punch, thereafter putting a little steam on board. They organized themselves, making Major Stevens president, Dr.—vice—etc. & at it they went, hauling others out of their bunks to make them go on deck, drink a cup of punch & propose a sentiment, which was replied to by cheers. They kept up till daylight, when one of the drunken rowdies who held the pail sang out 'Land!'—where? was the exclam[ation]. 'at the bottom of this pail'!"[88] Passengers on some voyages gave liquor to the crew, causing problems for the officers. *Apollo's* mate had to jump into the forecastle and use fisticuffs to recover a keg of brandy one morning.[89]

Two diversions eagerly embraced were whaling for porpoises and dolphins from the bowsprit stays, and fishing for sharks from the sides. On board *Robert Bowne,* the passengers particularly relished the flesh of a harpooned porpoise. "Don't know how it would relish to a landsman; but to the passengers . . . it was a court dainty, fit for a Emperor. So would have stewed dogs and cats, or even genuine 'Old Horse'—barring the hoofs."[90] The passengers and crew of the bark *Orion* constantly whaled for porpoises during their voyage to California, prompting passenger Seth Draper to comment that "hardly a day passes but that we have had a visit from some of the monsters of the deep. . . . We have caught a number of porpoises, certain parts of which serve to make a very palatable dish, as fresh provisions are becoming quite scarce with us."[91] Fishing for sharks, while providing not as much gustatory delight, did add an element of adventure. On board the ship *Cheshire* in 1849, passenger Edwin Franklin Morse excitedly told the story of sharks caught with huge iron hooks baited with salt pork. One was caught and hauled aboard with ropes under the mate's supervision:

> Just as the huge man-eater rose over the side, it flopped around suddenly and caught the mate across the body with its powerful jaws. It ripped off his waistcoat and clothes as if they had been paper, but fortunately it did not reach the flesh. . . .; if he had been a little nearer, it would have snapped him in two. It took a great deal of clubbing about the head to put the big fish out of commission. They cut the shark up, kept the huge jaws with the rows of cruel teeth, and some of us men took pieces of its skin, which was as rough as emery paper.[92]

The sport was aptly summed up by Cyrus W. Pease after a successful day's whaling on board the ship *Walter Scott* sailing from Edgartown, Massachusetts: "Sea monsters are natural enemies of all New Bedforders, Nantucketers and Vineyarders and we feel ourselves bound in honour to attack them upon every suitable opportunity—but the secret of it is, it is the most rare, wild and exciting sport that can be conceived of."[93] Be it for sport or for fresh meat, forty-niners regularly harvested the sea for porpoises and other monsters of the deep as they made their way to California.

In calm seas during hot weather, many passengers amused themselves by swimming around the ship, diving from the sides and sporting in the water. However the seafaring sons of Martha's Vineyard on board the ship *Walter Scott* were a different bred. Tying a rope from the bowsprit, they dangled fifteen feet down into the water. Cyrus Pease was the first to try it and exclaimed, "It was rapturous—The sensation produced by the eccentric and peculiar motion of the ship I cannot describe. It was like that a man feels when he is under the influence of morphine, as seated on some cloud, he is whirled round in the eddying vortex of a whirlwind. . . . It was a moment of intense delight." Rigging a canvas seat under the bowsprit, the passengers and crew enjoyed their novel amusement. So did the captain, who was the "first to be soused" on the new seat. Other amusements aboard other ships included setting ablaze barrels of tar and gunpowder or participating in shooting matches. On the bark *San Francisco* in August 1849, "a junk bottle is made fast to a float and towed astern and our marksmen, fully equipped with rifles, muskets and pistols are blazing away as if in earnest. The aforesaid bottle after undergoing as much anxiety as bottles can and dodging about the wake of the barque as much as the man at the helm will allow, finally came in safe from its precarious situation shining like a dollar and ready for another trial."[94]

Other amusements included music and dancing. Singing, especially hymns, filled part of the bill. Many passengers as the voyage progressed discovered they had numerous musical instruments on board. On the ship *London* of Liverpool, a band was formed with "2 flutes, 2 Cornopeons . . . & our cook rattled away on one of his tin boilers that he kept between his legs."[95] On the ship *Apollo*, Joseph Perkins Beach remarked, "We muster a violinist, two flute players, a flageolet, several accordion players & two instruments and a jews harp—all pretend to understand singing, but scarcely anyone really does."[96] The decks of many vessels were the stage for regular concerts as well as impromptu performances, including those when passengers joined sailors in traditional dogwatch musical displays. The most popular songs were penned by argonauts recounting their adventures, the most famous being "Oh, California!" (to the tune of Stephen Foster's "Oh, Susannah!"), which was written for the voyage of *Eliza* of Salem. On board the ship *Capitol* of Salem, a lesser-known ditty was penned on the subject of a leather bucket that was used to draw water for bathing. The crew drew the water early in the voyage, but after a disagreement between the captain and the passengers the latter had to fend for themselves. When the bucket fell overboard and was lost, the ship's wags wrote a parody, "The Old Leather Bucket," which included the stanza "How eager each mortal did stand to receive it, As poised on the rail their basins did dip, Not the bell for breakfast could tempt them to leave it, 'Twas filled with the water old Neptune did sip," and the refrain, "The old leather bucket, the recent lost bucket, the slab-sided bucket, Which lay on the rail."[97]

Celebrations of holidays and shoreside political events occupied considerable attention. Although passengers and crews did not usually celebrate holidays at sea during the nineteenth century, "one major divergence from this general trend occurred among the thousands of gold seekers in the hundreds of vessels that sailed . . . around Cape Horn to San Francisco in 1849." Historian Charles Schultz ascribes as a possible motive the fact that "the Forty-Niners made strong efforts to live aboard ship just as they did ashore, possibly influenced by the fact that very few of these pioneers had ever been to sea before."[98] The continuation of important, almost religious rites and celebrations (particularly the most common and most sacred of all—being Independence Day, or the Fourth of July) was a ritual that reaffirmed the bond with the land and the landsman's society for the argonauts.

Seafaring Fourth of July celebrations included speeches, flag-hoisting, banquets, fireworks or the firing of guns, and merry-making through the night. After Thanksgiving on some vessels and Christmas on most, the next holiday observed often was Washington's Birthday. On board *Robert Bowne*, passengers were mustered on deck by the captain, who read the Declaration of Independence, "a national song was sung . . . a prayer offered . . . oration by Mr. Grant (Captain's Clerk) . . . the singing of the 'Star Spangled Banner.' wound up the ceremonies."[99] The same day was ushered in on the ship *Sutton* with a salute by passengers' pistols and other firearms.[100] Many Irish passengers celebrated St. Patrick's Day. On board *London*, Thomas Kerr and his companions drank two bottles of wine and two bottles of champagne graciously provided by the skipper, "tho we had not the real shamrock to drown."[101] Shoreside political events were celebrated also at sea, including the inauguration of Zachary Taylor and some elections that were conducted as unofficial "straw polls." On the ship *Henry Lee*, an 1849 election of state officers was held and "all business was suspended. Each candidate was zealously supported."[102]

But by far the favorite pastime—and a show of how most passengers failed to come to terms with life at sea—was fighting with the captain of the ship. The rough-and-tumble world of a ship and the extreme authority of a ship's master outraged the sensibilities of many passengers. A number of masters were surly and combative, and mistreated their passengers. By contrast, some skippers got along well enough with passengers, a number even receiving signed testimonials and compliment cards at the end of the voyage.

Jacob D. B. Stillman, aboard *Pacific*, said the captain would not even discuss passenger complaints. When a committee of passengers complained about the food, the captain "abused us roundly, and told us if he had any more trouble with us, he would fire the magazine and blow us all to hell together."[103] On another occasion the captain told Stillman he was withholding pickles and vegetables until the passengers got scurvy. Stillman also complained about the way the ship was worked: "The master damns the mate, the mate damns the second mate, and the second mate damns the sailors, who damn each other and the cook. . . . In short, kindness is a thing I have not seen on board our ship. . . . Our Captain, having passed his life among seamen, is incapable of treating passengers any other way. . . . If a ship-master ever exhibits any gentlemanly spirit, he owes it to something else than the education he receives at sea."[104] Stillman and his fellow passengers triumphed over their captain, who was removed from the ship by the American Consul at Rio de Janeiro. The consular correspondence and official records for Rio and Callao are filled with numerous complaints from passengers, and more than one skipper was removed from command, indicating that not all complaints were invalid.

Some passengers sought revenge on masters they felt had mistreated them by not providing adequate or wholesome food (by far the most frequent complaint) or by being rude and brutish. Garrett Low, on board the former packet *Washington Irving*, wrote a detailed journal of his voyage that included every crime of Captain Plumer's. One scandalous tale involved the master's refusal to repair a fresh-water distilling machine in hot weather. According to Low, two young unescorted sisters on board, Fay and Lilly Barkley, caught the captain's eye. "Captain Plumer wished to lie with Fay and would not release the parts to repair the distilling machine until he did!" To Low and his fellow passengers' chagrin, Lilly Barkley slept with the captain. This and other details of a decidedly scandalous voyage (including several evenings with a passenger's wife) were carefully recorded by Low).

Passenger Joseph Lamson made his tale public, much to the anger of *James W. Paige*'s captain and several of his friends. To a nation that had learned about life at sea through the writings of Richard Henry Dana and felt sympathy for flogged and mistreated seamen, Lamson appealed to public sentiment, leveling a particularly damning criticism of Captain Jackson: "He hates Dana and his 'Two Years Before the Mast,' because Dana's sympathies are enlisted on the side of the oppressed seamen, and against tyrannical ship-masters."[105] Some of the best invective toward masters came in poetry such as that from the passengers of the bark *John G. Colley*. The long testimonial, done in the style of an "epic poem," (but close to doggerel) was titled "A Tribute to those Life-Lasting feelings of Disgust, Contempt, and Scorn Unanimously Entertained, By the Passengers, Officers, and Crews, of the Bark *John G. Colley*, For Captn. William Smith . . . He was the mildest manner'd man That ever scuttled ship or cut a throat." It detailed a number of the skipper's alleged crimes, including nearly wrecking the ship, drunkenness, cruelty, blasphemy, cursing, not providing adequate food, abusing an ill sailor until the man died, and being a former slaver captain.[106] The enmity between masters and passengers on the numerous voyages to California was unparalleled in the history of the two groups.

GETTING READY FOR THE DIGGINGS

Within a few weeks of a vessel's arrival at San Francisco, passengers and crew readied themselves for the coming adventure. Sailors cleaned, painted, and repaired the ship for arrival. On board the brig *Osceola*, only 800 miles from San Francisco, the crew "has been reeving new signal-halyards, repairing the side-ladders, and doing other odd jobs, in order to get the brig "ship-shape" before reaching port."[107] On board the bark *Orion*, passenger Seth Draper described the crew "busily employed painting and fitting ship, scraping, tarring, and setting up rigging."[108] On board the brig *North Bend*, passengers packed "their different articles that have been lying about the vessel promiscuously for four or five months. Some are shaving for the first time since they left Boston."[109]

The most common passenger activity, next to packing trunks, patching clothes, and making themselves "presentable," was making "articles to facilitate operations in the diggings." On board the ship *Henry Lee*, the members of the Hartford Union Mining and Trading Company turned their vessel into a floating factory. The passengers installed benches on opposite sides of the house over the main hatch, put a turning lathe forward of the mizzenmast, cleared midships for a portable forge, and turned the hurricane deck into a tailor's bench. Two boats, suspended from their davits, were "occupied for knitting fish-nets and making pouches for shot and bullets, and sheaths for knives, and belts for pistols." Vices were installed on deck for "filing locks, dirk and bowie knives, or stamps, or other iron work as the mania of the times directed." One participant described the scene:

> While these various departments were in operation, the puffs of the bellows, with the dingy smoke rising and curling above, the

heavy blows of the blacksmith. . . . were seen and heard. Soon the iron is shaped into a crank for a gold-washer. Next in view is the tinner, with his furnace, coppers, sheet-iron and tin, making another part of the washers, and canteens for the company. Opposite him is the joiner, engaged in mortising the frames for the same; while a machinist at the lathe is turning and finishing the cog-wheels. . . . Others are making carts, wagon bodies, wheelbarrows, axe-helves and other articles. . . . Thus the work, day after day, goes merrily on.[110]

The impending arrival weighed heavily. On board the storm-beset brig *North Bend* just a day from San Francisco, passenger Charles Ellis grimly noted, "We fully expected to make the harbor on Thursday morning but regrets are useless. . . . God only knows what is best for us & at present perhaps while we have been delayed by head winds & calms others have rushed on & made their fortunes & some to destruction."[111] On the bark *LaGrange*, passenger Asa Kitfield soberly studied, "reading about Oregon and California by Thornton, an emigrant to Oregon overland." When standing off the Golden Gate in the evening, awaiting sunrise to enter the harbor, Kitfield stated "When I look back on our long voyage and see how we have preserved and have been permitted to behold the long-wished for land, my heart is filled with gratitude."[112]

CARGOES BY WAY OF CAPE HORN

In addition to passengers the vessels that sailed around the Horn to California carried a variety of cargoes, much of it speculative merchandise. The afore-mentioned *Apollo* cleared New York with "adventures of valuable machinery, consigned . . . by parties in this and other cities."[113] The machinery was probably mining equipment carried on speculation. Other cargoes were even more speculative. Gathered by merchants not knowing what would be in demand in California several months hence, the cargoes consisted of small quantities of everything they could think of." When outfitting the 127-ton brig *Tigress* of Boston, the owners scoured hometown stores, sending all the "old odds and ends" that had accumulated and not sold for years.[114]

In addition to haphazardly assembled eclectic cargoes and otherwise unsalable merchandise sent on one-way speculative voyages, every conceivable item available on the market in New York, Boston, London, and a variety of lesser ports was shipped to San Francisco. As California merchants communicated the needs of the San Francisco market, eastern merchants attempted to meet demand by regularly dispatching ships. Building supplies—notably brick, ironwork, glass, and lumber—were usually lucrative cargoes, along with prefabricated wood and iron buildings. Yet even seemingly salable cargoes were often worthless upon arrival in San Francisco.[115]

The uncertain nature of speculative Gold Rush cargoes ruined more than one merchant. Joshua Norton attempted to corner the rice market by buying up all available rice in San Francisco. His capital invested, Norton was about to cash in when two ships loaded with rice arrived, ruining the market, his fortune, and his mind. The deranged merchant—and his particular delusion—later gained notoriety as San Francisco's famed "Norton I, Emperor of the United States and Protector of Mexico."

The needs of the California market gradually became clear, as reflected by high freight rates for lumber and other commodities well-received at San Francisco, particularly for vessels that could quickly bring a cargo to market before prices or demand fell. The need for quick passages on the California trade added a new and romantic chapter to the annals of American shipping. To bring the goods that San Francisco wanted to market, a specific type of vessel previously developed for the China tea trade came into play as the preeminent vessel of the post–rush period. That vessel type was the fabled clipper ship.

CLIPPERS TO CALIFORNIA

Clippers, fine-lined hulls with an emphasis on a streamlined shape, a large sail area, and a daring and skilled master who could wring a fast passage out of a ship, boomed because of the Gold Rush.[116] The rush for speed under sail in America and Great Britain produced increasingly faster vessels. The clipper was a development of the 1840s in response to the China trade. California gold and the need for quick passages to the new "El Dorado" inspired a boom in clipper construction that witnessed the increasing fineness of lines coupled with larger hulls. A race to complete clippers for California ensued through the early 1850s; "shipowners were now in a great hurry to get fast sailing ships quickly in the water in order to reap the benefits of the booming trade with California." "Measurement goods" commanded a freight of $1 per cubic foot, and $60 to $70 per ton was charged for bulkier cargoes."[117]

Clippers were hastily built to replace ships lost to the Gold Rush and to make fast passages to California, Australia (after gold was discovered there in 1852), China, India and the British Isles, particularly after the repeal of Britain's Navigation Acts in 1849 opened Britain to American ships. The fast lines of the clippers shortened the distance to California. Passages dropped from 125 days to 116 days, and then down to the record 89-day, 21-hour passage of *Flying Cloud* from New York to San Francisco from June 2 to August 21, 1851.[118] The speed and relatively predictable nature of clipper arrivals led to the beginning of regular supply-and-demand trade with California though speculation remained an active feature of the market. Clippers carried expensive items and previously unavailable perishables from the East, although some older, slower ships also brought perishables, including ice.

One of the early clipper departures for San Francisco was the 520-ton, Baltimore-built *Architect*, which sailed from New Orleans on January 18, 1849 and arrived at San Francisco on June 28. Principally carrying passengers eager to rush to the gold fields, *Architect* was an exception: most of the clippers that sailed to San Francisco carried few passengers. During the six-month period between June and December of 1852, for example, the average number of passengers carried by 11 clippers was five per vessel; the greatest number carried was 67 passengers brought by the clipper ship *Tornado* on July 1, 1852; the smallest number was one passenger on the clipper *Mandarin* on November 1, 1852.[119]

High-duty freight consisted of smaller, valuable items and was the principal clipper cargo. The cargoes of the clippers *White Squall* and *Witch of the Wave* were typical. When *White Squall* arrived at San Francisco on July 29, 1852, after a 110-day passage from New York, the clipper carried, in addition to five passengers, soap, medicine, coffee, liquor, wallpaper, books and a piano.[120] *Witch of the Wave*, arriving October 19, 1852 after a 116-day passage from Boston, brought "fish, clocks, drugs, finishing nails, 48 dozen coffee mills, varnish, farming tools, 14 bbls. potash, 6 ploughs . . . 100 reams paper . . . lard, cordials, lobsters, 490 cases powder, 19 cases shot, 10 cases scales, 200 ox bows, and assorted goods" along with sixteen passengers.[121]

English writer Frank Marryat, visiting San Francisco in 1851, lamented that Great Britain's ships could not compete with American clipper ships "that could perform a journey round the Horn in a space of time that would enable them to land a cargo, not only clean and in good order, but with a certain degree of regularity. . . ," while

> the ships that have sailed from English ports for San Francisco have been selected from a particularly inferior class of tubs, principally from the erroneous supposition that any thing was good for the diggings. . . . The expensive, dashing clipper leaves New York and, after a three month's passage, lands her cargo clean and dry in San Francisco. . . . The English ship . . . after a

passage of from eight to ten months, arrives . . . with *her* cargo. The market has not only gone by for the articles she brings, but these, from long confinement, and her unseaworthy properties, are landed in such an unprepossessing state as to be almost unsaleable.

Marryat observed that American clippers discharged at San Francisco, sailed to China, loaded expensive teas, and returned to New York full, "having accomplished a rapid voyage around the world and, in all probability, cleared a large portion of her . . . cost" while English vessels "can find no cargo to take home from San Francisco . . . so she either goes home empty at a great expense, or . . . is knocked down at auction for less than her value, and is converted into a floating store-ship."[122] With the introduction of the clipper ship, California was linked to the established world markets in Europe and the United States. While the clippers regularly brought freight, passenger service by way of Cape Horn was a short-lived phenomenon of the Gold Rush. Another oceanic link between the Atlantic and Pacific coasts, the route by way of Panama and Nicaragua, became the dependable link for passengers.

Chapter Two
VIA THE ISTHMUS

The California gold discovery revived a centuries-old sea route linking the Pacific and Caribbean oceans, as tens of thousands of gold-seekers crossed the narrow breadth of Central America at Panama and Nicaragua and booked passage in ships to San Francisco. The forty-mile-wide Isthmus of Panama had served as a major link in Spanish trade and commerce from the sixteenth century. The route faltered with the decline of Spain's American empire in the nineteenth century. By the 1830s, however, renewed interest in Panama by South American, British, and United States politicians, businessmen, and entrepreneurs increased Panamanian transit.[1] The war with Mexico and the conquest of California in 1846 heightened U.S. interest in Panama. In 1847 Congress responded to the need for better communication with the new Pacific territories by subsidizing two steamship companies to serve the Panama route. The United States Mail Steamship Company and the Pacific Mail Steamship Company were born.[2]

The government financed the two lines in return for their carrying U.S. mail and permitting the use of their steamers as auxiliary warships in the event of hostilities. The contract to carry the mail between Panama and the Oregon Territory was granted to Arnold Harris of Nashville, Tennessee, "a person with influential political connections" who had placed the winning bid. Harris had no intention of creating his own steamship line, however, and assigned his contract, at a profit, to William Henry Aspinwall, the principal partner in the firm of Howland and Aspinwall, the largest import-export house in New

York. Howland and Aspinwall ships traded around the world, calling at England, the Continent, the Mediterranean, South America, the Caribbean, and China.[3] The venture into steam navigation was risky business. Facilities for the provisioning, coaling, and repair of steamers did not exist north of Panama on the Pacific Coast, and returns would be small because travel by that route was still minor.

Aspinwall negotiated with the Post Office Department to confirm the details of his contract. His steamers would have to be in the Pacific by the Spring of 1848, and would touch at various Mexican and California ports. With the details confirmed, Aspinwall, G. G. Howland, Henry Chauncey, and Edwin Bartlett organized the Pacific Mail Steamship Company, chartered and incorporated by the New York Legislature on April 12, 1848, for "the purpose of building, equipping, furnishing, purchasing chartering, and owning vessels, to be propelled solely by steam or other expansive fluid or motive power, to be run and propelled in navigating the Pacific Ocean."[4]

Three small steamships were ordered by the new company. Two of the vessels, *California* and *Panama*, were contracted for with William H. Webb of New York. The third, *Oregon*, was ordered from the New York shipyard of Smith and Dimon. *California*, launched on May 19, 1848, and the first Pacific Mail steamer to depart for the Pacific, cleared New York on October 6, 1848.[5] By the time it reached Panama, gold fever had set in and the small vessel, built to accommodate sixty passengers, was crowded with more than 360 eager gold-seekers. *Panama* and *Oregon* soon arrived and were also overcrowded, voyage after voyage. The press of business nearly overwhelmed Aspinwall. In January 1849 he confided to a friend:

> I fear I have lost all character with you as a correspondent. I must get Louisa to exculpate me by letting you know what a snarl I am in from this California fever. I am half ruined by postage & have two clerks to answer letters & these have proved so inadequate that I have had to resort to printed circulars—In this state of things the letters which I reserve for myself occasionally, as now, get far behind.[6]

The situation in Panama required finding a solution to the problem of the inadequate Pacific Mail steamers:

> From early morning until late at night the frontage of the harbor was crowded with anxious searchers for means of exit from the place . . . there was much discontent and uneasiness, and, of course, much unhappiness. . . . A steamer arrived . . . but would take only those who had purchased through tickets. There

were a few taken, however, at exorbitant rates who happened to have plenty of money, but the balance of us were as lonely as ever.[7]

Many stuck in Panama booked passage on sailing vessels that called. Joseph Crackbon, a San Francisco-bound passenger on the brig *Sylph* noted, "I am fairly disgusted with Panama, and never left any place more willingly." Crackbon admitted, "I have no idea of being contented with *any place*, till I have been to *the mines* and got my pocket full of rocks." Crackbon and his fellow passengers put up with considerable discomfort to flee Panama: *Sylph* sailed with 182 persons, "rather more than we can accommodate."[8]

Another sailing vessel caught up in the Panama Route was the whaling ship *Niantic* of Warren, Rhode Island. Early in 1849, *Niantic* abruptly ended a voyage to the Pacific whaling grounds when Captain Henry Cleaveland stopped to provision the ship at Paita, Peru. Learning of the California gold discovery and the detention of thousands on the isthmus, Cleaveland landed his whaling gear and laid in supplies, lumber, and 150 mules for a Panama pack train. Arriving at Panama on April 7, 1849, *Niantic* lay at anchor for the next three weeks as the crew labored to build bunks in the hold and ready the ship for passengers. Signing on 249 passengers at prices ranging from $150 to $250 each, Cleaveland was ready to depart on May 2. Clearing Panama, *Niantic* made a 62-day passage to San Francisco.[9] The vagaries of sailing made some passengers wish for a steamer. As *Niantic* lay becalmed, passenger Elliot Cook wrote, "I thought laying idle in Panama was the worst thing possible, but being becalmed at sea in the tropics is a—I had almost said a dam'd sight worse."

To meet the demand and profit from the business going to occasional callers at Panama, Aspinwall obtained the British steamer *Unicorn* from the Cunard Line. *Unicorn*, a 648-ton sidewheeler, was built at Greenock, Scotland as a coastal steamer running between Glasgow and Liverpool. In 1840 the steamer was purchased by the British and North American Royal Mail Steam Packet Company, (later the Cunard Steamship Company, Ltd.) for coastal service on Canada's atlantic shore in conjunction with the company's transatlantic steamers. Reboilered in 1848, the tiny steamer was sent into the Pacific in 1849 after being chartered by a desperate Aspinwall.[10]

Meanwhile, Aspinwall searched for suitable larger vessels to augment the Pacific Mail fleet. His search led him to the office of Samuel L. Mitchill of the New-York and Savannah Steam Navigation Company, who sold him the company's new steamer, *Tennessee*. Then running between New York and Savannah, she became the first American steamship whose service was interrupted in order to be sent to Panama. Built in 1848 by William H. Webb, the 1,194-ton steamer made only a handful of coastal voyages for the owners before Aspinwall snapped it up.[11] Approved for the government by the Navy's Board of Naval Constructors for service under the Pacific Mail's contract, *Tennessee* was provisioned and prepared for a Pacific voyage by way of the Straits of Magellan. On November 22, 1849, sailing was advertised for December 1.[12] *Tennessee's* departure was delayed, however. Stormy weather kept the officers from loading the last of the provisions and coal. Nearly a hundred people had booked passage, but as the steamer sat at the wharf, many departed for home. When *Tennessee* was finally ready to sail on December 5, she carried only fifteen passengers.[13]

During an uneventful passage to Rio de Janeiro, *Tennessee* passed the equator on December 23. Arriving at Rio on December 31, 1849, she remained for two weeks replenishing coal. The steamer cleared on January 14, 1850, and battled winter storms in the straits to reach Valparaiso on February 16. After a ten-day layover, *Tennessee* cleared Valparaiso on February 16, 1850; "She takes but few passengers as few are willing to run the risk of getting from Panama. It is the report here that there are 3,000 persons at Panama waiting for a passage up."[14]

Tennessee arrived at Panama on March 12, 1850, after a passage of fifty-seven days (at sea) from New York. The passage had been fast, notwithstanding a delay in the straits. Passengers had been waiting for at least a week, including a large number who had booked passage to Panama on *Cherokee*, operating on the Atlantic side of the Panama route. Tempers were short in overcrowded Panama, and any delay incited angry demonstrations:

> The tardy arrival of the Tennessee gave rise to some indignation meetings, but one laughable event occurred. While the feeling was at its height, a meeting was being held on the plaza, sundry resolutions—having for their purport to take the "Panama" steamer, and go to your city [San Francisco] without leave or license—were being passed, when a party came from the walls and said the Tennessee had just dropped her anchor. Immediately all thoughts of the Panama were done away with and indignation stock fell 100 per cent. Where before there were to be seen nothing but frowns, now all were smiles, greeting passed between men who had met and passed fifty times a day with a mere nod, as would pass between intimate friends that had not met for years—or in other words, all before was night, now all was morning.[15]

Panama welcomed *Tennessee* "with demonstrations of joy." The Panama *Echo* of March 16, 1850, noting the ship's arrival, stated:

> This great leviathian of the Pacific came careening up in majestic style, towards the anchorage . . . and as she neared the place of mooring, the batture was lined with smiling countenances and sparkling eyes and stalwart arms, all ready to join in the loud huzza—hail, all hail; the welcome of the glorious ship, old Tennessee—and the chorus of that beautiful melody, "Away down in Tennessee, A li, e li, u li, e . . ." was instantly on the lips of the gratified concourse who were assembled to witness the ship's swanlike approach to the harbor![16]

Additional vessels followed as Aspinwall bought other steamers, some still in the stocks, and contracted with New York shipbuilders to expand his fleet. By 1851 the Pacific Mail fleet boasted fourteen vessels, starting with the large "flagship" of the company, the 2,500-ton *Golden Gate*, the three pioneers *California, Oregon* and *Panama*, the ships *Tennessee* and *Unicorn*, the 1,200-ton steamers *Republic* and *Northerner*, and six smaller steamers—*Columbia, Antelope, Carolina, Columbus, Isthmus*, and *Fremont*. Linking the two coasts with the United States Mail steamers, the Pacific Mail ships ran biweekly to San Francisco and connected with steamers linking San Francisco to Astoria, Oregon. A typical advertisement for the line, published in 1851, announced that the U.S. and Pacific Mail companies, "Forming the only through line for California, and Oregon, via Chagres or Navy Bay," connected New York to Chagres and Panama City to San Francisco, with two steamers, *Falcon* and *El Dorado*, operating between New Orleans and Chagres. Fares ranged from $200 steerage to $315 first class, children under twelve years traveling for half fare, and "landing and transit of the Isthmus at the expense of the passengers."[17]

THE ISTHMIAN CROSSING

Much like the Cape Horn passage, a journey to California via the Panama Route was characterized by common experiences attendant to each voyage. After booking passage on a steamer or sailing vessel to the Caribbean shore of Panama, passengers landed at Chagres, and crossed the isthmus by mule, on foot, or in small native canoes that carried them part way across on the Chagres River. The canoes were poled upriver by native boatmen and at night were pulled up the bank with passengers camping alongside huge fires lit by their guides. They listened all night long, as Charles Winslow complained to his wife, to the "screeching of parrots, the clattering of woodcocks, the gibberish of monkeys, & the howling of tigers."[18]

American entrepreneurs placed seven small steamers on the Chagres River between 1849 and 1851, starting with the 247-ton wooden sidewheeler *Orus*. Faster than canoes, the steamers were not always able to ascend the river's shallow depths to reach the head of navigation at Gorgona. A village of about 100 houses, Gorgona was situated on the banks of the Chagres. Surrounded by mountains over which the trail to Panama City and the Pacific Ocean passed, the village lay "in a natural amphitheatre perpetually reflected from the sparkling streamlet." Travelers usually stayed the night at small hotels or boarded in the homes of residents. After staying in Gorgona, and perhaps "becoming tired of eating mule steaks, dead pork, and iguana pie . . ." Panama-bound travelers walked over the mountains or booked passage with a mule train:

> With our mules in a string we plunged at once into a narrow, rocky path in the forest, where palm-trees and creepers shut the light out overhead—splashing through gurgling, muddy streams, that concealed loose and treacherous stones—stumbling over fallen trees that lay across our road—burying ourselves to the mules' girths in filthy swamps, where on either side the dead and putrid mules were lying amidst lightning, thunder, and incessant rain, we went at a foot-pace on the road to Panama.[19]

The ancient Pacific port of Panama City lay at the end of the road from Gorgona. Newly arrived travelers enjoyed narrow streets hemmed by balconied homes, local customs, ornately ornamented cathedrals and churches, and the activities of other impatient gold-seekers. In the early months of 1849, the lack of vessels calling at Panama to sail on to San Francisco resulted in a population boom. The gold-seekers whiled away the time strolling about town, exploring the nearby countryside, working to raise money for passage in arriving vessels, or drinking to excess and fighting among themselves. The accommodations added to their displeasure. "He keeps the best hotel in the place . . . they are all miserable poor affairs, poor food, badly cooked, no beds, eight to twelve dirty cots in a room, and everything else to match; board from eight to twelve dollars a week."[20]

Tropical disease was rife among the crowded lodgings of the forty-niners. Cholera, malaria, and the effects of "dissipation" killed off hundreds in Panama, and funerals were a daily sight. "Two American funerals to day, one Man and one woman a Mrs. Hardy. She has left a Husband here and a young child. It would have been mercifull to his family had he thrown them into the sea at New York instead of bringing them here to die by inches in this climate."[21] Still, the American population of Panama continued to grow in the first months of 1849. "The crowd at Panama was daily augmented by the arrival of passengers from the Atlantic, and the question 'how to get away'? became a very serious one."[22]

Under these circumstances, the angry demonstration of *Tennessee* passengers over a tardy arrival is clearly understood. Edward Hotchkiss, a twenty-seven-year-old merchant from New Haven, Connecticut, noted in a letter home to his mother, "If Howland & Aspinwall only knew the imprecations that were daily showered on their heads it would give them a shock to say the least." Hotchkiss was among the angry passengers who had held "indignation meetings," telling his mother about one meeting and stating "H & A are very much to blame in issuing tickets so long before hand, there are passengers here from New Orleans that have been waiting for the Tenessee [sic] 6 weeks." The problem of not enough steamers, was, however, in time answered with the boom of vessels in the Pacific Mail fleet and the various "opposition steamers" that were built or chartered.[23]

The difficulty of crossing the isthmus by canoe and muleback, or worse, by foot, early compelled William Henry Aspinwall and his partners to plan for, lay out, and construct a railroad across Panama's swamps, jungles, and mountains. Commenced in 1849, the Panama Railroad's broad-gauge track stretched atop pilings driven across swamps, and climbed through mountain passes for forty-seven miles. Starting in the small port of Aspinwall (Colon), the railroad ran along the shores of Navy Bay past Gatun and ascended the river to follow the same path prerailroad travelers had taken. The first locomotives and cars, built by Niles and Co. of Cincinnati, were brought by ship and reassembled in August 1851. In early 1852 the trains ran as far as Gatun—twelve miles from Aspinwall and at the mouth of Navy Bay. By July 1852 the line ran twenty-three miles into the jungle to Barbacoas. Bridging the 300-foot-wide Chagres at Barbacoas, the line was slowly built up into the mountains through 1853.

Disease and death plagued the railroad builders, as it did the later canal builders, and only after hundreds of deaths did the railroad finally reach the summit of the coastal mountains overlooking Panama City in January 1854. There, 242 feet above sea level and eleven miles from Panama, thirty-seven miles distant from Aspinwall, the vast Pacific finally came into view. Crossing deep swamps and scaling the mountains, the last few miles were built; "on the 27th day of January, 1855, at midnight, the last rail was laid, and on the following day a locomotive passed from ocean to ocean."[24] As the first transcontinental railroad in the Americas, the Panama Railroad revolutionized isthmian travel. Instead of landing in canoes or wading ashore on native backs at Chagres to pole and hike across, by 1853 passengers landed at spacious piers in Aspinwall. There people, mail, and baggage were loaded into the waiting cars and run across the isthmus, by 1855 making the entire transit in a few hours. After 1855 passengers disembarked at the Panama City terminal, built next to a large pier where small steam tugs transported them to the waiting steamship.

THE VOYAGE TO SAN FRANCISCO

The voyage of a Panama steamer to San Francisco offered little variety in the routine. The first voyage of the steamer *Tennessee* from Panama to San Francisco was typical in many respects. Eager passengers at Panama with tickets were joined by the less fortunate who, working their way north in the steamers, formed the backbone of many Pacific Mail crews. Among the latter was thirty-one-year-old James Rogers, who had been in Panama nearly five months when *Tennessee* arrived. His finances exhausted, Rogers was fortunate to be hired as a waiter on board to work his passage to San Francisco;

> They ship sailors, waiters, bakers, butchers, cooks & these on various terms. Some ship to stay by the ship until she returns here and goes back to California the second time, depositing $100 with the agent as a pledge that they will faithfully perform their part of the contract; and they get a specified sum per month. . . . Others ship for the trip up to San Francisco and for twelve days after arrival, depositing the $100 pledge, and get their month's wages if they stay by the ship the twelve days. . . . I shipped for the trip up and twelve days, giving my *word* as a pledge . . . and am to have $20 per month as wages.[25]

John B. Peirce, a merchant from Salem, Massachusetts, and Henry Peters, of New York, had a slight wait at Panama compared to James Rogers and were delighted when *Tennessee*, for which they were ticketed, arrived. On the evening of Friday, March 22, *Tennessee* came up to Panama, anchoring off the city at 6:00 P.M. The next morning passengers began to come aboard with their baggage. *Tennessee* was scheduled to depart on Sunday, March 24, for San Francisco.

The steerage passengers came aboard on Saturday, March 23. Steerage passage to San Francisco cost $150, and those passengers slept forward of the engines, below deck in the hold:

> They cleared out the run or cellar under, down below all the others and fitted up . . . berths, and many a poor fellow when he came on board and was shown his shelf in the cellar—damp, dark, stench as it is—turns up his nose and says this is surely not what I bargained for.[26]

On the morning of Sunday, March 24, the cabin passengers came on board. Cabin passengers slept above deck in the houses in 6-by-5 staterooms with three bunks. When *Tennessee* hoisted anchor and steamed from Panama on March 24, 1850, 164 cabin passengers and 387 steerage passengers were on board, the largest number of passengers thus far carried to San Francisco on a single vessel.

Some unfortunates—usually steerage passengers—were unable to obtain berths and slept on deck; "the purser has meted out an old mainsail for them with a perquisite of five or ten dollars he hopes will satisfy them."[27] Accommodations were better in the staterooms; Henry Peters wrote after his first night at sea that a difference from muggy Panama was welcome. "Such a night's sleep as I had has not blessed my weary frame for many a day; a fine cool air blew in at our port all night, and it was really delightful to lie in one's berth and feel it."[28]

There were no complaints in the cabin about the food. Edward Hotchkiss remarked, "We all have our appointed places at meals & the fare is very good."[29] Henry Peters was pleased to find "at supper everything was clean, and the eatables in abundance; good butter and potatoes were indeed a luxury to us."[30] John B. Peirce, despite complaints of overcrowding, also voiced his approval of the meals:

> Is not a monopoly worth having? Well can they afford to give us chickens, Turkey, Goose, Duck, Beef, Pork, Lamb & Kid all fresh, Beef, Ham, Pork & Fish salted, Rasins [*sic*], Prunes, Almonds, Filberts, Preserves, Tea, Coffee, Loaf Sugar, Pies, Puddings, Cakes, Cheese, Butter, Sardines, Green Peas, Green Corn, Green Beans, Pickles, Oranges, Bananas, Hot Cakes, Honey, Jams, Buckwheats, Eggs, Omelets, &c, &c. Well can they afford us the luxuries of the table, they are well paid, and I don't complain of our living, it is good enough and too good.[31]

Meals in steerage were "served out in messes and regular sailor fare. It is dealt out and their mode of feeding is the soup house style." Each passenger approached the bar with tin pot and pan in hand and was served salt beef, duff (a boiled pudding made from suet, flour, and dried fruit), coffee or soup.[32] R. R. Taylor, on board the steamer *Panama* in August of 1849, complained; "We get stinking salt pork & Beef & hard, black bread served up in tubs on deck, & each one grabs what he can & eats it the best way he can. . . . sitting on a cask on deck with a piece of half raw, musty, fat, boiled pork."[33]

The voyage to San Francisco took twenty days. Most steamers stopped at San Blas or Acapulco, Mexico, to take on coal and provisions. At Acapulco the passengers were allowed to go ashore and stretch their legs for several hours. On the voyage, passengers promenaded the decks watching the ocean and looking for whales, porpoises, and passing ships. Almost every night the decks were crowded with passengers escaping the stifling heat below. "It is curious to walk over the deck at night; men are lying about in every place large enough to hold them; hammocks are swung across the vessel and fastened to every stanchion and rope, each occupied by its owner who is rocked to sleep by the motion of the vessel."[34]

Entertainment of various sorts occurred. Among the passengers aboard *Tennessee* on the first voyage to San Francisco were "twelve or fourteen women of bad character" and "a little knot of gamblers, with their women." Every night the gamblers opened a faro bank in their cabin. "A thousand dollars passes out or in to the bank in less time than it takes me to record it. I have seen a man in half an hour win and lose over three thousand dollars, and when he left had lost in all eleven hundred and forty-five dollars."[35] Among the "motley company, on a strange pilgrimage," as John Peirce called his fellow passengers, were clergymen, doctors, lawyers, merchants, and several missionaries with their wives and children. Edward Hotchkiss noted, "It seems quite pleasant to hear the prattling of children around the decks, & to hear a woman speak was quite a novelty when I first came on board."[36] With the large number of clergy on board, regular religious services offered an alternative to the fast life. "The congregation as usual at sea are very attentive & show more devotion than at home."[37] Some passengers passed the time writing home, but as Edward Hotchkiss lamented in a letter to his mother on March 31: "One needs the power of abstraction to write where I am, amidst the crying of babies, chattering of children, men playing cards, and the continual tramp of people over my head."[38]

Off the coast of Southern California, tropical weather ended as the nights grew cool. Overcoats and blankets were hauled out, and sleeping on deck ceased. By this time "all hands are pretty well tired of steam boating with such a crowd as we have here. There will be few sad hearts when San Francisco heaves in sight. We have tried all kinds of amusements until everything is worn out."[39] John B. Peirce, writing to his aunt just a day out of San Francisco, noted that *Tennessee's* passengers looked forward to the end of the voyage "as a relief from the crowded cage in which we have been prisoned, wave tossed and nauseated, with disgust for twenty long days and nights."[40]

The anticipation of reaching San Francisco excited all on board. James Rogers and his companions in the crew shared the excitement. "After we had cleared away breakfast, all discipline in the steward's department quickly relaxed when it was known that the entrance to the greatest harbor in the world was fully in view . . . we . . . passed slowly along the whole line of shipping at anchor, and came to anchor ourselves."[41] *Tennessee* dropped anchor at noon. As soon as the anchor was down, the steamer was surrounded by boats "twenty deep," crowded with eager San Franciscans "who came to meet friends, others came to see the strangers, some men expecting their wives, such kissing and hugging and such endearing epithets one rarely sees or hears as passed from one to the other as the crowd rushed on board."[42]

The route taken by the steamers to and from Panama almost never varied. The 3,220-mile trip from Panama Bay to the Golden Gate included stops at intermediate ports such as Monterey and San Diego, California, and Acapulco, San Blas, and Manzanillo, Mexico. These intermediate stops allowed the Pacific Mail Steamship Company to provision (particularly to recoal), while encouraging regular coastwise travel on its steamers. Passengers on the steamers were assured of regular sights on their voyages north and south.

Pacific Mail generally expended a large amount of money each voyage to provision the steamers. *Tennessee's* provisioning records indicate a variety and a considerable amount of expenditures for food. After arrival at San Francisco on May 20, 1851, the company expended $11,039.95 on the vessel. Costs other than provisions included miscellaneous hardware, casting and other metal work for machinery, stationary, including ledgers, ticket books, passenger lists, manifests and other forms, fees paid to agents to round up passengers and crew, and laborers to work overhauling, cleaning, and painting the ship. Other expenses included replacing crockery and tinware broken or "borrowed" by passengers. Bedding was also expensive. More than 15,040 pounds of hay filled the mattresses on *Tennessee*.[43]

Prior to each voyage to Panama, the Pacific Mail steamers journeyed to Benicia for repairs that could not be done in San Francisco and for coaling. Additional coaling stations were located at Acapulco and at Panama. High prices, the lack of industrial facilities, and a short supply of coal and other items presented obstacles to Pacific Mail's regular operation of *Tennessee* and its other steamers. These difficulties were overcome, and with the exception of occasional hardships, the passengers who came and went to California via the isthmus in Pacific Mail steamers traveled in style and relative comfort.

ISTHMIAN COMPETITION

The profits to be made on the Panama route, and the seeming inability of the Pacific Mail Steamship Company to adequately handle the large number of persons awaiting passage to San Francisco, inspired a number of entrepreneurs to compete for the business of isthmian travelers. A number of sailing vessels continued to sail between Panama and San Francisco, many as a one-time arrangement and others making repeat voyages. True competition to the Pacific Mail, however, came from organizers of "opposition lines" of steamships, and proved, in the words of historian John Haskell Kemble, to be "bitter and ruthless. . . . the chief characteristic of steamship operation on the Panama route," replete with fare wars, angry denunciations, and lawsuits.[44] The earliest competitors of the Pacific Mail were the New York firm of J. Howard and Son, southern shipping magnate Charles Morgan, and the United States Mail Steamship Company, which was apparently not content with just the Atlantic side of the operation—but then the Pacific Mail was not content to operate solely in the Pacific. The feud between the U.S. and Pacific Mail resulted in both sending steamers to encroach on the other's territory and only ended when the two companies traded the steamers plying each others' waters and exchanged stock. The two companies began cooperating with one another, selling jointly issued tickets.[45]

The competition posed few problems for most argonauts. Many welcomed the fare wars. In June 1851, a Panama correspondent to the New York *Herald* wrote that "competition is, as a matter of course, very great, and passage to San Francisco can be had for a mere song."[46] A large number of steamships were introduced into the Pacific by the various competing lines, among them some famous vessels—*Brother Jonathan, Monumental City, Yankee Blade,* and *Samuel S. Lewis.* While welcomed by some, the opposition steamers were condemned by many, particularly as they suffered a spate of disasters and passenger complaints. Songster John A. Stone, disgusted with all parties concerned, penned a popular ditty, "Humbug Steamship Companies,"

They have opposition on the route, with cabins very nice,
And advertise to take you for half the usual price;
They get thousands from the mountains, and then deny their
   bills,
So you have to pay their prices, or go back to the hills.
You are driven round the steerage like a drove of hungry swine,
And kicked ashore at Panama by the Independent Line;
Your baggage is thrown overboard, the like you never saw,
A trip or two will sicken you of going to Panama.[47]

Despite these sentiments, people traveled on the opposition steamers through the 1850s.

A number of other individuals and firms competed with the mail steamship companies in 1849, 1850, and later, but the most troublesome was "Commodore" Cornelius Vanderbilt of New York, who, after trying to compete with the Pacific Mail in Panama, opened a new route by way of Nicaragua. Although California-bound immigrants had crossed Nicaragua as early as 1849, the heyday of the route was 1851–1855. Wider than Panama, Nicaragua nevertheless had the more easily navigated San Juan River and Lake Nicaragua, which reportedly made for an easier passage confined more to steamer than mule or canoe, although both were frequently employed on the Nicaragua route as well as in Panama. While hoping to take over the lucrative California trade from both the Pacific Mail and the Isthmus of Panama, Vanderbilt also planned to locate and build a transisthmian canal in Nicaragua and thus capture a prize already more than decade along in discussion and dreams. Commencing operations in December 1850 with the steamer *Prometheus*, Vanderbilt ordered the 613-ton sidewheel steamer *Independence* built by William H. Brown in New York for the Pacific. Launched with the engines and boilers in place and with steam up on Christmas Day 1850, Vanderbilt's new present steamed for the Pacific on January 13, 1851. Followed by the 1,003-ton sidewheel steamer *Pacific*, purchased from the United States Mail Steamship Company, *Independence* inaugurated through service on the Nicaragua route. *Pacific* arrived first, however, and in July 1851 the line officially opened.[48]

Gradually the Nicaragua route was monopolized by Vanderbilt, who employed seven steamers by early 1852. The line prospered, offering serious competition to the Pacific Mail. Although the number of passengers going by way of Nicaragua never surpassed those passing over the Isthmus of Panama, considerable business was lost to Vanderbilt; in 1851 only 4,971 passengers crossed Nicaragua as compared to 29,653 crossing Panama, but in 1852 the gap narrowed with 17,403 Nicaragua passengers to 33,108 Panama passengers, closing with 23,957 to 27,246 in 1853.[49] Part of Vanderbilt's failure to make more of Nicaragua was his inattention to passenger comfort. Passengers protested unsanitary and unsafe conditions on the Nicaragua steamers; they held a parade in San Francisco in which was carried a Vanderbilt effigy with a placard labeled "Vanderbilt's Death Line" hanging from its neck. Ill-feeling bolstered by several unfortunate disasters—the loss of the steamers *North America, Samuel S. Lewis,* and *Independence,* the latter with considerable loss of life—did little to help. The Nicaragua route all but closed when filibustering Yankee invaders plunged the country into turmoil. In 1856, only 8,053 passengers crossed Nicaragua, as opposed to 30,335 who went through Panama.[50]

In addition to Nicaragua, another route was a 213-mile passage acros Mexico's Isthmus of Tehuantepec. Gold-seekers sailed on regularly scheduled packets to Tehuantepec through 1850 and 1851. From Veracruz the national highway made its way over the mountains into the Valley of Mexico and thence to the Pacific, where vessels were engaged at Ventosa or Mazatlán, a regular port of call for both Panama and Nicaragua steamers. After 1851 steamers continued to make irregular trips to Tehuantepec or Veracruz; in 1853 the American steamer *Albatross*, laden with freight and passengers bound to San Francisco was wrecked (the only loss on this route) on a reef several miles south of Veracruz.

THE STEAMERS

Three steamers, *Winfield Scott, Samuel S. Lewis* and *Golden Gate*, that were employed in the isthmian routes had representative, somewhat typical careers that provide a more detailed sense of the activities and travails of pioneering steamer operation in the Pacific.

Winfield Scott. As the number of steamers sent to California from the Atlantic increased, new vessels were laid down to replace them. A product of the veteran New York shipyards of Westervelt and MacKay, *Winfield Scott* was named for the popular Brevet Lieutenant General Winfield Scott who had led the U.S. Army to victory over Mexico in 1847–1848. Launched on October 27, 1850, *Winfield Scott* was a 1,291-ton wooden-hulled, sidewheel steamer described as "very sharp . . . her lines partake somewhat of the 'hollow' kind, beautifully swelling to her extreme width, and as beautifully tapering off again as they approach her stern." The vessel's three decks housed cabins, salons, and wide, well-lighted and ventilated corridors. *Winfield Scott* easily accommodated 315 passengers below decks, and the dining salon handled 100 persons at a single seating.[51] It was propelled by a pair of side-lever steam engines manufacatured by the T. F. Secor Company of New York. Built for trade with Southern cotton ports, it steamed to the Pacific Coast at the end of 1851 to profit from the Gold Rush after only a year's operation between New York and New Orleans. She was intended to run between Panama and San Francisco in opposition to the Pacific Mail Steamship Company. Joining the steamer *United States*, the steamer became part of Davis, Brooks and Company's newly incorporated New York and San Francisco Steamship Line. *United States* operated between New York and Chagres; passengers hiked overland across the Isthmus to connect with *Winfield Scott* on the Pacific side.[52]

Winfield Scott left New York on January 26, 1852. Just twenty-one days and fifteen hours later she arrived in Rio de Janeiro—the shortest passage yet made to that port, according to the press—and on February 26 steamed for Valparaiso, Chile, on the Pacific. Navigating the Straits of Magellan, *Winfield Scott* arrived in the Pacific in short order, and soon steamed into Panama Bay. Departing Panama with additional passengers, she arrived in San Francisco on April 28, 1852. The steamer was graciously greeted by the town. It was noted that *Scott's* passage from New York to Panama—forty-eight days, ten hours—was the quickest on record.[53]

Her speed soon became her hallmark, and she became a popular vessel on the Panama Route. Passages cost $350 for a first-class cabin berth, $255 for a second-class cabin berth, and $200 for a steerage berth. Fresh meat was provided for the passengers by means of pens "forward the wheelhouse" on deck, where cattle, sheep and pigs were kept. Fresh vegetables were procured from stops along the way (usually Acapulco, Mexico). Other "refreshments" were also available; passenger L. M. Schaeffer, on board *Scott* for the first trip from San Francisco to Panama, remarked upon a "little crib" on the larboard side of the steamer near the foremast that "attracted" more visitors than any other part of the vessel, being the place for retailing the 'ardent'; twenty-five cents would procure a glass of brandy, *plain*, thirty-eight cents *brandy with ice.*"[54]

Between April 1852 and April 1853, *Winfield Scott* made several voyages for the New York and San Francisco Steamship Line. In October 1852 she was joined by the steamer *Cortes*, which became her running mate. The two steamers were intended to voyage with others, since the New York and San Francisco Steamship Line was planning to expand. That move was forestalled in the summer of 1853 when *Cortes* was purchased by Vanderbilt to run between San Francisco and Nicaragua, and *Winfield Scott* was purchased by the Pacific Mail Steamship Company.[55] The Pacific Mail had retained its first place in the Pacific, but at great cost, since many opposing companies, notably the New York and San Francisco Steamship Line emerged. The purchase of *Winfield Scott* both replaced the recently wrecked Pacific Mail steamer *Tennessee* and bolstered the Pacific Mail fleet, whose steamers were too small and too old to keep pace with the modern vessels coming into the trade. Entering the Pacific Mail rolls on July 20, 1853 (having been purchased on the eighth of the same month), *Winfield Scott* made only a few more voyages until wrecked on Anacapa Island off the California coast later that year.

Samuel S. Lewis. The screw steamer *Samuel S. Lewis* was built at Kensington, now part of Philadelphia, Pennsylvania, by Theodore

Birely and Son in 1851. Designed by Captain Richard F. Loper, *Lewis* resulted of Loper's experiments with screw propulsion and marine steam engines.[56] Loper and two associates, E. Lincoln and Samuel Reynolds, intended for *Lewis* to operate in the California trade, carrying immigrants and high-valued freight in the lucrative boom of steam transportation to the Pacific Coast following the gold discovery. Before the steamer was launched, it was purchased by the Harnden Express Company of Boston to operate on the Atlantic Ocean between Boston and Liverpool.[57]

Samuel S. Lewis underwent trials at Philadelphia on September 4, 1851, and sailed for Boston on September 13. Three days later the steamer participated in a grand jubilee on Boston Harbor to celebrate the completion of the first railroad linking Boston and Canada. President Millard Fillmore and other dignitaries including Daniel Webster toured the harbor aboard *Lewis*. Steaming from Boston on October 4, 1851, for Liverpool under the command of Captain George A. Cole, she lost the propeller in a gale and had to continue the voyage under sail. In England a new propeller was fitted and the ship set out for Boston, only to run out of coal. Finally arriving in the United States on January 3, 1852, her transatlantic career ended when the owners' business failed.[58]

Sold in 1852 to an agent of Cornelius Vanderbilt, *Samuel S. Lewis* was readied for a new career in Vanderbilt's "Independent Line." *Lewis* was to work the Pacific side of the Nicaragua route with the steamer *Independence*. Steaming from New York on March 5, 1852, she sailed into the Pacific, touching at Rio de Janeiro before navigating the Straits of Magellan. After stopping at Valparaiso and Panama, *Lewis* arrived at San Juan del Sur, the Pacific terminus of the Nicaragua route, where several hundred had waited for three weeks for passage. From San Juan del Sur, the vessel steamed to Acapulco, arriving at San Francisco on July 7, 1852, 112 days from New York, with 653 passengers.[59]

The San Francisco *Daily Alta California* greeted the new steamer lukewarmly. "She is a large fine looking vessel, possessing apparently all the requisites for a good safe sea-going steamer."[60] Vanderbilt's steamers were not noted for good service, and the deaths of nineteen passengers by disease enroute to San Francisco was not the best introduction for *Samuel S. Lewis*. The steamer operated between San Juan del Sur and San Francisco for more than a year. Its career on the Pacific was marked by problems. In the fall of 1852 *Lewis* was libeled for overloading, and in January 1853 *Lewis* was described "by the most reliable authority to have arrived here in the most filthy condition; so much indeed as to create nausea to those who visited her. She is in a very leaky condition, and has several feet of water."[61] The San Francisco *Daily Alta California*'s editors condemned the ship, stating "the lives and property of the public should not be trifled with . . . the present condition of the ship . . . is calculated to induce sickness and death, especially where human beings are packed together in dense masses."[62]

On January 4, 1853, *Samuel S. Lewis* broke down off San Francisco and was towed into port by the steamer *Goliah*. A week later the *Daily Alta California* reported that the ship was to be "thoroughly overhauled and repaired. . . . New engines are being put in her, and new propeller paddles to replace the old ones. The copper will be stripped off, seams recaulked, new copper put on, and in time the ship made as good as new. We are really glad that such is to be the case."[63] The ship was repaired under contract by the Pacific Mail Steamship Company at its Benicia depot near San Francisco. The old engines were repaired, not replaced, despite the newspaper's hopes. In late March 1853 *Samuel S. Lewis* departed San Francisco for San Juan del Sur, but was wrecked on the return voyage in the early morning of April 9, 1853. The steamer ran aground on Duxbury Reef several miles north of the Golden Gate and was a total loss, breaking up within twenty-four hours.

Golden Gate. Built to be the "queen steamer of the Pacific," *Golden Gate* was the product of New York shipbuilder William H. Webb, who had earlier constructed *California*, *Panama*, and *Tennessee*, all members of the Pacific Mail fleet. Originally ordered by the United States Mail Steamship Company, the steamer was taken over by the Pacific Mail Steamship Company following an 1851 agreement of the two companies to merge operations and cease competing with each other.[64] *Golden Gate* was built specifically with the lessons of gold rush traffic to Panama in mind. Large and spacious, the 3,000-ton steamer's 269-foot-long wooden hull accommodated 800 passengers, eliminating the overcrowding that plagued other Panama steamers.[65] Powered by two oscillating engines, *Golden Gate* was laid down on July 1, 1850. Launched on January 21, 1851, the vessel was fitted out through much of the year, steaming out into New York harbor for trials in the summer.[66] Departing New York in September 1851, *Golden Gate* made a 64-day passage to San Francisco, arriving on November 19.[67]

Golden Gate was heralded by the San Francisco press as "the largest and swiftest steamer in our waters."[68] Called "the finest specimen of naval architecture on the Pacific," she was joined within a few years by other large steamers built specifically for the Panama route, such as the 2,182-ton *John L. Stephens*, the 2,181-ton *Golden Age*, and the 1,616-ton *Sonora*, all to help secure the Pacific Mail's domination of the Panama route and Pacific coastal navigation. In two short years *Golden Gate* cleared an $800,000 profit for the Pacific Mail.[69]

Arriving in California after the initial gold rush, *Golden Gate* was packed full of passengers on nearly every voyage to and from San Francisco. On March 1, 1852, an article in the San Francisco *Picayune* noted that the arrival of *Golden Gate*, along with the steamers *California* and *Independence* at the end of February, had brought more than 1,800 persons to California in one voyage. One of the steamer's greatest achievements, however, was setting a new record for the passage from San Francisco to Panama in April 1853. She made the passage hence to Panama in 11 days and 14 hours time from port to port, and deducting for stoppages, in 10 days and 20 hours running time, a feat unparalleled in the history of steam upon the Pacific."[70] *Golden Gate's* record remained unbroken until 1855.

Golden Gate's career was plagued with accidents and other bad luck. Chartered to carry U.S. Army troops to San Francisco in 1852, the ship picked up a cholera-ravaged contingent of soldiers from the Fourth U.S. Infantry that had hiked across the isthmus. Among them was Captain U. S. Grant, future president of the United States. Loading regularly ticketed passengers at Panama between July 17 and 20, *Golden Gate* later moored off Tobaga Island in Panama Bay when cholera broke out among the 650 troops. In all, 82 soldiers and 2 passengers died on the steamer. The captain emptied the ship, sending healthy passengers north in other ships. The epidemic ended after 29 more deaths. *Golden Gate* was fumigated and proceeded to San Francisco with 450 soldiers, including Grant, arriving on August 19, 1852.[71]

In July 1853 *Golden Gate* was taken out for a two-month service overhaul at Pacific Mail's Benicia depot because "this vessel has been running *sans* intermission for two years, and since her arrival in the Pacific, has been carrying the mails and passengers between San Francisco and Panama."[72] Reintroduced to service, *Golden Gate* suffered a crippling mishap when the shaft cracked enroute to San Francisco on January 10, 1854. After drifting powerless for four days, the shaft was severed, allowing the steamer to limp on one engine and one paddlewheel to San Diego with "shattering vibrations . . . sudden lurches forward, and . . . crab-like scuttling" as the passengers went on strict rations of food and water.[73] Reaching San Diego, *Golden Gate* took on provisions and was limping to San Francisco when she went aground at Point Loma. Wedged on the rocks, the steamer could not be pulled free. Two days later the passengers were taken off and brought to San Francisco with baggage and mail. At the end of the month, *Golden*

Gate was finally pulled free and reached San Francisco on February 4, 1854.

The steamer's shaft snapped again in 1857, but the greatest misfortune to befall *Golden Gate* was final destruction by fire on July 27, 1862, off the coast of Mexico. Departing San Francisco on July 21 with 242 passengers and a 96-person crew, *Golden Gate* was steaming off Manzanillo when a fire broke out near the galley at five o'clock in the afternoon on the 27th. Passengers and crew panicked. As *Golden Gate* raced for shore, flames swept the decks, driving passengers forward to the bow and aft to the counter. Only four lifeboats were launched and many passengers threw themselves overboard. Passenger Andre Chavanne, clinging to a rope tied astern, saw a group of 150 people on the bow "straddling the bowsprit . . . a few hanging to chains. The coal bunker ports, close to the water line, had been opened by the stokers and engineers, who were hemmed in by the flames and were endeavoring to escape through those dangerous openings."[74] In all, 175 drowned, burned to death, or were crushed and mangled as they jumped and were swept into the paddlewheels.[75] The blazing hulk finally came ashore at Manzanillo and there, broadside to the beach, burned until the steamer sank.

SIGNIFICANCE OF THE PANAMA ROUTE

Introducing regular steamship service into the Pacific, the Panama and Nicaragua routes opened a major oceanic link between the two coasts, paving the way for the first transcontinental railroad in the Americas and, ultimately, the canal. Panama bore the brunt of hosting the majority of Americans abroad, and it was at Caribbean island nations or on Panamanian shores that many Yankees had their first experience of a foreign land and people. Panama was also the stage for the striking examples of early imperialism as the United States made Panama a virtual American colony fifty years before the canal zone. The same endeavors turned Nicaragua into an American-inspired strife-torn war zone in the 1850s.

The Panama route was significant for other reasons. On Panama steamers and across the isthmus California's wealth poured east, and mail and newspapers forged a regular link between California and the rest of the world. Expensive freight and express, usually high-duty quality goods, were shipped via the isthmus until clippers took over. Although many chose to come to California by way of Cape Horn or overland, nearly everyone who returned home went via Panama or Nicaragua, and those who decided to make their way back to California did so on the Panama-route steamers. Favored route of government

officials, the noted, well-to-do, or persons of ill repute for passage to
California, the isthmus was also a democratic route to the United
States. In all, 808,769 persons traveled via the isthmus between 1848
and 1869, when the transcontinental railroad linked the 2,400-mile
breadth of the United States.[76]

Transporting the Wealth. Between 1849 and 1853, Panama steamers carried nearly $64,000,000 in gold via Panama.[77] Gold shipments
on the steamers often totaled more than $1,000,000 per voyage. In
exchange for transporting gold, the Pacific Mail Steamship Company
received as much as 5 percent of the amount shipped. By 1850, the rate
dropped to 2½percent, as more "treasure" was shipped.[78] No major
robbery occurred on a Pacific Mail steamer because gold shipments
were secure in iron-sheathed strong rooms and padlocked wooden
chests. Armed express company agents who traveled with the shipments also ensured security. To further protect the company from theft
or loss at sea, the Pacific Mail carried open policies of insurance by each
steamer, each covering shipments of "gold dust" to the United States or
to the Bank of England up to 500,000 pounds sterling.[79] The payment
of primage to captains who safely brought the gold through doubtless
reinforced shipboard discipline.

The steamers also carried specie from Panama to San Francisco.
Very little money was in circulation in California during the early years
of the Gold Rush. Until the U.S. Mint was opened in San Francisco in
1854, gold nuggets and dust served as the circulating medium. However, the Customhouse and businesses in Europe and on the eastern
seaboard demanded payment in specie. Private concerns minted coins
and gold slugs for exchange, and a variety of foreign coins were
imported, tending to make business transactions an interesting lesson
in supply and demand:

> Mr. Hudson paid us off every Saturday night, and it was laugha-
> ble to see the kinds of currency tendered and accepted as a matter
> of course. He would come with a bag filled with roleaus (?) of
> silver coin, foreign coins of every description, simple slugs of
> gold stamped with their weight and value, Miner's Bank coins,
> etc. Everything went in those days, and in whatever shape wages
> came, there was no grumbling, as there was not sufficient coin in
> circulation to supply the demand.[80]

United States currency was imported to California via the isthmus
to meet the demand for coin. After crossing the isthmus, chests of
specie were loaded on the steamers for the voyage to San Francisco.
The Pacific Mail steamships frequently carried specie to California for
merchants, banks, and express companies; on arrival at San Francisco

on November 7, 1850, for example, *Tennessee's* manifest listed "coin in the amount of $2000 for A. Droullard" and on February 26, 1852, *Golden Gate* arrived at San Francisco with an unspecified amount of gold coin.

Express. Express companies prospered along with the Pacific Mail Steamship Company on the Panama route. A number of firms did business via the isthmus, transporting specie, cargo, mail, and passenger baggage between New York, Panama, and San Francisco. Freight rates were high: in 1853 freight costs to Chagres were $.70 per square foot, and freight from Panama to San Francisco ran $100 per ton.[81] The high cost reflected twice loading and thrice discharging the cargo, and shipping it by mule or canoe across the bandit-rife isthmus. As a result, light, expensive commodities that could return a good profit by commanding high prices in San Francisco were carried on the Panama steamer. A manifest of cargo shipped to San Francisco on *Tennessee* dated May 30, 1851, lists cases of pistols, glassware, muslin, linen, hats, "fancy goods," watches, jewelry, "camera & fixtures," playing cards, plated ware, cigars, drugs and "Two boxes American gold coin," most of it shipped in care of Adams and Company. When *Tennessee* arrived at San Francisco on September 4, 1850, she brought 97 packages of "machinery," another valuable commodity. The amount of freight carried on each voyage varied. On March 4, 1852, *Monumental City* arrived at San Francisco with 111 packages of merchandise;" *Panama* arrived on May 27, 1852, with 177 "packages of merchandise," and on July 10, 1852, *Tennessee* arrived with 419 packages of merchandise.

Passenger baggage transported in the Panama steamers was often sent in the care of express companies. Leaving baggage in care of the express companies was a boon for some, because "passengers are required to pay the expense of conveying themselves and their baggage to the Steamer."[82] A typical receipt for baggage, issued to Mrs. Anne Brown in Panama on November 4, 1852, indicates the terms of a contract with Adams and Company:

> Received . . . the sum of $20 for payment of Transportation Bill to Panama, and Shipping Charges on Baggage, to be received from Mr. John Woolsey and forwarded by us to Messrs. ADAMS & CO., of San Francisco, subject to whatever charges may be incurred there. The Baggage to be shipped by first Steamer leaving this Port, if room on board for same. If the Baggage is delivered to us by the Forwarding Agents here, the owner will find the amount of the transportation, with memorandum, and half our commission returned at San Francisco office.[83]

Losses and damage by seawater or isthmian humidity were not paid for, unless caused by carelessness on the part of the express agent, and the company disavowed responsibility for "damages by rain or weather, highway robbery or bad roads." As for Mrs. Brown, she learned her lesson the hard way—her trunk was thrown overboard on the passage to San Francisco during a storm.

Mail. The most important service performed by the Panama steamers was their service as a regular connection to the rest of the world. On the isolated western shore of the continent, any link to the familiar world back home was welcome. The Panama steamers were the chief source of news from the rest of the world to California, either through recent passengers, newspapers, or letters. Newspapers from eastern cities were always of interest. Cooke, Kenny and Company of San Francisco, for example, advertised on January 20, 1853, that they had "received Per Steamer Tennessee . . . Whig Review; New York Illustrated News; New Orleans Picayune; Gleason's Pictorial; Papers from all parts of the United States of the latest dates" all for sale at their store at 94 California Street.[84]

Pacific Mail received a subsidy of $199,000 per annum from the U.S. government to carry the mail to American territories on the Pacific coast. In March 1851 the subsidy was increased by $149,250 to total $348,250. The U.S. Navy's representatives inspected each steamship to ensure it met government requirements. The mail was loaded in New York, transshipped by mule across Panama, sent to San Francisco, and distributed at the San Francisco Post Office to lines of men that stretched for blocks.

Letters from home carried in the Panama steamers were practically devoured. One man, writing to his wife, told her:

> If you could have seen us when we received our letters, you would have laughed and perhaps called us fools—such hoorahing, jumping, yelling and screaming. . . . You will take good care and write often when I tell you that I live upon your letters, with a small sprinkling of pork and bread."[85]

The influx of mail was tremendous. *Tennessee* brought eight tons of mail in 100-pound sacks to San Francisco when she arrived on July 20, 1851, the largest amount of mail then brought to San Francisco by a single vessel.[86] On another voyage, *Tennessee* brought 113 bags of mail. The volume of mail often overwhelmed the primitive system used to transport it to the steamers. In January 1851 the editors of the San Francisco *Alta California* complained:

We are again constrained to notice another failure in the receipt of the regular mail. We are authentically informed at the post office that sixty-nine bags still remain on the isthmus, that should have been received by the Tennessee. The steamer was detained a number of days in order to procure and bring them up. A sad dereliction of duty is perceptible in the region of Granada [Panama].[87]

Pacific Mail and its steamer captains made every effort to ensure that the mail was on board when the ship left. Augustus Ripley, who left San Francisco on *Tennessee* in April 1851, noted his departure was delayed because "the mail-agent & mails had not come on board. We was [sic] thus detained some 2 hours. They finally came 52 bags of mail matter & 30 boxes Treasure (Gold Dust) . . . weighed anchor & put to sea."[88]

Sometimes the best efforts of the Pacific Mail failed. When *Tennessee* arrived at San Francisco on June 20, 1850, "Much disappointment was manifested when it was ascertained she had no mails, but it was in a measure allayed by the knowledge that the California with any quantities of letters and newspapers might be expected in a couple of days. Every one consoled themselves with " 'There's a good time coming, boys, wait a little longer.' "[89] The post office accepted letters up to a few hours before sailing, when envelopes specially marked for the departing steamer were placed on board. Mail was also carried on the steamers by express company agents. Often more efficient and quicker in delivery—but at a higher price than the U.S. mail—the express companies used Panama steamships to go "through ahead of the mails." In transporting this vital commodity the Panama route saw its finest service.

Training the Steam Navy. When Congress authorized the franchisement of mail steamers in 1847, it specifically stated that "the said steamships shall be commanded by officers of the United States Navy not below the grade of lieutenant, who shall be selected by the contractor, with the approval and consent of the Secretary of the Navy, and who shall be suitably accommodated without charge to the government."[90] Service on a mail steamer provided invaluable experience in marine steam navigation for young naval officers during the period of decline of the sailing navy and the rise of naval interest in steamships. Unfortunately, not enough naval steamers were available for all officers of promise. The construction of mail steamers under government contract and supervision, including inspection of the vessels by navy officers at the New York Navy Yard, created a new fleet of steamers similar in many respects to navy steam warships (without armament).

Lieutenant David Dixon Porter, one of the "pioneers in the mail steam service," as he described himself, stated in June 1850 that "the [mail] service will be creditable to the navy, and of infinite advantage to young officers."[91] Other officers and government officials agreed; in December 1849 it was announced that the steamer *Ohio*, recently built for the United States Mail Steamship Company, "will be commanded by Lieutenant Schenck of the United States Navy. She will also carry four midshipmen of the Navy; and together with the *Georgia*, now nearly finished, will form a steam naval school for the young officers of our service."[92] Porter, then in command of the Pacific Mail steamer *Panama*, crossed the isthmus and made his way to New York to take command of *Georgia*. Porter, the most famous mail steamer commander, rose to the highest rank in the navy and gained fame during the Civil War. Following the capture of New Orleans, a major editorial in the San Francisco *Daily Alta California* reminded readers that the "hero captor" had commanded the mail steamers *Panama*, *Georgia*, and *Crescent City*, particularly noting that the "pioneer passage of the *Panama* was attended with incidents which displayed, on the part of her commander, courage, caution, patience, and thoroughly competent qualifications to the post."[93]

Another notable officer was James F. Schenck. Entering naval service in 1825, he served with distinction in the Mexican War, participating in the conquest of California. In May 1849 Schenck assumed command of *Ohio* and served as a mail officer. He earned the gratitude of his fellow officers in the mail service in 1851 when he protested a Navy decision that placed him while in command of a mail steamer either "on other duty" or awaiting orders, and hence not authorized to receive his annual pay as a naval officer. Appealing this decision, Schenck was able to receive an opinion from the attorney general, who accepted his argument. Secretary of the Navy William Graham accordingly ordered in November 1851 that the lieutenants commanding the mail steamers, and the passed midshipmen serving with them, were entitled to full pay.[94] In 1859 Schenck returned to naval service as commander of USS *Saginaw*, joining the U.S. West Gulf Blockading Squadron at the outbreak of Civil War. Promoted for gallantry to captain and then commodore, Schenck figured prominently in the capture of Fort Fisher, North California, in January 1865. Assigned to the command of the U.S. Naval Station at Mound City, Illinois, in May 1865, he ended his career as a rear admiral before retiring in 1869.[95]

William Lewis Herndon, another notable officer, commenced his naval career in 1828. After posts that included considerable sea duty and command of the revenue cutter *Jefferson* and USS *Wave*, Herndon was ordered to lead an expedition to explore the headwaters of the Amazon River and the Amazon River basin in 1851. Herndon's expedition and the subsequent publication of his observations, maps, and plates won fame for the young officer. His work forms an important chapter in the annals of naval exploration at a time when such endeavors were mostly government-financed military tasks. Detached to command the U.S. mail steamer *George Law* in 1855, Herndon's promising career was cut short when he was lost at sea as the ship, renamed *Central America*, sank in a hurricane off South Carolina in September 1857. The only naval officer lost while serving on a mail steamer, Herndon is honored by a memorial at the United States Naval Academy in Annapolis.[96]

Thomas A. Budd, one of the first officers to enter the mail service along with Porter, joined the navy in 1829, was promoted to passed midshipman in 1835, and earned the rank of lieutenant in 1841. Seven years later he assumed command of the first Pacific Mail steamer, *California*. Under his command *California* became the first American steamship to navigate the Straits of Magellan. Serving on the Pacific throughout the Gold Rush, Budd, like David Dixon Porter, enjoyed long service in the mail steamers, resigning from the Navy in 1853 to pursue private opportunities. With the outbreak of the Civil War, Budd again applied to the Navy, was appointed acting lieutenant, and received command of the gunboat *Penguin*. He was killed in action in a skirmish at Mosquito Inlet, Florida, on March 23, 1862.[97]

Going Home. Next to the mail the most significant freight carried by the Panama steamers was homebound argonauts. After the construction of the Panama Railroad made the Panamanian transit easier, the Panama route became the favored means of going home from California. Between 1849 and 1859, one-fifth of the immigrants who reached California decided to return home. Most chose to leave by way of Panama, but some went by way of Nicaragua.

Daniel Wadsworth Coit, writing to his wife from San Francisco on September 15, 1850, told of two men returning to Massachusetts. One had "met with incredible success" in business. The other was a young man from Boston who had barely made enough in the mines to survive and had arrived in San Francisco to seek his way home "with simply the clothes on his back." Coit overheard San Francisco banker Lucien Skinner, principal of the firm of Wells and Company and a friend of the young man's father, talking to the man:

. . . reflect what must be *his* feelings on returning to his family
. . . my attention was called to him from a conversation between
him . . . and Mr. Skinner. . . . "Well," said Mr. Skinner, "I have
taken a passage for you on the *Tennessee*" (steerage, I suppose, of
course), "but I suppose you'll want clothes, too, won't you?"
"Yes, sir," said the young man, in a voice hardly audible from
shame and mortification. (He had on simply a pair of thin
trousers, with a check shirt and a California hat.) "Well," said
Mr. Skinner, "come in by-and-by and we'll see you provided."[98]

Other cases were less extreme. Robert Beck, heading home on *Northerner* in November 1850, remarked that "after a sojourn of 14 months
in San Francisco" he left California "in hopes of regaining health and
strength in my native air and midst the smiling scenes where we spent
my boyhood days."[99]

Sailing day for home was always hectic and emotional. Walter
Pigman, leaving San Francisco on *Republic* in February 1851, found
the scene of his departure one of "bustle and confusion. . . . A crowd
throngs the pier and landing and you may see friends bidding one
another goodbye; some had to stay, and others could set sail for their
far-off homes. As we looked back from the deck of the ship we could
see the signals waving—fluttering handkerchiefs in the breeze, as long
as we could see the port."[100] Lieutenant George H. Derby, leaving
aboard *Northerner*, described the scene much the same:

> As the last line fell from the dock, and our noble steamer with a
> mighty throb and deep sigh, at bidding adieu to San Francisco,
> swung slowly round, the passengers crowded to the side to
> exchange farewell salutations with their friends and acquaint-
> ances. 'Good bye, Jones,' 'Good bye, Brown,' 'God bless you,
> old fellow, take care of yourself!' they shouted. Not seeing
> anyone that I knew, and fearing the passengers might think I had
> no friends, I shouted 'good bye, Muggins,' and had the satisfac-
> tion of having a shabby man much inebriated, reply as he swung
> his rimless hat, 'good bye, my brother.' Not particularly elated at
> this recognition, I tried it again, with 'good bye, Colonel,'
> whereat thirty-four respectable gentlemen took off their hats.[101]

Parting was often sad and tearful, as opposed to the joyful greeting of
each incoming steamer.

Differences in passengers heading to California or leaving the
Golden State were commented on sharply by archaeologist Heinrich
Schliemann, who compared the passengers on his Panama-bound
steamer to those on San Francisco-bound steamers anchored nearby at
Acapulco. The passengers on the San Francisco steamers were "danc-

ing and singing all the day long on deck, talking of nothing but the golden mountains they were going to accumulate in California." On Schliemann's ship, though,

> . . . no body of us sung or danced. . . . Because the mind of the most part of us was taken up by the consideration what long and sour faces the friends at home would make on seeing them return with disappointed hopes and empty pockets, whilst those few of us who had realized fortunes . . were absorbed by . . . how to bring the money safely home. [102]

The Gold Rush reestablished one of the world's most important oceanic routes. The significance of Panama, made clear by the volume of Gold Rush traffic and the establishment of the Americas' first transcontinental railroad, was underscored in the twentieth century by the United States' construction of the Panama Canal. While the transit of goods, people, and mail established the Panama route during the Gold Rush, the introduction of Panama to the world's shipping lanes was the eminent contribution of the California gold discovery to world maritime history. The penultimate contribution to maritime commerce by the Panama steamers was their boost to Pacific steam navigation. Introduced in the 1830s and early '40s by the Hudson Bay Company's *Beaver* and the pioneer vessels of the Pacific Steam Navigation Company, early steamers were candles in the wind. The influx of steamships of all types on the Panama and Nicaragua routes provided the means for expanded steam service up and down the coast and out into the Pacific. The first steamer to cross the Pacific was *Monumental City*, a Panama route veteran. Hawaii's first steamer was the Pacific Mail's *Constitution*. From California, ocean steamers spread out to conquer an ocean.

Chapter Three

THE PORT OF SAN FRANCISCO, 1849-1851

Because of several fortuitous factors, San Francisco became the great entrepot of the Gold Rush. The founding of the town as a commercial center in 1835 and its subsequent growth during the Mexican War had made it the largest settlement on San Francisco Bay. By 1847–1848 San Francisco dominated the bay, whose rivers drained the Sierra foothills and the heart of the gold country. Between 1849 and 1851, hundreds of oceangoing ships and steamers discharged cargo and passengers at the city's wharves and piers. From San Francisco, the argonauts bound for the goldfields made their way into the upper reaches of San Francisco Bay and entered the river systems. Running up the Sacramento or San Joaquin, they sailed and steamed to the river ports of Sacramento, Marysville, and Stockton, the jumping-off points for the mines.

San Francisco boomed from the Gold Rush traffic passing through the city; businesses flourished serving the needs of the recently disembarked passengers. Miners weary of primitive conditions returned to the more civilized entertainment and accommodations of San Francisco thereby aiding the city's economy. Many San Francisco merchants sent vessels to various ports for merchandise: foodstuffs from Hawaii and other Pacific islands; fruit and beef from Mexico; manufactured goods from South America, China, and other parts of the United States; and lumber from the Pacific Northwest began to arrive regularly. The city grew as an active port and was described in July 1849 as an "animated" place "propelled by the most indomitable perseverance."[1]

San Francisco expanded rapidly in response to Gold Rush migration and trade. The population increased quickly between 1848 and 1850. It was estimated at 2,000 in February 1849, 3,000 in March, 5,000 in July, and 12,000 to 15,000 in October of the same year. The population fluctuated between 20,000 and 40,000 in the spring of 1850. The city's "nucleus of tradesmen, craftsmen, and others working in service industries supported a comparatively high floating population" as miners arrived in the city in the fall and winter months "either heading home or seeking a more comfortable winter abode."[2] As a result, the village of San Francisco became a city in the space of a few months.

San Francisco was ill-equipped for immediate urbanization and for its new status as the principal American port on the Pacific. The city was located in one of the worst sites imaginable for growth. Hemmed in by steep and unstable sand-dune promontories and shallow Yerba Buena Cove, which was primarily a mudflat at low tide, San Francisco struggled to overcome its geographic obstacles. At the same time, the city attempted to create requisite facilities to cope with the tremendous influx of shipping.

The task was made easier by Gold Rush capital, energetic activity, and the never-ceasing flow of passengers and cargoes. Beginning in 1849 and running through the mid-1850s, San Francisco was built out over Yerba Buena Cove, eventually filling in its shallow waters to establish a waterfront bristling with piers, wharves, docks, and a host of maritime businesses to serve the vessels arriving off the city. The clogged harbor, packed with idle, practically deserted vessels, was cleared and made orderly with the establishment of harbor regulations and the appointment of a harbormaster. Merchants established a system of marine intelligence, with lookouts reporting the arrival and departure of vessels. By 1853 San Francisco was a major metropolis and an active and significant port that would outlast the temporary excitement of gold fever.

MARINE INTELLIGENCE

Early in 1849, as the first indications of the tremendous influx of shipping that would change San Francisco grew, the *Daily Alta California* asked that shipmasters provide "any information of a public character which they may be enabled to give us on arrival. . . . Lists of passengers we will always be happy to insert."[3] The significance of the maritime trade ensured early efforts to document it. The most important step taken in documenting harbor shipping was the establishment of the office of harbormaster. The harbormaster recorded arriving and departing vessels, regularly providing the newspapers with the name of the vessel, the port it was from or clearing to, and in the case of arrivals, the time of the passage, number of passengers, and a synopsis of the cargo.

The harbormaster, collector of the port, pilots, tugboat men, and commercial shipping merchants, as well as the residents of the town, learned of arrivals from a marine lookout perched at the summit of Loma Alta, the sand-shrouded rocky promontory that marked the northern end of Yerba Buena Cove. The hill afforded a clear view of the Golden Gate, and with a telescope a sharp observer could easily discern the rig, flag, and in some cases (such as warships or steamers) the type of vessel. Until the lookout was established, vessel arrivals were heralded only when the ship rounded Clark's Point and dropped anchor off the waterfront or were spotted by a chance observer on the hills above the town. In February 1849, a naval officer at San francisco drew up a suggested "code of signals" to that ships in the stream could signal vessel arrivals to shore. The plan was eagerly received: "Several of our largest commercial houses have approved the suggestion, and expressed themselves ready. . . . There can be no doubt that such an undertaking is demanded by the great and growing commerce of this Port, and we sincerely trust that our citizens will take the matter in hand."[4]

The matter was taken in hand with the construction of the marine lookout atop a better vantage point, 284-foot-high, appropriately named Loma Alta ("tall hill"). The lookout station, a small two-story rectangular frame building, was erected atop Loma Alta in September 1849. From the roof a large flagstaff with wooden semaphore arms "telegraphed" the news of a vessel's arrival, nationality by flying the appropriate flag and ship type to the town below. Because of the station, Loma Alta was quickly dubbed Telegraph Hill, a name that stuck.

Bayard Taylor reported in September 1849 that the lookout on the hill first would come down and report "an inward-bound vessel, which occasions a little excitement among the boatmen and the merchants who are awaiting consignments."[5] When this method proved inefficient on days when more than a dozen ships arrived, the system was changed. When a vessel was spotted coming through the gate, the lookout rang a bell and rigged the semaphore arms to signal the type of vessel. This alerted the harbormaster and other officials, as well as enterprising merchants who rowed to the incoming vessel in a white-hall boat to ascertain the cargo and perhaps strike a deal for a scarce item at a lesser price than ashore. The most eagerly sought signal, however, was for the Panama steamers, which not only brought the greatest number of passengers but also the mail. Business in town would be suspended and the post office immediately besieged. Ships in the harbor apparently joined in the signaling. The *Alta California* on December 26, 1850, warned a "malicious scamp" on a vessel in the harbor to stop "firing cannon . . . in imitation of the arrival of a steamer from Panama" since he was known, and a repetition of the prank would bring "upon himself unpleasant consequences."

The proprietors of the lookout were George F. Sweeney and Timothy E. Baugh. To improve their service, Sweeney and Baugh opened a second lookout station in April 1850 outside the harbor at Point Lobos, the south head of the bight leading to the Golden Gate. With a telescope, the Point Lobos lookout had several miles' visibility on a clear day. Vessels were spotted far out to sea. The Point Lobos lookout rigged his semaphore, which was then read by the Telegraph Hill lookout, who signaled the Merchants Exchange downtown, which then signaled merchants from its own flagstaff. So that merchants could read the semaphore signals, a broadsheet was printed and distributed around town. "The plan is a plain and suitable one, and will be found very valuable for every Counting House in the city."[6] In March 1851 the editors of the San Francisco *Daily Evening Picayune* sang the telegraph's praises, noting that everyone in San Francisco "cast sharp glances" at it, particularly on "the days of anticipated steamer arrivals."[7]

A legendary San Francisco tale illustrates the prominence of the telegraph station. According to San Francisco pioneers T. A. Barry and B. A. Patten, by spring 1850 "everybody in San Francisco knew the signal for a side-wheel steamer . . . two outstretched, uplifted arms—two long, black boards, one on each side of the long, black signal pole." This fact was demonstrated during a performance of *The Hunchback* at American Theater. In an emotion-packed scene, an actor walked on stage at the end of an argument. "The actor's figure, dressed entirely in black, stood in bold relief against the white . . . scenery. . . . Throwing up his arms, he exclaimed, "'What does this mean?' 'Side-wheel steamer,' roared an immense voice from the gallery. The effect was electrical. Shouts of laughter and round upon round of applause interrupted the play for some minutes."[8]

Sweeney and Baugh prospered and by 1852 moved to new quarters at 123 Sacramento Street.[9] Another sign of their prosperity was the installation of a magnetic telegraph line (using electrical impulses) between the Point Lobos station and their offices on Sacramento Street in 1853. The first electric telegraph system in San Francisco, the line was dedicated in a well-attended ceremony on September 22, 1853.[10] The old "Inner Signal Station" was soon vacated because it was no longer necessary. The "Outer Signal Station," however, remained in use, twice surviving a change of sites and buildings until it was closed in 1961, overshadowed by modern radio-telephone communication and radar.[11]

A BUSY WATERFRONT

The sheer number of vessels lying at anchor off San Francisco made a lasting impression on many Gold Rush visitors and firmly established San Francisco as a maritime city. It also conferred a negative image of the port to wary shipowners reluctant to send a ship for a prolonged layover. In the summer of 1849, as the first onslaught of Gold Rush arrivals began, the harbormaster counted 72 vessels at the port.[12] By October 30, 1849, the San Francisco *Daily Alta California* counted 308 vessels at anchor "in the Port of San Francisco," although some were not laid up but merely between voyages, such as a few dozen coastal and Hawaiian traders, naval vessels, and the Panama steamer *California*.[13] In the June 6, 1850, edition, the *Alta* counted 509 vessels in port, a few dozen between voyages. By November 1851, the *Alta* published the deputy harbormaster's enumeration of 452 vessels in the harbor, which included 242 American-registered vessels, 36 vessels hailing from Great Britain, and 11 French, 10 German, 3 Swedish, 3 Austrian, 5 Chilean, 2 Dutch, 1 Italian, and 1 Austrian-registered vessel. The *Alta* also counted 148 storeships.[14]

Despite the large number of laid-up vessels on the San Francisco waterfront, the statistics of arrivals and departures indicate an active port. Initially marine news focused largely on the arrivals—very few vessels departed San Francisco in 1849. The formal recording of arrivals commenced on March 26, 1849, and seven vessels arrived in the next five days. The enumeration of arrivals (Table 1) for the remainder of the year shows a sharp peak in the summer months. Listed arrivals in 1849 totalled 782, including several repeat visits by coasters, Panama steamers, and Hawaiian traders.[15] In January 1850 the harbormaster reported that the aggregate tonnage of arrivals from April 12, 1849, to January 29, 1850, stood at an amazing 284,238 tons and was comprised of 805 vessels, 487 American and 318 foreign.[16]

A record of departures kept from the end of September through the end of October 1849 is particularly illustrative. Sixty-three vessels

Table 1

1849 Arrivals

Month	Arrivals
April	64
May	43
June	74
July	93
August	112
September	128
October	90
November	82
December	89

exited during the month, all for Pacific ports except one bound for London. Twenty-five vessels sailed for South American ports, primarily Valparaíso or Callao, with ten vessels clearing for the Hawaiian Islands, nine to the Oregon territory, and the remainder to Panama, Hong Kong, Mexican ports (usually Guaymas or Mazatlán), and California ports (usually San Pedro, the harbor of Los Angeles).[17]

Arrivals declined slightly in 1850, with a total of 650 vessels recorded (592 American and 58 foreign registered) between January 1 and December 26. The monthly figures show a more equal spread of arrivals, with a slight summer peak (Table 2).[18] An interesting observation by the editors of the *Alta* was that "of the whole number . . . but a small portion have cleared direct for California, either from points in the United States or in Europe. The largest number have merely touched here, having cruising on indefinite voyages in the exploration or trading service."[19] In October 1850, the Sacramento *Transcript* reported that 1,301 vessels had cleared ports in the United States, in a "fleet" comprised of 414 ships, 360 barks, 276 brigs, 217 schooners, 2 sloops, and 32 steamers.[20]

In 1851 departures began to outstrip arrivals. By September of that year, "the clearances of some time past have been almost as numerous as the entries. . . ."[21] More than a thousand people left for the eastern seaboard by way of Panama at the end of August, and at the end of September the San Francisco *Daily Herald* observed "Our port is now being perceptibly thinned of shipping. . . . From the 1st to the

Table 2

1850 Arrivals

Month	Arrivals
January	55
February	46
March	54
April	50
May	75
June	85
July	62
August	54
September	39
October	49
November	55
December	32

21st of September, 51 vessels, besides steamers, sailed whilst the arrivals only amounted to 28."[22] The *Herald* viewed the change as entirely healthy, because an active harbor no longer clogged with laid-up ships would inspire more arrivals, and "ship owners will send out their ships with greater confidence, convinced that at last some of the difficulties are removed."[23]

The *Herald* was partially correct. Statistics show a continued influx of vessels after 1850 that bolstered the port and the maritime economy of San Francisco as the tide of maritime immigration slowed and regular voyages for import and export commodities began. Shipping statistics published in January 1854 in the San Francisco *Daily Herald* record 650 arrivals in 1849, 1,521 arrivals in 1850, 977 in 1851, 743 in 1852, and 862 in 1853, with the majority of vessels arriving from foreign ports after 1850.[24] The *Annals of San Francisco*, however, tabulating arrivals and clearances in San Francisco in 1851, noted 847 arrivals and 1,315 departures, with 1,147 arrivals (primarily American, British, South American, Mexican, Hawaiian, French, and German) and 1,625 departures in 1852.[25]

CREATING A WATERFRONT

One of the immediate problems was a lack of piers and wharves to facilitate the loading and discharge of vessels and a scarcity of buildings for storage of merchandise. In 1849 a large portion of the city's population was living in tents because there were not enough buildings. William Shaw, an English gold-seeker, stated: "When I first arrived in [San] Francisco, the streets were piled with merchandise of every description; high tiers of goods formed barricades before many houses, as warehouse room for stowage adequate to the shipping discharge could not be had. . . . Fronting the harbor . . . cases, casks and bales, to the amount of thousands of pounds value, lay . . . exposed to the weather."[26]

The residents of San Francisco responded with ingenuity and expanded into the bay. San Francisco lay inshore of Yerba Buena Cove, a mile-wide, 336-acre shallow body of water and tidelands bordered to the north by Loma Alta and to the south by Rincon Hill. The stagnant waters of Yerba Buena Cove were too shallow to permit deep-draft vessels. This obstacle was first tackled with the construction of wharves and by the use of lighters at high tide. The problem was ultimately resolved by the extension of the city out to deeper water—the "stream"—where vessels anchored.

The submerged lands of Yerba Buena Cove were the property of the U.S. government, which held title to all submerged and tidal lands in California in trust for the future state. In 1847, when alcalde Edwin Bryant requested permission to sell submerged land in Yerba Buena Cove to private investors, Military Governor Stephen Watts Kearny agreed after reserving certain areas for the United States. Kearny stipulated that the remaining property be subdivided and sold at public auction to the highest bidder, with the proceeds being used "for the benefit of the town of San Francisco."[27] The "beach and water lots" were surveyed in July 1847 and divided into 444 lots, each measuring 137 feet, 6 inches by 45 feet, 10 inches. The sale was advertised three months in advance with a prophetic announcement: "The site of the town of San Francisco is known by all navigators and Mercantile men . . . to be the most COMMANDING COMMERCIAL POSITION on the entire western coast of the Pacific Ocean, and the Town itself is no doubt destined to become the COMMERCIAL EMPORIUM of the western side of the North American continent."[28] The auction was held on July 20, 1847, with about 200 lots sold at prices averaging seventy-five dollars each.

The sale of the water lots benefited San Francisco by providing revenue for the city government. More important, it provided the means for the ultimate expansion of the city beyond its constraining cove to a deep-water anchorage. The city retained lots on which the various streets would run, if they were extended into the dove. Those lots running on an east-west axis were leased to entrepreneurs who built the wharves, which were the first structures to bridge the shallows of Yerba Buena Cove. Many lots were granted by civic authorities in 1848 and 1849, but another water-lot sale was held on January 3, 1850. The city had already expanded to the limits of the lots surveyed in 1847, so 328 additional lots were laid out. The auction brought exorbitant prices on 343 lots sold.[29] Additional lots were sold by court order to satisfy judgments against the city, the first in 1851 when 96 lots were sold for the benefit of Dr. Peter Smith. Smith, proprietor of the city hospital, was to be reimbursed by the city for caring for the indigent. When he did not receive compensation, he successfully sued and received a $19,239 judgment. The city, unable to pay, lost the water lots to Smith, for whose benefit they were sold at auction on September 19, 1851, to the chagrin of the city and many citizens, who saw valuable municipal property fall into the hands of a few speculators as San Francisco "was plundered of her inheritance."[30] After seven sales of city water lots were held, the California legislature stopped the practice. Additional lots were auctioned, however, this time by the city's "commissioners of the Funded Debt," in 1852, when property deeded by Justice of the Peace G. O. Colton in 1849 and 1850 was determined to be invalid because the lots had been deeded and not publicly auctioned as the law demanded.[31] The water lots, which in 1847 had not been enthusiastically sought, comprised by 1849 some of the most desirable property in town.

The water lots gave rise to an interesting maritime phenomenon of the gold rush. Conflicting titles and clashing interests between wharf companies and waterfront developers led to the employment of "hulk undertakers," who scuttled ships on the water lots to help establish title. The sinking of a vessel on a lot placed an "improvement" on the property. The best-known hulk undertaker was Captain Fred Lawson, who purchased three blocks of the notorious Dr. Peter Smith water lots in 1851. The blocks, bordered by Vallejo, Broadway, Front, and Davis streets; Pacific, Jackson, Davis, and Drumm streets; and Washington, Clay, East, and Drumm streets, were at the time submerged in water thirty-five feet deep and were used as slips for vessels, particularly for the Pacific Street wharf. The title to the lots was questionable (although later upheld by the California Supreme Court), hence Lawson got a bargain price of $3,500 each. Lawson said he "was not the only one who laid claim to the property," and he decided that the best way to establish a "perfect title was to float a ship in and sink her on the spot."[32] He had helped beach vessels for storeship conversion in 1849 and used this experience to guide him. The situation led to open warfare on the waterfront, and to a free-for-all between lot owners and other companies seeking to build wharves to serve the large numbers of vessels.

After sinking some vessels to establish his own title, Lawson was approached by others to do the same for them. The firm of Palmer, Cooke and Company asked Lawson to scuttle two vessels on a lot they claimed. He asked $5,000 for the job and was refused. The man then hired by Palmer and Cooke sank the bark *Cordova* and the brig *Garnet* after nearly loosing *Cordova* when she broke adrift. When the two were finally scuttled, they went down on lots belonging to the Pacific and Broadway wharf companies, forcing Palmer and Cooke to purchase the lots for $100,000! Palmer and Cooke, obviously displeased with the less than satisfactory results, next engaged Lawson to scuttle the former Russian collier *Rome* at Market and East streets. The job was by far the quickest he had performed, having been hastily hired in the morning to sink the ship before 1:00 P.M. the same day. When Lawson delivered, he was paid the same $5,000 fee he had asked for the previous job.

Lawson scuttled five vessels—*Elizabeth, Noble, Hardie, Bethel,* and *Inez*—on his lots, though not without some difficulties with the Pacific Wharf Company. The wharf companies, who held title to adjacent lots, were obviously not enamored of developers who bought up lots next to those held by the companies and occupied space with pilings and buildings that could otherwise be put to use as mooring space for vessels alongside the wharves. Lawson fiercely maintained his right to do as he wished with the property by driving pilings and sinking his ships. Heavily ballasting the vessels, Lawson would pierce the hull, plug the holes, then pull the plugs to quickly sink a ship in a precise location. Lawson explained his process and some of the requisite difficulty when he discussed scuttling the 207-ton bark *Noble* in early 1852:

> I put in plenty of ballast and scuttled her. . . . She cost me $500, I slipped her in very quietly one bright moonlight morning about 3 o'clock. Before I could drop her to the bottom the Pacific Wharf Company had the [steamer] Antelope astern, and before I could prevent it she had fastened a line to my boat and began to steam

away. She didn't take me too many feet, though, for with a cutlass I cut the line and with pistol in hand ordered them to keep off. They did so.[33]

On another occasion, while scuttling the ship *Bethel,* Lawson tied the ship to the wharf to hold position while it sank. The wharfinger tried to cut the line, so Lawson shot the knife from the wharfinger's hand.

Lawson's pile-driving activities also ran into difficulties. The piles he drove during the day were yanked out at night by crews employed by the wharf company. "I got a little tired of this," the captain later noted, so he brought in the ship *Inez* and sank her so close to the dock that the bowsprit "struck the wharf as she was settling and broke short off. . . . The crash informed the opposition of what was going on, but they were too late."[34] On another occasion, Lawson was employing a gang of 400 men to drive pilings when "suddenly we were fired on and one man was instantly killed." A gunfight erupted, ending without any other deaths but with one additional casualty—Lawson. While shouting orders, with his mouth open wide, Lawson was shot in the face, the bullet passing through his cheeks, missing his teeth and tongue. Lawson's beard hid the wound, and to the end of his days he sported on either side of his face "a hole . . . large enough to admit the end of the little finger."[35] Lawson was not deterred and returned to work the next day with a handkerchief binding his wound. To stop the battle, Lawson cut the anchor cables of five vessels moored alongside the wharf and towed them off his property before driving his last pilings. In the end, he won his battle with the wharf company, as did other property owners, but the loss was only a temporary victory; the wharves gradually extended into deeper water beyond the area of questionable titles and extensive development.

Waterfront real estate was valuable because frontage along the bay meant immediate access to discharging vessels. To reach these ships, many wharves and piers were extended across Yerba Buena Cove. The construction of wharves coincided with efforts to solve the shortage of buildings and the problem of millions of dollars of unprotected merchandise lying in the open on the wharves. The use of storeships, and the construction of shacks and warehouses on pilings along the waterfront and next to the wharves and piers, created not only colorful disputes such as Captain Fred Lawson's but also a unique city described as "a Venice built of pine instead of marble. It is a city of ships, piers, and tides. Large ships with railings, a good distance from the shore, served as residences, stores, and restaurants. . . . The whole central part of the city swayed noticeably because it was built on piles the size of ships' masts driven down into the mud."[36] Because the shallow waters of Yerba Buena Cove prevented large vessels from directly discharging their cargoes on the shore, one of the top priorities of city government was the construction of wharves and piers to cross the cove into the deeper water of the anchorage.

Prior to the Gold Rush, goods were landed by boat on the beach near the foot of Clay Street. The first wharf to be built was a landing constructed in 1847 along the line of Broadway Street at Clark's Point, a promontory at the base of Telegraph Hill at the northern end of Yerba Buena Cove that allowed deep-water access to vessels. Other wharves followed as the city, unable to finance wharf construction, leased the submerged rights-of-way for city streets to entrepreneurs and companies at favorable terms. After several false starts, the first wharf to bridge the shallows of Yerba Buena Cove was completed in the summer of 1849. With assistance from the municipal government, including a right-of-way into the cove between Clay and Sacramento streets (a private venture), the Central Wharf Joint Stock Company was formed in April 1849. On April 19, the San Francisco *Daily Alta California* reported that $100,000 had been raised in a forenoon for the wharf. "This is a very gratifying evidence of the interest, wealth, and enterprise of this community, and we have no doubt that the work will be undertaken with the same energy and carried to a speedy conclusion. The necessities of commerce, and the prosperity of the place, demand that such should be the fact."

In the first week of May, advertisements called for proposals to build a 36-foot-wide, 700-yard-long wharf. Work began on July 7, 1849, and by August 31, an advertisement in the *Daily Alta California* noted that "piles for its support have been driven for a distance of three hundred feet, and about one half that distance is already completed and planked." On September 20, the *Alta* noted that Central Wharf "has so far progressed as to admit small vessels and scows coming alongside." The wharf was extended through 1851, being praised in November 1850 as the first to be built "at a time when this port was quite destitute of every kind of facility for landing goods."[37]

The success of Central Wharf inspired the city to order wharf construction at the foot of every street, commencing with Market, Broadway, and Pacific streets. When municipal enterprise failed, five-year private contracts were let to build the wharves, and contractors paid a percentage of their profits as rent. Meanwhile, several private wharves were also built. One such wharf, built near the foot of Sacramento Street, was Howison's Pier, which was commenced early in 1850 (the Sacramento Street Wharf was not built until 1851). The foot of Sacramento Street had already "stood prominent as a reception point for merchandise" in 1849 and early 1850.[38] With the construction of Howison's Pier, Sacramento Street became the mercantile center of gold-rush San Francisco.

Other wharves built on city-street alignments between 1850 and 1853 were on Jackson, Clay, Vallejo, Market, Pacific, and Washington streets. As early as 1850, more than a million dollars had already been expended to build nine wharves that ranged in length from 250 to 975 feet, with a total wharfage of 6,000 feet.[39] This included wharves built on private property along the base of Telegraph Hill. Among the wharves was one at Clark's Point, with a stone pier just below it built by J. H. Merrill. Other Telegraph Hill wharves included Frederick Griffing's, Law's, Buckelew's, and Cunningham's wharf, which was advertised in October 1850 as being "now in order:"

> . . . having twenty-six feet of water at its end, and sufficient at the sides for the largest class vessels, offers great inducements to them to land there, as by doing so they will be able to discharge in one-half the time and at much less expense than they would be put to it by lying in the stream. . . . A spacious shed and fire proof building are connected with the wharf. . . . Goods landed or stored on this wharf, will have the advantage of being shipped by first class steamers to Sacramento city and the mining districts, free of all costs of cartage.[40]

Some wharf companies moored storeships alongside to store goods. Others lined the shallows along the wharves with buildings. In August 1849 the *Alta California* noted that near a private wharf at the foot of Pacific Street built by DeWitt and Harrison, the firm of Cross, Hobson and Company was "erecting a large building . . . which is to answer both as a storehouse and wharf" while "Messrs. Northam and Gladwin have also erected a large warehouse at the foot of Pacific street, which will answer the purposes of a wharf also."[41] The construction of wharves and buildings erected on stilts over water inspired tremendous maritime trade in Douglas fir pilings cut on the northwest coast and brought to San Francisco, some from as far away as British Columbia.

By 1850–1851, William Heath Davis claimed that Central Wharf was a significant feature of the city and "presented a scene of bustle and activity, day after day."

> The Central Wharf . . . was the thoroughfare for communication with vessels, and was crowded from morning 'til night with drays and wagons coming and going. Sailors, miners, and others of all nationalities, speaking with a great variety of tongues, moved busily about; steamers were arriving and departing, schooners

were taking in merchandise for the mines, boats were crowding in here and there—the whole resembling a great beehive, where at first glance everything appeared to be noise, confusion, and disorder.[42]

As early as 1850 a few north-south-axis streets were laid across the cove on pilings. Sansome and Battery streets were gradually extended to Market Street, though at first as narrow plank walkways without railings, erected atop a row of pilings. "Along this narrow way, pedestrians passed and repassed in the dark, foggy nights, singing and rollicking, as unconcernedly as if their path was broad Market Street, instead of an unprotected four-foot wide plank walk, with drowning depth of water awaiting the unwary traveler who might miss his footsteps."[43]

The shallows alongside the wharves were gradually filled in as the high sand hills and drifting dunes in the city were torn down and cast, along with San Francisco rubbish and garbage, into the bay. Several disastrous fires aided the process. In May 1851, after the worst conflagration the Gold Rush city faced, the San Francisco *Daily Herald* noted, "It is probable that the water lots will not be built upon again unless filled up, as the water in many cases is so low and the piles so numerous that the pile drivers cannot be used to prepare the superstructure."[44] Steam shovels were employed to systematically fill in Yerba Buena Cove, with much of the old waterfront disappearing by 1851, when a line limiting the extent of fill was established by the California legislature. In all, some twenty-one million to twenty-two million cubic yards of fill created much of what is now downtown San Francisco and extended the city's waterfront to a more desirable, if less sheltered, locale out in the bay.[45]

A waterfront location was ideal for most merchants because of the need for immediate access to discharging ships in the rapid pace of the Gold Rush market. Of twenty-one shipping and commission merchants listed in the 1850 San Francisco City Directory, a majority—fifteen—was listed within the nine-square-block area bounded by Montgomery, Jackson, Front, and California streets. Four were located on Sacramento Street, five on Montgomery, and four clustered around the intersection of Jackson and Sansome.[46] To increase business opportunities, the only logical place to build was out to the waterfront. The construction of Central Wharf and Howison's Pier at the already busy foot of Sacramento Street spurred hasty development along both wharves.

Construction was suspended until the end of winter 1849–1850, an extremely wet and muddy winter that curtailed most activity in San

Francisco. Spring 1850 was marked by a burst of pent-up energy as the city expanded. The hasty construction of buildings was noted in the San Francisco *Picayune* of August 10, 1850: "A CRASH—The frame of a building in course of erection on Howison's pier, fell this morning, with a great crash, carrying with it several workmen, who were engaged above, but fortunately injuring them but slightly. It will be probably put up next time with more regard for strength than speed."

By early 1851 a series of structures stood along Howison's Pier, then a 40-foot-wide, 1,100-foot-long pier at the foot of Sacramento Street. Here the city's maritime merchants established themselves in a compact area centered on Central Wharf no farther west than Montgomery Street and extending to the actual waterfront on East Street. Howison's Pier and the intersection of Sacramento and Battery streets in 1850 was described in a reminiscent account: "The corners of Sansome, Battery, and Sacramento streets were originally on piles— little piers just large enough to accommodate the stores and premises forming the junction of the streets. At high tide goods could be lightered from the shipping to the stores, and from the stores to the Sacramento and Stockton steamers."[47]

The area aptly illustrated the "Venice built of pine" aspect of the Gold Rush waterfront. In addition to the piling-supported stores and shops, four storeships were moored near Battery and Sacramento streets; the closest was *Apollo,* which had been hauled to the northwest corner of Battery and Sacramento streets in January 1850. Between Battery and Front streets on Sacramento lay *Thomas Bennett,* hauled in during March 1850. To the south, at the corner of California and Battery streets, *Tecumseh* and an unidentified brig were moored. On Battery and Clay stood *General Harrison;* a block farther inland, at Clay and Sansome, stood the first storeship to be hauled ashore (in August 1849), *Niantic.*

In October 1850 the San Francisco *Picayune* reported that "The click of the hammer, and the whir of the saw are continually heard. Large substantial warehouses, with numerous floating depots for the storage of merchandise, line our wharves and waterfront. . . . Masses of building materials are scattered through our streets."[48] The *Picayune* described one building just completed, the Cross, Hobson and Company warehouse at Sansome and Battery streets:

> This magnificent warehouse is supported by clusters of piles of the most solid quality and of the largest size, driven to a stone ledge. It extends one hundred feet in length parallel with Pacific; and has the breadth of twenty-five feet fronting on Battery street. It will be four stories high and possess a capability of sustaining

as great a weight as any of the "merchant palaces" of its size to be found in the Atlantic States. . . . The columns supporting this elegant structure weigh not less than three tons each. The beams and flooring are of solid iron.[49]

The waterfront lost its Venice-like quality in 1851 when a major conflagration leveled San Francisco. The fire began about midnight on May 3, 1851, and lasted into the evening of the next day. The most destructive of several fires to devastate San Francisco, it consumed more than 2,000 structures, including the storeships *Niantic, Apollo,* and *General Harrison.* The heat of the fire was intense: iron buildings melted, brick crumbled, and people trapped inside supposedly "fire-proof" buildings were literally baked to death.[50] Wooden buildings elevated over the water on pilings were burned when flames blew underneath them. Four days after the fire, the waterfront was "a melancholy array of charred posts. All the sleepers are burnt off, and in many instances the piles are burnt down to the water's edge."[51] In the aftermath of the fire, fill dumped over the ruins buried the old waterfront. Some buildings continued to be erected on pilings, but the lessons of the fire dictated new methods of construction. More substantial brick buildings gradually replaced wooden structures.

ESTABLISHING A MARITIME MERCANTILE COMMUNITY: THE SHIPPING AND COMMISSION MERCHANTS

Maritime trade and commerce created and sustained San Francisco. Although in 1849 some vessels bypassed the city to sail directly to Sacramento and the other interior river ports, San Francisco became the hub of the Gold Rush by 1850. Deep-draft oceangoing vessels discharged their cargo at San Francisco and small, shallow-draft sailing craft and steamers transshipped the merchandise to Stockton, Sacramento, and various landings and towns up the Sacramento and San Joaquin rivers.

Initially the arrival of shipborne goods at San Francisco was a haphazard, often chaotic affair. Some shipments brought goods that exceeded the demand, such as tobacco, iron, cement, salt beef and pork, shoes, and other bulk commodities. "The cost of storage being greater than their actual or prospective value, they could be turned to no better use than fillage. Thus entire lines of sidewalks were constructed of expensive merchandise in bales and boxes."[52] Another expedient means of disposing of cargo was by auction. An entire class of merchants—shipping and commission merchants—sprang into being in San Francisco in response to those conditions.

Dozens of shipping and commission merchants plied their trade in the city. Among the more notable was William Tell Coleman, who distinguished himself later as leader of San Francisco's three committees of vigilance. Years after the Gold Rush, Coleman explained the secret of his success as a shipping and commission merchant. "The early bird," he said, "was eminently successful in those times. Ships arriving overnight with desirable cargoes would be besieged by six o'clock next morning. . . . In all this there was little sharp practice, or dishonorable dealing. Business was carried on to a great extent upon honor. . . . but of course the shrewder sort, and those having the best knowledge of their business, would make money."[53] Coleman himself did well on his first transaction, purchasing a cargo of pickles from Captain Job Coleman (no relation) of the ship *Manchester*. The captain made Coleman pay an exorbitant price for his pickles, and also buy the remainder of his cargo. Coleman, realizing that pickles were a scarce item, advertised their availability in the early morning editions. When Captain Coleman landed his cargo the next day, William Tell Coleman's store was already crowded with eager buyers who purchased not only the pickles but also most of *Manchester*'s cargo, making the shipping and commission merchant a 100 percent profit.[54]

Other shipping and commission merchants included the firm of Turner, Fish and Company, 39 Sacramento Street, who advertised in early 1850 that "liberal advances made on merchandise to be offered for sale or left for storage. Sight bills on N. York for sale; gold dust bought at the market price."[55] Others included Hussey, Bond and Hale, who sold "vessels, lumber, provisions, flour, groceries and assorted cargoes" from their store on Howison's Pier.[56] Gildemeester, De Fremery and Company were also located on Howison's Pier. The firm of Osgood and Eagleston was located at Clark's Point, and one of its advertisements indicates the nature of the business:

John F. Osgood & John H. Eagleston of Salem, Mass., having associated themselves together for the purpose of transacting a general commission business in this city, have taken the new store at Clark's Point, where they offer for sale merchandise, just received per Osceola, as follows; writing desks, lounges, sofas, bureaus, card tables, beds, pillows and bolsters, blankets, carpeting, shoes, rubber boots, fine clothing, comforts, cashmere shawls, sperm candles, adamantine candles, mason's brushes, hair, doors, laths, pickets, saleratus, butter crackers, American segars, Spanish segars, Haxall flour, in half and whole bbls., cases of oysters, lobsters, turkey, chickens, pickles, sour krout, cabbage, onions, milk, plum cake, cook stoves, iron houses, 10 × 12, 12 × 15, 15 × 20, complete, cement, lime, and bricks.[57]

Every day the San Francisco newspapers were filled with advertisements from shipping and commission merchants, usually starting with the typical announcement, "Cargo of Ship ———, Just Arrived, from ——— . The subscribers offer for sale the following merchandise now landing from the above vessel, viz. . . ."

WATERFRONT SERVICES

Several concerns commanded the attention of both the town's merchants and shipmasters: the necessity of providing adequate measures to pilot vessels to a safe anchorage; the efficient loading and discharging of ships; the providing of crews for departing vessels; and the providing of necessary services and supplies to maintain a vessel in working order, be it repairs, sails, or the provisions supplied by a ship chandler. These needs were quickly met by a number of individuals who scrambled to establish waterfront service industries. Pilots formed companies, the legislature regulated and controlled the practice, and individually founded businesses handled cargo on lighters and at the docks. Shipping agents established offices to find crews; ship chandlers opened shops; and sailmakers, ship carpenters, and blockmakers opened shops and sail lofts. The first boardinghouses for sailors opened their doors, though some of the establishments were of dubious reputation. All in all, San Francisco's port received the much-needed support to service the ships and sailors.

Pilots. Guiding vessels across the occasionally rough outer bar, through the narrow gap of the Golden Gate, and to safe anchorage off the city was a difficult responsibility for ships' captains visiting the unfamiliar port. The first pilot, William A. Richardson, met incoming ships in the 1820s and 1830s that signaled him by firing two guns.[58] What worked well in the 1830s did not work at all in 1849. As the number of arriving vessels jumped to several per day, enterprising individuals entered the business as harbor and bar pilots.

The lack of an organized board, licensed pilots, or regularly established fees was a major concern of arriving shipmasters in 1849. The experience of Captain Henry Cleaveland, sailing through the gate on July 5, 1849, in the ship *Niantic*, was probably typical:

> . . . a pilot boat came alongside. "Do you want a pilot?" was the call. "Are you a regularly organized Board of Pilots?" was the Captain's query. "No, but we expect to be," was the reply. "Expectations won't save my ship," said Captain Cleveland. "What do you charge?" "Ten dollars a foot," said the pilot. . . . "What shall I do, Mr. Freeman," asked the Captain. "Tell him to go to Hell," said the Mate. "I have been in here before, and can do it again."[59]

The first Gold Rush pilots used a small Boston pilot boat, *Anonyma*, which arrived at San Francisco on June 27, 1849. James Fowler and Captain Kelly, two passengers on board, used the vessel for two months as a pilot boat before withdrawing her for river trade. Once they departed, San Francisco had no regular pilot service through the end of 1849.[60] The lack was severely felt, particularly after the near-disastrous stranding of the bark *Arkansas* in December 1849. Noting the "wreck," the *Alta California* also commented on the arrival of the ship *Boston*, which had been lost in the fog and anchored in a dangerous locale. The newspaper added this comment: "An organized Board of Pilots would materially relieve the difficulty and danger to which inexperienced shipmasters are frequently subjected in entering this harbor."[61]

Several San Francisco merchants petitioned Brevet Brigadier General Bennett Riley, military governor of California, to appoint pilots in December 1849, because "such appointments would promote the commercial interests of said port."[62] The California legislature, meeting in advance of California's admission to the United States, passed an act to appoint pilots on January 8, 1850. The governor was empowered to appoint twelve pilots, each required to pay $10,000 bond. The pilots were to keep at least "one boat or vessel for six pilots, in good condition and seaworthy, sufficiently large to cruise in heavy weather, to be exclusively employed as a pilot boat." The pilot boat had to cruise at least ten marine miles seaward from the San Francisco headlands. The pilots received eight dollars for each foot of draught for each vessel they piloted, with an additional six dollars a day for every day the ship was detained by headwinds, bad weather, or any other condition beyond the pilot's control.[63] General Riley promptly appointed six pilots described as "experienced and competent men" whose "knowledge of the harbor is perfect; and years of duty at the wheel, upon the rugged coasts of the Atlantic, has amply qualified them for the task. . . ." The six men, who had been recommended by San Francisco merchants and government officials, were George Simpton, Lewis Coxetter, Robert Wagstaff, Charles J. Wright, Charles Richardson, and Richard H. Leach. Purchasing the small schooner *Rialto*, the six quickly set about their new duties.[64] By February 4, 1850, advertisements noted that masters of outgoing vessels requiring pilots needed only to inquire of the pilot association's agent, B. Kelly, at the corner of Montgomery and California streets.

On February 25, 1850, the legislature passed another act establishing the Board of Pilot Commissioners for the Port of San Francisco.

Comprised of two resident merchants, two experienced and resident shipmasters, and the harbormaster, the board had the power to appoint and suspend pilots, collect fees, and maintain records of pilot boat arrivals and departures. Prospective pilots were now required to be examined by the Board of Pilot Commissioners. To be appointed, American citizenship was required and pilots had to pass a rigid examination "touching . . . qualifications concerning . . . knowledge of the management of square rigged vessels; of the tides, soundings, bearings and distances of the different shoals, rocks, bars and points of land, and night lights of the harbor and bay."[65] In 1850, six more pilots were appointed, operating in the boat *Relief*. In addition to the licensed "Outer Bar" pilots, the harbormaster employed five harbor pilots, and eleven pilots for the San Joaquin and Sacramento rivers kept an office in San Francisco.[66]

There were problems early on with the pilots. The bar pilots relinquished a vessel to the harbor pilots only when in the harbor; this practice angered many masters, who felt that pilots should stay with a ship until it was properly moored. The use of two pilots was onerous given the amount of money charged. The situation was one of "thorough, unqualified extortion," and shipmasters petitioned that pilots not receive their fee until a ship moored or went to sea, "as is usual in other ports."[67] The largest complaint, however, was the lack of pilots. In November 1850, the *Alta California* commented that it had often "heard complaints of the frequent impossibility of procuring pilots when most wanted," and supported a petition signed by merchants, shipmasters, and others "connected with the commerce of San Francisco" to the Board of Pilot Commissioners, nominating six more pilots. The petition stated that on the day of signing, six vessels had entered the harbor without obtaining pilots.

Another problem—unauthorized pilots on the bar—arose in 1851 when William Neal and Henry Van Ness, river pilots, and William Long, a harbor pilot, were caught in a "willful and obstinate infringement upon the rights of the Sea and Bar Pilots . . . by setting up an open opposition to them and piloting into and out of the harbor . . . sundry vessels." The Board of Pilot Commissioners revoked the three men's licenses.[68] The board also increased the number of pilots, and by 1852 two companies—"Old Line Pilots" and the "Opposition Line Pilots"—had formed, employing twenty-five men and five pilot boats: *Relief, Fanny, Sea Witch, R. B. Potter,* and *Favorite*.[69] By 1853 the port had three pilot lines with thirty-five pilots, twenty-four seamen (to sail the pilot boats) and eight boats employed by the Old Line, Opposition

Line, and Merchant Line.[70] The pilots, who operated as cooperatives with an agent handling their business affairs, maintained separate companies until they joined forces in the 1860s.

Lightermen and Boatmen. A problem most shipmasters faced on arrival in San Francisco was finding a mooring on the city's piers. The crowded waterfront often prevented ships from discharging at the few piers that stretched far enough into the stream to reach deep water. To land cargo quickly, most skippers had to depend on ship's boats or lighters, broad, flat-bottomed craft employed in the harbor specifically to load and discharge cargo. Lightermen found frequent employment, as did the boatmen who ferried passengers and visitors to vessels moored off the waterfront. The lightermen and boatmen fared better because many masters were unable to discharge their vessels with the ship's crew. Desertions and recalcitrant crews depleted the labor force usually available on board ship, compelling some masters, like that of the ship *Probus,* to virtually enslave their crews. Adolphus Windeler, a seaman aboard *Probus,* recorded his captain's plight in late December 1849:

> Brought one load of goods ashore & made two dollars. 5 of our [crew] deserted, in afternoon the captain made the following bargain with us. We the undersigned are to have 3 dollars a day besides our wages for discharging the cargo, and what is made in the longboat by carrying the cargo ashore, is to be divided amongst all hands & to be paid every Saturday night, A. Windeler & the rest of the crew.[71]

Windeler and the rest of the *Probus* crew finally came to a parting of the ways with their skipper and came ashore. There Windeler and some of his shipmates worked at odd jobs, including once helping discharge the brig *David Henshaw,* which involved taking fifty-six barrels of salt pork to the storeship *Salem* for five dollars a day plus board.[72] Windeler found, however, that odd jobs were hard to find on the waterfront. The lightermen had moved into the gap left by the sailors and were busily engaged with the ships in the harbor, hence jobs were scarce since the trade was "sewn up." On another morning, Windeler woke early to stand in line for a job "to fill a ballast lighter, but did not get it."[73] Bayard Taylor, describing the town in September 1849, stated that one of the first sights at sunrise was lighters "warped out from ship to ship" and running to shore to meet "carts and porters . . . busy on the beach."[74] These flat barges, poled along the shallows, carried the bulk of freight, while narrow whitehall boats ferried passengers.

As Augustus Windeler's experience indicates, most of the light-ermen were also in the ship storage business, being the owners, lessees, or employees of storeships or of vessels converted into floating ware-houses. One prominent lightering firm, Mohler, Cadue and Company, was in the "ship-storage business," owning the brigs *Piedmont* and *Casilda,* which were moored close to its offices on Howison's Pier. "It was very convenient for lightering goods to the up-river steamers, saving wharfage and drayage."[75] Other lightermen with storeships included L. L. Batchelder, who had the ship *Trescott;* Charles Read, with the storeship *Elizabeth;* Captain G. Chase, who owned *May-flower* and *Gold Hunter;* and M. R. Roberts, who owned *Alman-darina.*

By 1850 "nearly all the business was done by the lightermen into storeships, the city front and harbor having a large number of them."[76] The San Francisco City Directory for 1850 lists twenty-three light-ermen, including Mohler, Cadue and Company, who advertised the services they provided; "Ships discharged, supplied with water, and ballasted at the shortest notice."[77] The ships were discharged by horse-power. Double teams of horses provided the lift for cargo slung out of the ships' holds or off decks. "At the first sound of the boss stevedores, "go ahead," off they went until the next yell, "high," stopped them, and at a third call the sling load of merchandise would be slung out."[78]

The *Alta California* claimed that steam-hoisting engines were not introduced until two stevedoring brothers, Bill and Fred Morton, used one in July 1852 when they discharged the clipper *Tornado.* Steam technology was available in San Francisco as early as 1847; the failure to employ it may have been a result of lack of wharf space and reliance on the lighters, on which no steam "donkeys" were apparently in-stalled.

Of the twenty-three lightermen, eight organized into four part-nerships, with one company headed by Theodore Allen said to be "in the front rank" by 1850.[79] In addition to the independent lightermen and stevedores, various shipping and commercial merchants had others in their employ, the firm of Flint, Peabody and Company being one example. By 1882, when the *Alta California* published a reminiscence of the "old-time stevedores, Another Important Class of Pioneer Men Along the Wharves," it listed fifty-six men who had been employed as lightermen and stevedores in 1849 and 1850, including several who were still actively employed in the business some thirty-two years later. According to the *Alta*'s account, some lightermen monopolized the trade with vessels from specific ports: Stewart Menzies, Richard Lowrie, and James Childs, who served British vessels; Dave Bujac, "stevedore for all French ships"; James Chase, "an active stevedore of German vessels"; and Tom DeVries, who also sought a German clientele and was eventually in partnership with Chase.[80] Lightering paid well: in December 1850 lightermen commanded three to four dollars per ton of forty cubic feet.[81]

The 1850 city directory also listed twenty-seven boatmen, most clustered at the principal landings in the town—Central Wharf, Clark's Point, and the Sacramento Street Wharf. According to one account, the boatmen lived a hard life, "called up, as they were in early days, at all hours of the day and night, and not stopping for sea or weather. . . . 'First come, first served,' was the rule, and the first . . . boatman aboard 'took the cake.' "[82] The boatmen were in a position to make a lucrative living; *Niantic* passenger John M. Cushing, in July 1849, described his ship surrounded by boatmen who were charging ten dollars a head to ferry passengers ashore.[83] In addition to passengers, the boatmen also carried small orders of fresh meat, clothing, and supplies from a ship chandler to ships. The principal craft was the whitehall boat, a small, open boat built to carry several men, with sharp lines for fast pulling. Whitehalls, perhaps the most famous American rowing workboats, were employed not only by San Francisco's gold-rush boatmen as a "water taxi," but were also the principal tool of "ship chandlers, newspaper reporters, insurance adjusters and agents, pilots, and all others having business with shipping," as they were in other ports.[84]

By 1852 the San Francisco City Directory listed only seven lightermen, six individual stevedores, two stevedoring companies, and thirteen boatmen. The lightermen were for the most part located south of Market Street in Happy Valley. The area was a perfect location for the lightermen since Yerba Buena Cove south of Market was as yet not filled, unlike the waterfront north of Market Street, which had been almost completely filled in and lined with wharves by 1852. The decline in numbers for the three professions was not an indication of a dwindling maritime trade but rather indicated the maturity of the waterfront at the time, as demonstrated by a less-crowded waterfront, easier access, and more use of the city's now numerous wharves; crews not so eager to jump ship for the "diggins"; and the introduction of labor-saving steam hoists to the docks.

Shipping Agents. One of the greatest problems shipmasters faced at San Francisco was the near impossibility of keeping a crew. The discovery of gold spread gold fever among sailors as surely as it did among other professions. In late November 1848, Captain Christopher Allyn of the ship *Izaak Walton* wrote to his owners:

All hands have left me but two; they will stay till the cargo is landed and ballast in, then they will go. Both mates will leave in a few days, and then I will only have the two boys, and I am fearful that they will run. . . . As for the ship she will not lay here for a long time, but there's not the least chance of getting a crew. . . . A sailor will be up at the mines for two months, work on his own account, and come down with two to three thousand dollars, and those that go in parties do much better.[85]

The problem of keeping a crew persisted through 1849, 1850, and into 1851. Raising a crew to send a ship on a voyage was extremely difficult, particularly for prolonged deep-water voyages. Sometimes, by paying wages in excess of $200, coastwise vessels, including Panama steamers, did manage to crew their ships, although in many instances crews were formed by miners in distressed circumstances who sought free passage to or from California.

The traditional means of acquiring crews was to enlist the services of a shipping agent, who operated what amounted to seamen's employment agencies. Shipmasters did not ship a crew directly; they contracted with the shipping agent, who kept a list of men available and provided them before sailing, receiving a fee that generally ran to five dollars per man. The San Francisco City Director for 1850 lists only five shipping agents: C. A. Bertrand at Broadway and Battery near Clark's Point; Thomas Goin, offices at Central Wharf and Clark's Point; James Murray at Montgomery and Central Wharf; Joseph S. Spinney at the end of the Sacramento Street Wharf; and Wilson and Eagleston at Central Wharf. James Murray's name and payments for shipping of crews appear throughout the financial records of the Pacific Mail Steamship Company, as he apparently was the sole provider of seamen for the Panama steamers.

In 1851 and 1852 the business of shipping crews boomed. Desertions decreased, but vessel departures increased, so that in September 1851 the San Francisco *Daily Herald* noted, "We are informed that there is a great scarcity of seamen in our port at the present time and that vessels bound on an outward voyage are frequently delayed on this account. We are surprised at this considering the large number of this class who have arrived at this place, generally attached to the seafaring life, and the good wages paid which we understand are as high as $75 per month."[86] The *Herald* noted a few days later, "Directly the rains set in, this difficulty will then be removed, as numbers will flock down from the mines."[87] Not surprisingly, therefore, the 1852–1853 San Francisco City Directory lists sixteen shipping agents and offices, including Joseph Spinney, Thomas Goin, and James Murray. The majority of shipping offices at that time was located on Central Wharf. The services as advertised were simple: "T. J. Cundell, C. W. Anthony, E. T. Thebaud, CUNDELL & CO., Shipping Office, and Passenger Agents, Ships supplied with crews for sea and harbor duty. Cargoes discharged by estimate." Thomas Goin, advertising at the same time, promised "crews obtained for sea and harbor duty, at the shortest notice, and on reasonable terms."[88]

When crews could not be obtained by legitimate means, the alternative was the expedient means of kidnapping or shanghaiing a man for sea duty. The extent of the practice during the Gold Rush is unknown, though it is portrayed as widespread and is part and parcel of a latter-day view of the rough-and-tumble San Francisco waterfront of 1849–1850. According to the Reverend William Taylor, a San Francisco street preacher and seamen's rights advocate of the period, the practice was "ancient" but the term "Shanghai" was a "modern, California name," born of the Gold Rush. In an 1855 sermon, Taylor claimed:

> A few years ago, as many of you remember, it was very difficult to make up a crew in this port, especially for any place from which they could not get a ready passage back to this land of gold. Crews could be made up for Oregon, Washington Territory, the Islands, and the ports of South America; for from any of these places they could readily return. Even from Canton, they could stand a pretty good chance of a direct "run" back, but from Shanghae, they must make the voyage round the world. That was getting too far away from the "placers" of our mountains. Hence to get "crews" for Shanghae . . . they depended, almost exclusively, on drugging the men. Crews for Shanghae were, therefore, said to be "Shanghaed," and the term came into general use.[89]

Taylor told several stories of "sharks" or "crimps" shanghaiing sailors and unwary landsmen, including the sad saga of a German glazier who was "hired" to put glass in the stern gallery windows of a ship. As they rowed out, the shark offered the glazier an opium-laden cigar. When the glazier collapsed into the bottom of the boat, his pack of glass was thrown overboard and he was hoisted, supposedly drunk, onto the deck to be shipped before the mast. Worse yet, according to Taylor, he was kicked and cuffed throughout the voyage for having the presumption of "signing" himself on as an able-bodied seaman when he knew nothing of seamanship![90]

Shanghaiing continued in San Francisco long after the Gold Rush. The peculiar circumstances of the port during 1849 and 1850, combined with the sordid image of shanghaiing, indelibly etched a bad perception of shipping crews during the Gold Rush that in reality was usually a much more common and quieter business arrangement between a shipmaster and the shipping agent.

Miscellaneous Maritime-Support Service Industries. A variety of other maritime-support service industries slowly developed in the town through 1850–1851. Most were presumably started by former seamen who had "swallowed the anchor" to go gold mining. They probably found serving the active maritime trade in San Francisco a more lucrative profession than their past two endeavors, particularly in 1851–1852 as departures began to outstrip arrivals, indicating the unhealthy (to the maritime economy), enforced lay-up of ships as the gold excitement was ending.

This trend is reflected in entries in the San Francisco City Directory in 1850, when the listed miscellaneous maritime trades included William Lavers's "sailor's home" on Battery Street between Broadway and Vallejo. A few ship carpenters and caulkers were also listed in the 1850 directory, along with three sailmakers, including George Marstin "on board Bark Globe." By 1852, the number of miscellaneous maritime-related industries had increased, and several dozen newer individuals are listed in that year's city directory: carpenters, caulkers, joiners, and shipwrights working in the shipyards at Happy Valley; Joseph Eyre, a marine surveyor; a major sail loft operated by Captain Joseph Oat and C. G. Amory at 57 Front Street; and Fred Mitchell, a blockmaker at 16 Sacramento Street. The directory also listed Thomas Tennent, "Mathematical and Nautical Instrument Maker," at Commercial and Front streets. Tennent manufactured instruments and repaired and rated octants, sextants, and chronometers in addition to selling navigational charts. The large number of persons employed in shipping and port trades as reflected in the 1852 directory is another strong indication of the maturing of the port as the initial gold excitement died and the San Francisco waterfront settled down to business.

Chandlers. Among the oldest maritime industries were San Francisco's numerous ship chandlers, who were dealers in cordage, canvas, and any articles used to furnish a ship. Without chandlers to supply and provision ships in the harbor, San Francisco could not have sustained its status as an active and important port. The type of items chandlers sold to ships at San Francisco (or most ports, for that matter) are illustrated in the bill presented by New York chandlers Crosby, Crocker and Company to the master of the ship *Charles Crooker* on November 11, 1850. In addition to preserved or dried foods, the bill included a bale of oakum, two barrels of tar, tins of white lead, varnish, turpentine, and black paint, wicking, rigging leather, brick, one dozen corn brooms, matches, manila rope, tarred cordage, and copper tacks.[91]

Ship chandlers were an important part of the maritime activity of the port. Only three individuals appear as chandlers in the 1850 San Francisco City Directory: Thomas Bargin, "chandler," corner of Green and Powell streets; John W. Smith, "ship chandlery," Happy Valley; and William C. Hoff on Howison's Pier. Others undoubtedly also sold to ships, such as James B. Weir, a grocer and commission merchant on Clay Street near Montgomery, who advertised in the 1850 city directory that he had "constantly in store, and receiving daily, fresh supplies of goods suitable for traders. Also, ship and Miners' stores."[92]

One of the largest ship chandler's shops in San Francisco was located at the corner of Sacramento and Battery streets. High above the tidal waters of Yerba Buena Cove on pilings stood the two-and-a-half-story store of William C. Hoff and Henry Owner, ship chandlers. On the second floor, San Francisco's harbormaster, George Simpton, kept his office. Both establishments required ready access to the ships in the harbor, Hoff and Owner to provision and supply vessels, Simpton to greet arriving vessels and to indicate a safe berth for a ship to discharge its cargo or moor. A trapdoor in the southeast corner of the ground floor and the staircase beneath it led to the water and, most likely, a whitehall boat or two tied up to the pilings that allowed the proprietors and the harbormaster to quickly descend to the water and row out under the Battery Street Wharf to a waiting vessel. "Under the store the tide ebbed and flowed. From the rear of this and all the stores between California and Pine streets, lighters could be loaded or discharged.[93]

William Cebra Hoff, a native of Johnstown, New York, emigrated to California at age forty-three in the ship *Tarolinda*, arriving at San Francisco on July 6, 1849. In 1850 Hoff was listed at the "foot of Sacramento Street" in the San Francisco City Directory. He was not listed as such but may have already been a ship chandler, however, by 1852: "Wm. C. Hoff, shipchandlers, 27 Sac," was listed in the directory. Hoff was located in this building in the spring of 1850, at a time when the structures along Howison's Pier were first built, indicating that he was probably an original tenant, if not the owner. In the June 1850 fire several refugees found safe haven in the "rooms over Mr. Hoff's store, on the extreme end of Howison's Pier."[94] Hoff's store stood until the fire of May 3–4, 1851, destroyed it. The site was immediately filled when Hoff and Owner rebuilt on the spot, but its special physical connection with the waterfront was lost when the area was developed into a dryland mercantile neighborhood. Hoff and Owner, however, remained in business well after the Gold Rush.

The most significant ship chandlery was the firm of Folger and Tubbs. The principal partner in the firm, Captain William H. Folger, established the business in the fall of 1850 with twenty-two-year-old Alfred A. Tubbs, recently arrived from Concord, New Hampshire. Locating the business on a wharf close to the water, Folger and Tubbs built a store at No. 49 Pacific Wharf, near the future intersection of Pacific and Front streets. An 1851 catalog of its stock listed the company as "Importers and Dealers in Ship Chandlery, Ship Stores, Steamboat Stores, and Naval Stores." Every conceivable market was covered in the catalog. The primary item sold was rope, including manila, cotton, hide, hemp, and bolt rope, spunyarn, wormline, ratline, and houseline. Other goods listed included gin wheels, job hanks, log chips, clout nails, leading trucks, firmer chisels, long jointers, spoke shaves, salometers, "petticoat lanterns" and kedges, in short, "every conceivable item a ship would need to operate."[95]

The company was listed in the city directory in 1852 at 49 Pacific, where it remained and prospered through 1854. Alfred Tubbs, writing enthusiastic letters back home, convinced his older brother Hiram to come to California. Arriving unceremoniously on the wrecked Pacific Mail steamer *Tennessee* in March 1853, Hiram Tubbs became his brother's new partner. Captain Folger, ready to retire, sold his interest in the business in January 1854 to the two brothers for $1,528.67.[96] A dissolution of the Folger-Tubbs partnership was signed at the end of the month, and by year's end the two brothers had moved to larger quarters at 139 Front Street, between Jackson and Pacific. The brothers continued to prosper, ultimately establishing in 1856 the first cordage-manufacturing factory on the Pacific coast when they built a ropewalk in San Francisco's Potrero District. Their firm, the Tubbs Cordage Company, continued in business in San Francisco until 1987.

The maturity of the port was further reflected by a tremendous increase in ship chandlers by 1852. To service the numerous vessels actively arriving and departing on a waterfront previously clogged for two years by a fleet of "deserted" vessels, no less than nineteen chandlers emerged, most joining forces to form partnerships. Grouped together on the waterfront, the majority of chandlers was located on Sacramento Street. A typical chandlery was the firm of J. D. Farwell and James F. Curtis at 38 Commercial Street, which advertised in early January 1852 that it had extended the company store into a fireproof brick building that stood at the rear of its old shop on Central Wharf.

The company advertised in the January 7, 1852, edition of the *Daily Alta California* that it was prepared to offer a large "and complete assortment of Ship and Steamboat Chandlery and Stores, Naval Stores, India Rubber Packing, Cotton and Flax canvass, Hemp and Manilla Rope, Paints, Oils &c, and are receiving by Clipper arrivals, constant additions to their stock."

The vagaries of business constantly changed the number and names of the chandlers. The business, however, which had started small in 1850, grew to proportions commensurate with a major port as early as 1851–1852 and remained strong through the following decades. It ultimately spawned a major industry through the auspices of Messrs. Tubbs' ropewalk, for some time the only rope-manufacturing firm on the Pacific coast. The story of the ship chandlers, like the various other maritime-support services and industries, demonstrates that the boost the port received from their presence in 1849–1850 was paid off handsomely in the years that followed, as San Francisco consolidated its position as the principal American port in the Pacific basin.

SAN FRANCISCO ELECTS A HARBORMASTER

The random mooring of ships created a host of problems on the San Francisco waterfront. Vessels, particularly steamships commencing regular service between Panama and San Francisco, or between inland river ports and the city, could not reach the wharves to load or discharge. Closely moored vessels in the crowded confines of the cove were constantly going adrift and colliding with one another. What was needed was order afloat, order enforced by a harbormaster who would see to proper mooring and berthing and look after the port's interests.[97]

The Legislative Assembly of the District of San Francisco considered the appointment of a harbormaster during two weeks of meetings commencing on March 17, 1849. On April 3, 1849, it passed a law establishing the office and appointed Captain Edward A. King to the position. The assembly quickly moved to inform the newly appointed harbormaster of his responsibilities:

> In view of the approaching bad weather and heavy winds, as well as for the safety of private property and the promotion of the commerce of the town, the Council request the Harbor Master to have all vessels, not receiving or discharging cargoes, removed to Wood Island or to the south side of Rincon Point.[98]

The need for a harbormaster was quickly underscored during the winter of 1849. A French visitor, on board the ship *Georges* in mid-harbor, wrote in his journal on December 16, 1849, that he had seen "ships strain and drag their anchors so badly that we saw several collisions. From here we would see the *Ceres*, several hundred feet away from the ship where we had taken refuge, struck very violently by three large vessels and a section of her stern caved in."[99]

The first ordinance passed by the newly incorporated City of San Francisco regulated the duties of the harbormaster. Passed by the board of aldermen on May 15, 1850, and hastily approved by Major Jonathan Geary on May 16, ordinance no. 1 ordained that

> the Harbor Master shall have all the power and authority vested in the corporation of this city, to regulate and control the position of the steamers, sailing vessels, or other craft lying and situated in the harbor. . . . He shall, whenever it is deemed advisable, cause any steamer, sailing vessel, or other craft to change its position. . . . It shall be the duty of the Harbor Master to keep an open and free passage to all wharves of the city.[100]

The harbormaster was given the power to call upon the "mayor, marshal, and police of the city, to aid and assist him." When the appointment of Captain King was approved by the military governor of California, Brevet Brigadier General Bennett Riley, on June 19, 1849, the harbormaster was finally ready for business.

Edward A. King served as San Francisco's appointed harbormaster through the end of 1849. King's initial efforts focused on untangling the packed mass of ships on the waterfront. During the first week of November 1849, King ordered all "merchant ships in this harbor will clear hawser on or before the 15th instant, and cockbill their lower yards."[101] Clearing the crowded anchorage, replete with ships tangling in one another's moorings and rigging, was an impossible task for one man, so King's wise decision to order each master or owner to attend to his own vessel solved the problem for the entire harbor. The effort was not completely successful, though, as the number of ships increased dramatically in 1850.

King's successor, the first *elected* harbormaster, was James Hagan, who kept offices at Commercial Wharf and Clark's Point.[102] Apparently near financial ruin caused by having to personally fund his duties forced Hagan to decline to run for reelection in 1851. He was succeeded by George Simpton, an outer bar pilot on board the pilot schooner *Rialto* in 1850.[103] Upon assuming his new duties in December 1850, Simpton moved the office, serving notice in the March 28, 1851, edition of the *Daily Alta California:*

> For the convenience of ship masters, merchants, and others connected with shipping, an office has been opened at Messrs. Hoff

and Owner's store, on the wharf at the foot of Sacramento St., where all orders and applications may be left at any hour of the day. The Harbor Master can be found at this office between the hours of 10 and 12 N, and at the office on Cunningham's Wharf from 3 until 5 PM, and at his dwelling on the wharf, foot of Broadway, at all other hours. Geo. Simpton, Harbor Master.

Even with considerable authority conferred by the town council, the job of harbormaster was difficult. More than a year after the position was created, the harbor remained crowded as more vessels arrived, although it was noted that the harbormaster had made "a good beginning in opening an ample thoroughfare" through the crowded mass of ships to allow the passage of the Panama and river steamers.[104] During the winter of 1850, several accidents occurred as poorly moored vessels collided when they shifted in stormy weather. During one gale, the bark *Harvest*, breaking free, drifted into and sank one vessel before careening off and damaging several others.[105] The San Francisco *Picayune* noted on November 27, 1850, "We are sorry to say that there are now in this harbor quite a number of vessels badly moored, with anchors and chains so foul that they endanger the whole fleet. The Harbor Master, we understand, has been at the expense of removing and mooring several himself." Harbormaster Simpton endeavored to clear the port, notifying owners of "abandoned" vessels in December 1850 that "if they do not take care of them forthwith, he will do it for them."[106]

Although the law empowered the harbormaster to move any vessel and "have such position made at the expense of the City and cause suit to be entered against the owner, master, captain, or agent of said vessel for the costs of removal," the harbormaster usually bore the costs personally. It is not surprising that on March 3, 1854, the town council appropriated $1,110 for the relief of James Hagan, "late Harbor Master, for costs incurred by him in the performance of his official duties."[107]

Harbormaster George Simpton suffered a setback when his office was destroyed when Hoff's store burned and collapsed into the bay during the May 4, 1851, fire. The destruction of the office did not deter Simpton from remaining at Hoff's, however, and when Hoff and Owner rebuilt, Harbormaster Simpton remained a tenant. The published "Regulations of the Harbor and Port of San Francisco," dated October 1, 1851, lists Simpton's "Offices, on the corner of Sacramento and Davis streets, and at Hoff & Owner's Ship Chandlery Store, near Long Wharf." Simpton meanwhile vigorously pursued his duties, advertising in the San Francisco *Daily Herald* in June 1851 that any

vessels lying idle without persons aboard were to be removed immediately.[108] Simpton met, however, "with great difficulty and opposition from the owners and agents of these vessels when he has attempted
to remove them."[109]

The problem remained unresolved in August 1851, when it was
noted that owners were still resisting Simpton's orders to clear from the
waterfront and moor either in the lee of Rincon Point or in the stream.
The town council was urged to pass an ordinance to assist the harbormaster. The San Francisco *Daily Herald* reported that Simpton "has
labored most faithfully to discharge his duty, and has reduced the
harbor from the state of chaos in which he found it to a state of
comparative order; but there are . . . serious difficulties. . . . he finds
himself . . . wholly powerless to carry out the regulations."[110] The
harbormaster did receive help. Harbor regulations posted on October
1, 1851, stated that "disobedience to the orders of the Harbor Master,
in the discharge of his duty, will subject the offender to a fine of five
hundred dollars . . . according to law." As a result, by January 1852
only forty-six vessels were "more or less badly moored."[111] By the end
of 1852 energetic work, coupled with increased vessel departures, had
cleared the shipping lanes and much of the waterfront. Photographs
show the crowded graveyard of ships, most of which would never sail
again, at Rincon Point, and also document the active shipping and an
occasional storeship at the city's wharves. By 1853–1854, work to clear
the ship graveyard had commenced in earnest, firmly closing out the
pioneer era of the harbormaster's activities and clearing the last physical
reminders of the Gold Rush harbor.

The facilities and skills needed to transform San Francisco's small
anchorage into the most important American port on the Pacific were
hastily combined in 1849–1850 as shipping boomed on the waterfront.
Molded by the pressures of at times a dozen arrivals per day and the
needs of hundreds of vessels massed along the city's wharves, San
Francisco first became an instant port, then a city. The refinement of
both in the aftermath of a series of disastrous fires culminated after
1853 with the emergence of a world-class port worthy of the shipping
it hosted and supported.

Chapter Four
REGULATION AND INDUSTRIALIZATION

The problems of protecting and regulating maritime trade and commerce in California occupied the attention of the conquering United States even as the Mexican War continued. The naval force in California was by far the largest show of force made by the United States in California until the 1847 arrival of volunteer troops for the army. Even then with army officers governing the conquered territory, the navy remained the primary force guarding California's ports and the only means for regulating maritime commerce. The gold discovery exacerbated the problems of maintaining the Pacific Squadron in California. Desertions and discontent plagued the commanders of naval vessels, while the tremendous influx of vessels at California ports, including many foreign arrivals, emphasized the need for proper licensing, customs, and seagoing law and order. The navy quickly asserted itself, enforcing shipboard discipline on merchant vessels and patrolling coastal waters. Both army and navy officers served as collectors at the various ports, as California's military government collected revenues to use for conducting the affairs of the conquered province. The burden of these duties was largely relieved when the U.S. Treasury Department took responsibility, utilizing two important arms—the revenue marine and collectors of the port.

The need for regulating shipborne commerce was matched by the need for adequate protection for shipping. In the early 1850s monies were appropriated, plans drawn, and construction commenced on the first navigational aids built by the United States on the Pacific coast as well as seacoast and harbor fortifications to augment navy ships. As a series of emplacements and a mighty brick and granite fortress rose respectively on Alcatraz Island and at Fort Point on San Francisco Bay, the U.S. Navy began constructing a large naval shipyard and base at Mare Island on the bay's upper reaches. Shipbuilding and repair of merchant vessels also boomed, and small foundries specializing in marine boilers and steam engines were built on the shores of Happy Valley on San Francisco's southern waterfront. Derelict vessels clogging the waterfront were dismantled for their fittings and timber. At the same time, California gained its first major industrial complex at Benicia with the construction of a massive complex of joinery, shipwright, boilermaking, and engine-manufacturing shops, and a provisioning and coaling depot for the steam fleet of the Pacific Mail Steamship Company. By the mid-1850s, California boasted several maritime industries, a naval base, seacoast forts, lighthouses, and the extension into the state of customs, revenue, and marine laws of the United States.

COLLECTORS OF THE PORT

Isolated from the rest of the nation by the vastness of the continent, and lacking industrial and agricultural development, California thrived on foreign trade. The bulk of trade was also a financial boon to the United States, which had acquired California in 1848 at considerable expense because of the Mexican War. The active maritime trade in the new Pacific territory encouraged the substantial collection of duties on imported goods and merchandise. Congress, eager to collect revenue generated by California's Gold Rush trade and also desiring to establish American laws and regulations in the new territory, responded by extending U.S. revenue laws to California on March 3, 1849. The act set aside ports, harbors, and inland waters of California as a new federal collection district and established a port of entry at San Francisco with ports of delivery at San Diego, Monterey, and "as near as may be to the junction of the rivers Gila and Colorado, at the head of the Gulf of California." The act provided for the appointment of a collector of the Port of San Francisco, who, with three deputies at the other ports, was granted the power to establish collection districts, enforce customs laws, regulate foreign trade, and collect revenue.[1]

Within two weeks President Zachary Taylor selected the first collector of the Port of San Francisco, choosing James Collier, a native of Connecticut, veteran of the War of 1812, and a Whig party stalwart. Vessels and cargoes from foreign ports could land only at San Francisco, where they had to pay the necessary duties and only then proceed to a designated port of delivery. Collier's primary duties were to enforce this rule, to serve as agent for the collection of duties for the relief of sick and disabled seamen, and to establish lighthouses. As collector, Collier licensed vessels for coastal trade and oversaw the inspection and registration of vessels. He also served as a "depositary of public moneys" collected in California. Assistant collectors could be selected by Collier and placed at the designated ports of delivery, customs inspectors could be hired, and a warehouse could be rented to store cargoes at government expense. For these services, Collier received an annual salary of $1,500, a three-percent commission on all duties (not to exceed $3,000 per year), and an additional $400 per annum for other incidental duties. Collier was empowered to call upon the revenue cutter *C. W. Lawrence* to enforce the revenue laws. As for any unforeseen circumstance, "in view of the great distance of your district, and the consequent infrequency and uncertainty of regular communications, much must be left to your good judgement and discretion, which the department confidently expects will, within the limits of the law, be judiciously exercised."[2]

After making preparations, Collier and a group of young men he had selected as assistants (including two of his sons) made an arduous six-month overland journey to San Diego. There, Collier boarded the brig *Malek Adhel* and sailed to San Francisco, arriving on November 12, 1849. A considerable amount of work and an office in complete disarray greeted him. Just two weeks before his arrival, Acting Deputy Collector J. D. Carr and Appraiser Abraham Kentzing, Jr., had complained in a letter to Treasury Secretary William Meredith that "this office has never as yet been supplied with any locks for ship's hatches, nor any gauging or weighing machines, not measures of any kind, and this being a new country, it is impossible to purchase such things here."[3] They requested 300 to 500 locks, fifty pairs of scales and balances, gauging rods, and extra copies of the revenue and tariff laws of the United States. Collier added his voice to theirs in his first report:

> I am perfectly astounded at the amount of business in this office. . . . The amount of tonnage, however, on the 10th instant [November 1849] in port, was 120,317 tons, of which 87,494 were American, and 32,823 were foreign. [The] Number of vessels in the harbor on that day . . . 312, and the whole number of arrivals since the first of April, 697; of which 401 were American, and 296 foreign. This state of things, so unexpected, has greatly surprised me.[4]

Collier noted the clerks made more money than he did. He complained that the customhouse was an old adobe structure, "a long, dark one story building, in miserable condition" with most of the doors off their hinges and with a roof that leaked when it rained. With the gold-inflated prices of San Francisco, Collier reasoned that the costs of repair of the adobe or rent for a new customhouse were exorbitant and impossible to pay. Collier asked to build additional warehouse space because "in a commercial point of view, this port is equal to that of Philadelphia," and the "necessity of providing suitable buildings without delay must be seen and acknowledged."[5]

Collier found his duties overwhelming. He had not men enough to do the job; the coast was unguarded and smuggling was rife. He specifically mentioned the port of San Pedro. "I am fully of the opinion that more goods are landed at San Pedro than at any other point, excepting only San Francisco." Collier proposed that San Pedro be made a port of delivery and the proposed port on the Gila River be abandoned, erroneously believing the Colorado River would never be navigated. "I presume no white man could be found willing to become deputy collector in a port where a flag would never flutter." Collier also noted two major deficiencies that hampered his effectiveness— California needed a court to adjudicate seizures of vessels for revenue law violations and a marine hospital; "almost daily applications are made for relief or assistance by sick and disabled seamen."[6]

Collier begged for additional staff, claiming that "the situation of the bay, there being no wharves, renders it necessary for vessels to anchor some distance from the shore, and goods are landed by lighters and small boats, employed for that purpose. This together with . . . the high price of storage . . . either induces or compels the owners or consignees to keep their cargoes on board (the same being bonded) and consequently an officer must remain, for sometimes weeks, perhaps months, on board;—this will account for the large number of inspectors."[7]

Through 1849 and 1850 Collier struggled to remedy the problems he had inherited and to establish his authority. Both were not easy tasks. The lack of adequate storage space compelled the collector to least three storeships, *Elizabeth, Zuid Pool,* and *Knickerbocker,* for use as bonded warehouses. *Elizabeth* featured in an embarrassing incident for the collector in July 1850, when a customs inspector and Captain Webster of *Elizabeth* gathered a group of men and tried to remove the ship *Audley Clarke. Clarke* had anchored on a water lot where Collier was about to build a bonded warehouse, and the captain refused to move. While the dispute was being resolved, Webster and his companions forcibly boarded the ship and tried to slack her chains; "a general row" erupted that had to be broken up by the police, resulting in "a few blackened eyes, scratches and bruises" and a court appearance for all.[8] Eventually *Audley Clarke* was moved, but the problems of storage space and the need for a proper customhouse persisted. Collier did move out of the old adobe customhouse (renting it out for $9,000) and leased another building in the city for his own use.

Government officials in Washington, D.C., made arrangements to build a new customhouse. Lieutenant Colonel Charles Thomas of the U.S. Army contracted with twenty-seven men of Bangor, Maine— carpenters, masons, painters, wheelwrights, a cabinet maker, a turner, a brickmaker, and a blacksmith—to sail with the necessary materials, including bricks shipped as ballast, to San Francisco to build the customhouse. The government paid for their passage to California, gave them a fair wage, and provided for their subsistence. Sailing from Bangor on October 6, 1849, on the bark *Gold Hunter,* the "company of mechanics" arrived at San Francisco on March 26, 1850. By July 1850 they had completed a four-story customhouse, which stood until destroyed by the fire of May 3–4, 1851.[9]

Collier gained many enemies by his insistence on stopping foreign vessels from engaging in the internal trade of California, since law expressly forbade it. Urged not to cancel licenses granted by the U.S. Navy to foreign vessels because there were not enough American vessels to supply the needs of the inland ports, Collier was told, "Were the craft in question suddenly thrown out of trade not only would the owners thereof be great losers, but the now ill-supplied Emigrants, and the population of the great valleys of the Sacramento and San Joaquin would be subjected to the greatest extortion for all the necessities of life already frightfully deficient in the mining district."[10] Collier realized the need but strictly applied the law, noting, "I should exceedingly regret that the strict enforcement of the laws should inflict injury upon any portion of my countrymen, but I am not vested with discretionary powers upon such subjects. I must abide by the law whatever it may be."[11] On November 15, 1849, the new collector announced in the *Alta California:* "Notice is hereby given to all concerned, that Licenses granted to any ship or vessel [other than "ships or vessels of the United States entitled to be enrolled or licensed"] for carrying on trade in the Bay of San Francisco and its tributaries, or within said collection district, are hereby *revoked* and that said license is required to be surrendered."

Collier's strict view of the law also resulted in his enforcement of a law prohibiting the importation of bottled liquor in quantities of less than fifteen gallons. He placed a deputy at San Pedro to hamper smuggling at that port. He determined as well that vessels built in California but engaged in trade prior to the American conquest had not become "naturalized" by the treaty of peace ceding California to the United States and were not to be granted the privileges of American ships.

A deficiency Collier regretted was the absence of a U.S. District Court with authority to hear admiralty cases. Seizures for violations of law, and libels of vessels by passengers and consignees, had to be adjudicated in Louisiana or Oregon. The distances and difficulties led to the extralegal establishment of local- and state-convened admiralty courts that assumed authority for all maritime matters. Collier refused to accept their authority:

> I presume there is no port on earth where commerce is more embarrassed, or where more wanton sacrifice of property is sanctioned or tolerated. Hardly a ship enters the bay before she is waited upon by the sheriff, and an officer put on board by him. No matter from what country she may come, or to what nation she may belong, judgments are rendered and executions are levied within a week, and the ship advertised for sale. The exercise of jurisdiction by these courts in such cases I am apprehensive will be attended with difficulty hereafter. Much harm has already been done to foreigners, and much to our own countrymen. [12]

Feeling that due process of law was lacking, Collier held the registers and licenses of these vessels and refused to surrender them following a municipal court-ordered sale. His obstinacy resulted in a meeting of citizens and the lodging of a complaint with the secretary of the treasury by those who had profited from the irregular proceedings of the local courts. The matter was finally resolved in 1851 when the U.S. District Court for California's northern district was established in San Francisco, and President Fillmore appointed Ogden Hoffman of New York as the presiding judge. A strong advocate of passengers' and seamen's rights, Hoffman adjudicated 150 admiralty cases in his first decade on the bench. [13]

James Collier's critics and their constant allegations against him induced Secretary Meredith to send Special Agent Gilbert Rodman to San Francisco to investigate the collector. Rodman's reports attracted the attention of three secretaries of the treasury—William Meredith, Thomas Corwin, and James Guthrie—for more than three years. The reports were instrumental in ultimately securing Collier's removal from office. Rodman collected affidavits alleging fraud, embezzlement, and misuse of government funds and forwarded them to Washington. He intimated that Collier had pocketed monies from the rent of the old adobe customhouse, sold cargoes seized by the government and pocketed the receipts, and exhibited "gross misconduct and illegality" by having cronies within the banking firm of Wells and Company deposit $100,000 in the customhouse vaults to cover missing public funds while Collier kept Rodman otherwise occupied.[14]

Although the charges were never sustained, Collier lost his job. In response to needs Collier had repeatedly stressed in his official dispatches and demonstrated in the able conduct of his duties, Congress established on September 28, 1850, six collection districts in California, with ports of entry at San Francisco, Sacramento, and other locales.[15] President Fillmore nominated Collier for a new term of office as collector of the port for the San Francisco district, but the Senate refused to confirm his nomination and he was replaced by Thomas Butler King of Georgia in February 1851. James Collier left his successor in good stead; as one biographer has noted, the difficulties Collier faced upon his arrival in November 1849 had been adjusted at his urging by the secretary of the treasury and the recent legislation. Critics notwithstanding, Collier returned east to vindication and spent his last years as a banker. He died in 1873 at the age of seventy-four with his significant contribution to California's maritime trade and commerce all but forgotten.

THE REVENUE MARINE IN THE GOLD RUSH

The United States Revenue Marine, created in 1790 by Secretary of the Treasury Alexander Hamilton, performed duties in addition to the enforcement of revenue laws. Throughout its history the service aided vessels in distress, engaged in lifesaving and salvage, suppressed the slave trade and piracy, carried government diplomats and dispatches, and assisted the navy in wartime, "all with their many incidental adventures," eventually merging with other government agencies in the twentieth century to become the United States Coast Guard.[16] In 1844 the revenue marine, which had previously been supervised by political appointees with little or no experience and with many accompanying abuses, was professionalized by the appointment of Captain Alexander V. Fraser, an officer from the ranks, as commandant. Fraser had control of personnel, promotion, and discipline, but not of the individual vessels or cutters in the service that were subject to the supervision of the collectors of the ports where they were stationed. Incidents of interference and abuse continued with this arrangement, and friction between Fraser and powerful collectors arose, friction that four years later would result in Fraser's reassignment.[17]

In 1848 seven new cutters were ordered for the revenue marine, which had suffered substantial losses of vessels in the recent Mexican

War. One of these, *C. W. Lawrence,* built at Washington, D.C., by William Easby, was probably laid down in late 1847 or early 1848.[18] The first mention of the ship was in December 1847, when Baltimore sailmakers Kirby and Whittington were ordered to make "sails, Awning, Bags, Hammocks, Hammock cloths, Tarpaulins &c for the new revenue brig . . . have them ready for shipment to this City [Washington] on or before the first day of May next."[19] By July 1848 *Lawrence* was armed with ten guns—two 32-pounders, a long 18-pounder, and two 6-pounders in addition to carbines, percussion pistols, Colt revolvers, boarding pikes, and cutlasses.

Launched on August 20 and christened *Cornelius W. Lawrence* after the collector of the Port of New York, the brig was to be commanded by Captain A. V. Fraser on the voyage to San Francisco. Between August 20 and October 10 *Lawrence* was fitted out with supplies as final touches to her rig were made and the ship was painted black. On October 11 the revenue marine took formal possession and a thirty-five man crew came aboard. On November 1 the brig weighed anchor for the Pacific. After a stop at Norfolk, Virginia, for additional provisions, which included 1,825 pounds of black powder, the ship entered the Gulf Stream on November 17.

Lawrence encountered fierce storms within a week of entering the Gulf Stream. The ship's departure late in the year exacted a heavy toll and almost a year passed before she reached San Francisco. The voyage was nearly epic as storms and strong head winds damaged the ship and brought Captain Fraser's temper and sharp tongue into play. On December 22 a weary Fraser remarked on the strain of the voyage in a terse note to his officers:

> As a particular favor, it is requested that at least until the arrival of the vessel at Rio the duty shall be carried on quietly. Having scarcely felt any relief from the cares of the deck on this passage, it is absolutely necessary that I should obtain the rest which it appears predetermined to deprive me of.[20]

Land was sighted on January 16, 1849, and the following day *Lawrence* anchored at Rio de Janeiro. Lengthy shoreside repairs delayed the voyage for almost two months; work crews caulked leaky seams and removed and repaired damaged spars and rigging. When the work was completed on March 7, *Lawrence* again hoisted anchor and set sail for Cape Horn.

Fierce gales met the ship at the storm-tossed continent's end. For more than five weeks *Lawrence* tacked across the stormy passage, at times sighting the horn before being blown back into Atlantic waters. Finally entering the Pacific, *Lawrence* sailed north for a needed provisioning at Valparaíso, Chile, arriving on June 20, 1849. The ship was overhauled, cleaned, painted, and provisioned for the next three weeks, sailing on July 19 for the Hawaiian Islands, where Fraser was to deliver important government dispatches. Well out in the Pacific and off the coast of Peru, *Lawrence* helped another California-bound ship. On August 9 the bark *LaGrange* of Salem, Massachusetts, hailed *Lawrence*. *LaGrange,* 140 days out of Salem and bound for San Francisco with gold-seeking passengers, was "in want of coal."[21] After providing *LaGrange* with six bags of coal, Fraser chatted with her master about conditions in the California goldfields before she "filled away and made all sail."[22]

On September 2 the "island of Owyhee" was sighted. The brig reached the island of Oahu the next day and at 4:00 P.M. passed Diamond Head, anchoring three miles from Honolulu. The next morning *Lawrence* was "towed by the natives" into the harbor, anchoring at 9:30 A.M. For the next three weeks the ship was cleaned and overhauled for the last leg of the voyage to San Francisco while Fraser delivered the important dispatches. Several members of the crew deserted at Honolulu prior to sailing, compelling Fraser to ship seventeen islanders as crew members before *Lawrence* lifted anchor on September 28. On the voyage from Honolulu to San Francisco Fraser's relations with his officers, already strained by tensions engendered by the long voyage and the captain's strong belief that his young officers were untested political appointees, reached a climax. On October 20, as *Lawrence* neared the California coast, Fraser chastised his officers, saying they had neglected their duty to provide him with a report on the vessel's daily position despite the presence of "two sextants, several quadrants . . . and a nautical almanac."[23]

On October 31 land was sighted, and at 11:30 A.M. *Lawrence* "passed the fort at the mouth of the harbor, and stood up the bay" to anchor off San Francisco. The long voyage ended with *Lawrence* safely on station. The next day Fraser wrote to Treasury Secretary William Meredith to report his arrival, saying that he found "the presence of the vessel very necessary for the enforcement of the revenue laws."[24] Unfortunately Fraser also had problems with desertion. On November 5 the first man deserted, followed by others on November 8, 9, 17, and 22. On November 27 nine men left the ship, and ten left the next day. The high cost of living in the inflated Gold Rush market with limited salaries also created problems with the demoralized officers. Fraser lamented to his superiors that "the officers have intimated to me their intention to resign" and that he had "neither the power to arrest or punish deserters."[25]

The first lieutenant and two second lieutenants resigned, the last departing in March 1850, leaving Fraser "entirely unassisted in my duties."[26] Collector Collier came to Fraser's aid. Reporting to Secretary Meredith, Collier said:

> You have no doubt long been aware of the difficulty of keeping a crew on board of any vessel and especially government vessels at this station. The Revenue Brig Lawrence has encountered this difficulty and most of the crew have deserted. To that portion of them who have remained faithful, I have, after consultation with, and indeed after solicitation of Cap't Fraser, promised to raise their wages to $35 per month. This is but small compensation compared with that in the Merchant Service. They now give $100 per month.[27]

To further assist Fraser in carrying out his duties with a crew so diminished as to be unable to sail *Lawrence*, Collier chartered the small schooner *Argus* and purchased another, *Catherine*, to operate as auxiliary cutters. In the early months of 1850 while at anchor off Sausalito both vessels were overhauled and refitted with some of *Lawrence*'s armament and rig. Collier justified the action, pointing out that each vessel

> . . . can be kept constantly under way, in this bay, with three or four hands and will be able to render the most efficient service. The Lawrence will be kept in readiness should her services be required, but to keep her under way, would of course require a full crew which cannot be obtained without the payment of higher wages. By the course adopted the Department will save much more than the cost of the schooner, in the course of the year.[28]

Lawrence was kept "in readiness" on San Francisco Bay for over a year. Following the fitting out of *Argus* and *Catherine*, *Lawrence* was moved to a new anchorage off San Francisco, alternating between Clark's Point (at Telegraph Hill) and Rincon Point, and to the midst of San Francisco's crowded "forest of masts." *Lawrence*'s remaining crew members performed a variety of duties, boarding ships for inspection, quelling mutinous behavior, assisting ships in trouble, recovering boats adrift in the bay, and helping shorthanded craft get under way.

Smuggling was a major problem, because many merchants did not wish to pay duty on foreign goods imported to San Francisco. Compounding the situation, some citizens, including several influential local officials, felt it was wrong to collect revenue for the United States prior to statehood for California. Many measures, accordingly, were undertaken to avoid the payment of duties. Ships with foreign merchandise would bypass San Francisco and Monterey where collectors were on duty, sail into small ports such as Bodega Bay, and transfer their goods to smaller coasting vessels that brought the goods to market. Crew quarters on steamers and in sailing vessels were packed with illicit goods; false bottoms on crates and merchandise shipped as passengers' luggage were other ploys used. During the year *Lawrence* was anchored at San Francisco, officials boarded many ships searching for and occasionally finding evidence of smuggling or nonpayment of duties. *Lawrence* then seized the ship and confiscated smuggled merchandise, which was then to be sold at auction by the collector with the proceeds going to the U.S. government. The first vessel seized was the English ship *Valparaiso* on December 8, 1849. On December 17, *Lawrence* interrupted the schooner *Laura Virgin*'s rendezvous with the barque *Eliza* of New York, which was transferring liquor to the smaller vessel to avoid duty. Not every case involved smuggling, however, for on December 27 *Lawrence* intercepted a small boat headed for the barque *Boston,* only to find that lunch was being brought to *Boston*'s crew.

The difficulty of keeping a crew on ships anchored in the port during the Gold Rush compelled *Lawrence*'s officers to intervene for masters on numerous occasions. The first to need help was the commander of the ship *Magnolia* on December 19, 1849. Those who "refused duty" were arrested and placed in irons on *Lawrence.* (As *Lawrence* grew crowded, other prisoners, such as those from the ship *Robert Pulsford,* were ironed on board their own vessels.) By March 1850 twelve prisoners were in *Lawrence*'s brig. Security was embarrassingly lax. On March 25 "at 6 a.m. when all hands were called [we] found that all the prisoners had deserted."[29] *Lawrence* also rendered assistance to other vessels, helping ships short of hands get under way and picking up boats adrift in the harbor. During a two-week period in March 1850, for example, the brig's crew retrieved three boats.

Lawrence was at anchor on October 18, 1850, when the steamer *Oregon* arrived from Panama with the news that California had become a state on September 9. That afternoon *Lawrence* sent "2 small brass guns with 31 blank cartridges [California was the 31st state] under the charge of an officer with 10 men to assist the civil authorities in the celebration."[30] Eleven days later a formal celebration was held, with a parade, fireworks, and speeches. *Lawrence*'s officers and "as many men as could be spared went ashore to participate." The day was marred by tragedy. That afternoon as the steamboat *Sagamore* prepared to leave Central Wharf the boilers burst, ripping through the packed vessel and killing many of the passengers, throwing some into the water. *Lawrence* was anchored nearby, and the crew was returning from the celebration as *Sagamore* exploded. "The boats were instantly manned and officers were dispatched to render assistance." Rescuers plucked survivors from the water and took them ashore to the hospital. The boats returned three hours later "having picked up a number of valuable papers and letters, which were delivered to the consignee of the vessel."[31]

The crowded harbor brought more problems for *Lawrence*. On November 19, 1850, in the midst of a strong gale, the bark *Providence* lost both anchors and drifted athwart the hawse of the ship *Tiara*. Two boats were sent from *Lawrence,* and after working all night the officers and men were able to moor the two ships alongside each other.[32] *Lawrence* did not fare so well during her stay. Five times in a single year she was struck by another vessel. The ship *Thomas Hart* drifted across *Lawrence*'s chain, and when the tide turned *Hart* came back and "carried away our flying jibboom." The schooner *Alfred* ran afoul of *Lawrence,* carrying away the flying jib iron; the bark *Goose* "came in contact with us, thereby destroying carved work on L cathead." The ship *George Pollock* went afoul of the jibboom, and the ship *Amulet* struck *Lawrence* and "carried away the main gaff."

After a year of riding at anchor, his crew deserting and his ship rammed, Fraser complained to his superiors in October that "two years have now elapsed since my departure from the Chesapeake Bay, during which time I have scarcely been out of view from the vessel which I command."[33] Collector Collier sympathized with Fraser:

> . . . the detention of the Lawrence in this harbor since you first arrived as at my suggestion and was regarded by me not only advisable but indispensable—indispensable not only for the enforcement of the Revenue Laws of the United States but in preserving the peace and the maintenance of order in the bay— Few men, I hope, had more difficult or responsible duties to perform and no man could have more faithfully and promptly discharged those duties. When it is remembered that you have been in a harbor where from five to six hundred vessels were riding at anchor—in the midst of a great excitement—with crews insubordinate & lawless—without the aid of civil authorities or civil process & when day & night you have been called upon to render assistance & to aid Masters of vessels in suppressing mutiny & violence, surely it becomes me to bear willing testimony to the necessity of your presence & your promptness in the discharge of your onerous duties.[34]

A variation in the routine finally came for Fraser and *Lawrence* late in 1850.

On September 27, 1850, the revenue marine bark *Polk* arrived in San Francisco to augment but not replace *Lawrence*. A poorly designed steamer, shorn of her engines, unseaworthy, and poorly manned, *Polk* spent a three-year career on the bay until sold for use as a floating marine hospital. With the arrival of *Polk*, Collector Collier felt that *Lawrence* could be spared to go to sea "and proceed down the coast as far as San Diego, touching at the various intermediate ports . . . making such examinations of the harbours upon the coast as it might prove serviceable to the commerce of the Country."[35] Throughout October and November *Lawrence* was refitted, repaired, and made ready for sea. On December 15 the two 32-pound guns were taken out, to be stored at Sausalito. *Lawrence* was then provisioned, and on December 26, 1850, finally left San Francisco, clearing the Farallones that evening.

For the next few months *Lawrence* cruised the California coast, stopping to survey the harbor of Avalon at Santa Catalina Island. After a three-week layover in San Diego, she sailed on to the Sandwich Islands. After visits to Hilo and Honolulu, the brig departed on April 10, 1851, sighting Point Reyes on May 4. By that evening *Lawrence* was anchored one mile south of Rincon Point at San Francisco. That day a great fire had devastated the town and more than 2,000 structures had been destroyed. For the next month a party of *Lawrence* men was sent ashore each night to guard the vault exposed when the fire burned down the customhouse.

Once again *Lawrence* entered into the "regular" duties attendant to the station: boarding vessels, punishing recalcitrant seamen, and rendering assistance to vessels. Collector Thomas Butler King, Collier's replacement, was on hand to greet the ship. New orders also greeted *Lawrence*. Commencing on June 10 *Lawrence* was to send a boat with a commissioned officer in charge "to row guard around the harbor during the night to prevent smuggling."[36] In addition, state authorities had notified Collector King of their intention of enforcing a new state law forbidding any passengers from New South Wales to land in San Francisco (because anti-Australian sentiment was running high at the time); *Lawrence* was ordered to board all British vessels entering the harbor, "detain all passengers," and wait for the collector. More significant was the news that Fraser's request for a leave of absence had been granted. On June 7 he was relieved of command by Captain Douglass Ottinger, a revenue marine officer on leave who was privately employed on the coast as commander of the Pacific Mail steamship *Isthmus*. *Isthmus* arrived from Panama on June 6, and the next day Ottinger presented himself. Since he had just learned of his recall to duty, Ottinger was not ready to accept permanent command. First

Lieutenant Bennett was left in temporary command until Ottinger's return in September.

Under Bennett's command, *Lawrence* again readied for sea, sailing from San Francisco on June 18 for a cruise "to the northward" to investigate ports and coasting vessels for evidence of smuggling. Returning to San Francisco late in August, the brig remained for a short time, sailing again on September 15. Journeying to the south, *Lawrence* called at Monterey on September 17. Departing on the twenty-fifth, she went as far south as San Luis Obispo. Anchoring but "having seen nothing to indicate smuggling," the ship left and went north. Reaching Bodega Bay on October 7 *Lawrence* was unable to enter due to heavy seas and returned to San Francisco. On October 10 "Capt. Douglass Ottinger came on board and assumed command."[37] The next day *Lawrence* weighed anchor and sailed for Benicia, arriving on the twelfth. There the ship was overhauled once again.

Lawrence returned to San Francisco on October 20, where orders awaited Ottinger. *Lawrence* proceeded to Sausalito, where the 32-pound guns landed by Fraser were reemplaced on October 24. The next day *Lawrence* anchored off Alcatraz Island, where the crew drilled at the guns. Additional cannon were emplaced on the twenty-seventh, when two 12-pound guns were brought over from *Polk*, bringing the number of guns on board *Lawrence* to six: the two 32-pound cannon, two 12-pound cannon, and the two 6-pound cannon. *Lawrence* was ready for action.

Action came quickly. On October 29 the clipper ship *Challenge* anchored at San Francisco after a 102-day passage from New York. Captain Robert H. Waterman and his men had not seen eye to eye during the passage—many men had been battered and some killed by Waterman and his "bucko" mate. Driven to desperation, some of the crew had mutinied, attacking and stabbing the mate. The uprising was quelled but not forgotten. Upon anchoring, Waterman sent word to *Lawrence* that he needed help. "By request of Captain Waterman [we] sent a boat on board in charge of an Officer; secured seven men in Irons charged with mutiny and brought them on board."[38] *Lawrence* left for the bay on other duty, not returning to her anchorage until the next day. On October 31 *Lawrence* once again became involved with *Challenge*. Public sentiment had arisen in favor of the clipper's crew and against the master and mate. Threats had driven both men into hiding, and the possibility of the mob's destroying the ship was very real. The consignees of the ship wrote Ottinger on the thirty-first:

> Owing to a mob having taken forcible possession of the ship "Challenge" to our consignment and having threatened to injure

her in any way in their power even to scuttling her & we having
called upon the U.S. Marshall to protect the property of our
constituents; we now ask that you will with the force at your
disposal assist in protecting the ship and property on board.[39]

Ottinger, Lieutenant Richmond of *Polk,* and a force of men proceeded to *Challenge,* where they were joined by local officials, the
U.S. marshal, and members of the Committee of Vigilance (who were
in support of the legal authorities and opposed to the destruction of the
ship). They encountered a crowd of more than a thousand. The group
dispersed without incident, but not before some damage had been
done when the mob ransacked the ship searching for Waterman. *Lawrence's* men were stationed on board during the night. By morning the
threat had dissipated. Waterman and Mate James Douglass were ultimately brought to trial for murder. Ottinger was called as a witness in
the case, which finally ended on February 10, 1852, when both men
were found guilty of lesser charges of assault and fined—rather a quiet
end to an emotion-charged, notorious case.[40]

The *Challenge* affair was not the only excitement afforded *Lawrence's* crew. Rumors reached the collector that certain vessels were
illegally carrying munitions, weapons, and filibusters to Hawaii,
where they would take forcible possession of the islands. *Lawrence*
was ordered to search the suspected ships. The ship *Gamecock* of New
York was stopped when *Lawrence* fired a shot across her bow on
October 29 just after the brig left *Challenge.* The ship was searched but
nothing suspicious was found. Three other vessels, *Colonel Fremont,
Keoka,* and *Joe* had already been stopped, boarded, and searched on
the twenty-third. Nothing was found. The additional armament emplaced on *Lawrence* on the twenty-third and twenty-seventh had been
in response to a possible fight with the suspected filibusters:

> We keep a constant watch on the conditions and movements of all
> the vessels which you have named in your directions to me and
> have them under our eye several times during the night. Our
> boats are moving quietly around the shipping and I do not think
> that they can escape us; Our guns are kept loaded with 32-lb.
> shot and matches kept burning from dark until daylight.[41]

No evidence was uncovered concerning the suspected plot. Ottinger
said that he had heard the expedition had been broken up, "but as this
may be a Ruse I shall not lose sight . . . I am ready for getting away at
any moment."[42]

In early November *Lawrence* continued searching vessels for evidence of smuggling, and aiding masters. On November 9 a mass
desertion of the ship *Raymond* was thwarted. The next day Ottinger

and his crew arrested three men from a boardinghouse who had threatened the captain and mate of the British ship *William Money* with "violent personal abuse" while helping the crew desert. *Raymond* again hailed for assistance; the officers had also been attacked and the crew had deserted. Alarmed, Ottinger had the match fires lit and "depressed the guns for a close shot in case of an attack from boats."[43] He evidently feared that the men who had attacked the officers of *Raymond* might assault *Lawrence* to rescue their mates, who were ironed in the hold. The night passed without incident, and the next morning the three men were taken ashore and turned over to the civil authorities. On November 15 the clipper ship *Telegraph* and the ship *Flavius* were boarded and searched. They were the last vessels boarded by *Lawrence* in San Francisco Bay. Three days later *Lawrence* stood to sea, enroute to Monterey, where her mission was to pick up the collector and bring him to San Francisco. *Lawrence* arrived at Monterey on November 20, sailing the next day with Collector William H. Russell on board. On the twenty-second she anchored at Santa Cruz, where the schooners *Empire* and *Sarah Hooper* were boarded and searched. *Sarah Hooper* was found to be lacking a clearance certificate and was loaded with a "quantity of domestic and foreign goods." After reporting *Hooper* to the collector at Santa Cruz, *Lawrence* again stood for sea.

Sailing north for San Francisco, the brig encountered no difficulty, arriving off the Golden Gate on the evening of November 25 and anchoring near Point Lobos, the southern head of the harbor entrance. Unfortunately, the tide had ebbed and was running with a strong set to the south. Heavy seas ran from the west, almost directly toward land. After an hour at anchor, the vessel was swept by heavy seas and broke the anchor cable. Driven southerly toward the ocean beach of San Francisco, *Lawrence* was lost at 9:00 A.M., striking

> . . . in 3½ fathoms water, and in the next breaker came down with such tremendous force, that it appeared as if every seam and timber in her must have started. At the same time, tons of water fell on our decks. By changing the position of the sails, the ship's head was kept toward the beach and stern to the breakers. We then let go the bower anchor, to lighten her forward, as she was coming broadside to. The vessel then laid bows toward the land, continuing to strike very heavily, and force her way through heavy combing seas toward the beach.[44]

Discipline and order were maintained on board throughout the night despite "a short time when none could feel that they would see another day."[45]

The next morning *Lawrence* was hove onto the beach by a hawser carried ashore. The ship lay in 3½ feet of water at low tide that morning. High tide at 1:05 P.M. brought the brig even higher up on shore.[46] The launch and a cutter were lowered, and valuable items were transported to the beach. The wreck was stripped of guns, fittings, and equipment before being abandoned.[47] Ottinger justified his decision, noting repair costs would outstrip those of replacing the brig, and "the sailing qualities of the "Lawrence" were very ordinary, most of the Coasting Schooners, and some of the Merchant Ships, could pass us to windward, aside from the new class of Clipper Ships some of which beat us at the rate of four or five knots an hour."[48] Ottinger asked that *Argus* be detailed as a new revenue cutter, but the collector of the port for Benicia refused to part with the schooner. *Polk* was considered unseaworthy and not available for duty.[49] Another vessel, the schooner *Frolic*, was located and pronounced fit for service after Ottinger inspected her. Collector King purchased *Frolic* for $4,000 but eventually had to renegotiate when the Treasury Department disallowed the expense. *Frolic*, outfitted with *Lawrence*'s guns and equipment and manned by *Lawrence*'s crew, carried on *Lawrence*'s role.

THE NAVY IN THE GOLD RUSH

While the activities of the U.S. Navy in the Mexican War and the conquest of California have been described and assessed by participants and historians, the role of the navy in the Gold Rush has not been discussed, beyond the excellent account in Robert Erwin Johnson's history of the Pacific Squadron, *Thence Round Cape Horn*. The conquest of California was a naval event with landings affecting the conquest of Monterey, San Pedro, and San Francisco. During the war years of 1846–1848, vessels of the Pacific Squadron stayed for prolonged periods in California. Sailors and marines helped maintain the American presence ashore and participated in several actions, while the presence of the vessels provided a deterrent to any who might attempt to seize California by sea. After playing a prominent role in the Mexican War, the fourteen-vessel strong Pacific Squadron, which formerly had used South American ports, remained a major presence in California as the new territory responded to news of the gold discovery. As the major representative of U.S. strength in California, the navy was an important participant in the Gold Rush. The California experience was also significant to the navy. In the aftermath of the Mexican War the "relatively small force" of the navy was left with "the enormous task of defending a nation with two sea frontiers, 2,500 miles apart by land, but more than 14,000 miles apart by sea."[50] The importance of the new sea frontier was demonstrated by the maritime trade and commerce spurred by the Gold Rush and the rise of San Francisco. Protecting California, particularly San Francisco, and the ships that sailed through the Golden Gate to the far reaches of the Pacific led to the expansion of the Pacific Squadron, which led the United States into the role of mightiest naval power on the Pacific.

The navy gained two important prizes as a result of the Gold Rush. To provide the necessary support in California, the navy selected Mare Island on San Francisco Bay's northern reaches as the site of a permanent naval shipyard and station in 1850, verifying the permanence of the new expansion and commencing a long, significant career for that installation. Young naval officers on government-subsidized mail steamers provided the navy with a cadre of professionals trained in the new technology, as the beginnings of a steam navy materialized without enough steamers to train all men of promise. While only seven steamers were carried on the navy list in 1850, by 1860 there were twenty-six. The significance of most officers' careers was enhanced by their Gold Rush experience with steam.

When the Mexican War formally ended in 1848, the Pacific Squadron was deployed at four tasks: possessing California, protecting her shores from foreign intervention or seizure, blockading the Mexican Pacific coast, and capturing and possessing important ports and all of Baja California. With the end of hostilities, the navy lifted the blockade, returned Mexican ports that had been seized, and ferried troops and Mexican collaborators and their families to California. Commodore Thomas Ap Catesby Jones, having just assumed command of the Pacific Squadron, wrote to J. Y. Mason, Secretary of the Navy, from La Paz, Mexico, on the eve of his departure for California to recommend the "retention on this coast of all cruising ships of the Pacific Squadron," even going so far as to recommend how the ships could be kept in repair and provisioned without a return to the Atlantic.[51] Jones was quick to change his mind once he arrived in California. The province had always been prone to desertion among the ranks of both naval and merchant vessels, but the discovery of gold had given a fresh and compelling impetus to desertion. With crewmen finding every opportunity to jump ship, including "some of the best petty officers and seaman, having but a few months to serve, and *large* balances due them, amounting, in the aggregate, to *over ten thousand dollars*," Jones advertised "A new Gold Discovery"—namely $40,000 in rewards for captured deserters.[52] His efforts were for naught, as not a single deserter was apprehended. Secretary Mason, answering Jones's dispatches, noted that while "the efforts which you have made to prevent desertions & to apprehend deserters have been characterized by your usual energy, it will not be advisable to continue your large offers for the return of deserters."[53]

Jones lamented. "I fear for years to come it will be impossible for the United States to maintain any naval or military establishment in California." He nonetheless responded to the crisis as best he could. He restricted shore leave, kept line officers on board ship at all times, armed trustworthy officers of boat crews when necessity forced them ashore and, to the displeasure of the navy, discharged seamen whose terms of enlistment were up on the Pacific coast as opposed to the usual practice of waiting until the vessel's return to the East coast. Jones moored the squadron at Benicia away from the temptations of San Francisco, in hopes of discouraging desertion and bolstering the fortunes of the town in which he had heavily invested.[54]

While desertion slowly declined, the Pacific Squadron was shocked by a mutiny on board a boat from the U.S. schooner *Ewing* in September 1849. Requisitioned by the United States Coast and Geodetic Survey, *Ewing* was sent from New York to California in January 1849 for survey duties on the Pacific coast. Under the command of Lieutenant William P. McArthur, U.S. Navy, who joined the ship in San Francisco, *Ewing* was manned by a naval crew and subject to naval discipline.[55] Reaching San Francisco on August 1, 1849, the schooner did not assume survey duties until the arrival of Lieutenant McArthur in September. Four days before McArthur took command on the sixth, four crewmen stole a dinghy and deserted. Following McArthur's arrival, *Ewing* made a short cruise to Monterey, returning to San Francisco on the twelfth. *Ewing*'s officers hosted a dinner for a group of army officers and local citizens on the evening of the thirteenth. Passed Midshipman William Gibson volunteered to command the ship's boat that conveyed the guests ashore when dinner was over. He gave this account of the incident:

> Backing into a small wharf, where Sansome Street now is, a pistol in each hand, I landed my passengers and started to return. When about half way . . . I put back my pistols and resumed the yoke ropes. In a few moments, the after oarsman, John Black, with a hoarse exclamation, threw his oar out of the rowlock and himself upon me. Struggling to my feet, I found myself clutched by several of the others. Their first effort seemed to be to get possession of my pistols, but very soon one of them (Peter Black, I think) exclaimed, "Damn him, throw [him] overboard—that's the quickest way!" With this I found my arms free, and seized John Black by his neckerchief, dragging him overboard with me.

Twisting it with one hand, I attempted to draw a pistol with the other, but the man was too heavy for me, the rest were striking at me with the oars, and . . . I had to let go, wholly exhausted and half drowned. I saw a little way, saw them help Black into the boat and settle into their places and . . . they pulled off.[56]

Dragged down by his saturated clothing and swept out by the ebb tide, Gibson lost consciousness. His "apparently lifeless" body was spotted by the captain of a merchant vessel stepping from his ship's boat onto a ladder to board his vessel. "As he looked down to assure his footing he saw the upturned face of a man sweeping fast between the boat and landing step." Grabbing Gibson by the hair, he pulled the unconscious midshipman aboard, resuscitated him, notified *Ewing*, and sent the hapless officer to the hospital.[57]

A few days later, on September 14, a trusted crew of sailors under Lieutenant Washington Bartlett captured the five men from *Ewing* as they stopped to rest before heading up the San Joaquin River to Stockton in their boat. Subjected to a quick court-martial, the five mutineers and deserters—John Black, Jonathan Biddy, Henry Commerford, Peter Black, and William Hall—were sentenced to death for "Mutiny with intent to kill," "Desertion, with an attempt to kill, and running away with a boat, the property of the United States." Commodore Jones approved the sentences but three days later commuted those of Biddy, Commerford, and Hall to 100 lashes and confinement by ball and chain at hard labor, since the two Blacks (no relation) had instigated the mutiny and the attempt on Gibson's life. On the morning of October 23, 1849, with the crews of the assembled naval vessels present, John Black was hanged from the yardarm of *Ewing* and Peter Black was hanged aboard Jones's flagship, USS *Savannah*, as both vessels lay at anchor off Sausalito. Commodore Jones's address was read to the assembled crews, emphasizing "If there remain any among you who meditate desertion, let them ponder well and count the cost before making the attempt; they may escape as some have, but they may be apprehended, tried, condemned and executed, as you now have the most appalling proof before your eyes."[58] Desertions in the Pacific Squadron declined after 1850, and there was no repetition of the unfortunate actions of the men of *Ewing*.

The secretary of the navy felt that the number of desertions was abetted by Jones's insistence on keeping the Pacific Squadron in California, and he ordered the commodore to send the vessels on prolonged cruises. Jones acquiesced in sending out some of his ships but refused to depart himself. Recognizing that the navy represented the mightiest expression of federal power in Gold Rush California, Jones replied that the presence of his ships discouraged murder, rapine, and piracy inspired by the "madning effects of the Gold mania."[59] The commodore was correct, but his motives were not exactly pure. Heavily speculating in gold dust with government funds, and actively promoting the cause of his pet port, Benicia, Jones (as one biographer noted) had a difficult time separating his private and public interests. When finally relieved of duty in July 1850, he was court-martialed in Washington for fraud, attempted fraud, scandalous conduct, and oppression. Convicted on the latter three charges, Jones was particularly censured for his speculative use of government money and sentenced to a five-year suspension of duty without pay. Thus gold-inspired greed proved the undoing of the so-called "contentious commodore."[60]

Jones's successor, Charles S. McCauley, while keeping *Savannah* and one other vessel, *Warren*, at San Francisco through the Gold Rush years, did send the rest of the Pacific Squadron on cruises, with many touching at the Sandwich Islands and at Panama. The latter port was particularly important, and the necessity of showing the flag was highlighted by the tremendous traffic across the isthmus. In October 1850, for instance, McCauley wrote to Captain Charles Gaunt, who commanded USS *Raritan*, that his orders were to

> . . . sail for Panama, touching at Payta [Peru] on your way. At Panama communicate with Mr. Corwine U.S. Consul. The Isthmus is the great thoroughfare of emigration to California and Oregon, and the town is generally filled with our countrymen, to whom you will afford such protection and countenance as they may require and you can give them consistently with the laws of nations. The time of your continuance will be determined by yourself.[61]

In the years that followed, the Pacific Squadron continued the mission, effectively cruising the waters of the Pacific and protecting American commerce.

USS *Warren*. The presence of U.S. naval vessels on California's coast and particularly on San Francisco Bay proved a great boon to the region during the Gold Rush years. Commodore Jones supported the civil authorities whenever possible, and kept a ship at San Francisco on permanent station to serve as the port's guard ship. A veteran of the Mexican War, the second-class sloop of war *Warren* was laid down at Boston Navy Yard in 1825. Launched and commissioned in 1827, the 697-ton, 127-foot-long vessel served for three years in the Mediterranean, chastising pirates and protecting American interests. Decommissioned for repairs at Norfolk Navy Yard in 1830, the vessel subsequently served in the south Atlantic and the Caribbean before sailing to join the Pacific Squadron in 1843. *Warren* was an active participant in the naval conquest of California during the Mexican War. In the fall of 1846 *Warren* figured in a sad affair when her launch, bound from San Francisco to Sutter's Fort, disappeared with all hands, including two sons of Captain John B. Montgomery. It was determined that the crew had mutinied and murdered the officers, though no suspects were ever brought to justice, and the culprits vanished in the ensuing confusion of the Gold Rush migration.[62]

Receiving and storing goods on San Francisco Bay beginning in 1846, *Warren* took on a new role after the gold discovery. With the large-scale problem of desertion and mutiny occasioned by the Gold Rush, the navy and *Warren* played an important part in establishing shipboard discipline. Seamen accused of desertion, disobedience, recalcitrance, or mutiny were taken in irons to *Warren*, which, with her 190-man crew and twenty-four-pound guns, served as a floating guard ship. There the sailors and some officers of various merchant vessels were worked as "man-of-war's men" until released to the care of their captain or shoreside authorities. The vessel's new role commenced in the summer of 1849 when she moved from her anchorage of Benicia in the Carquinez Straits to a new mooring off Clark's Point at San Francisco.

The first recorded use of the vessel as a prison was in July 1849, when lawless ruffians known as the "Hounds," who had terrorized the town, were arrested and incarcerated on board *Warren*. Following that event, *Warren*'s log for late 1849 and early 1850 records numerous arrests and incarcerations. In the predawn hours of November 29, 1849, for example, the ship's log records that she "sent to the Hamburg Barque America a Sergeant, guard of marines and took from her Charles Helman (2d Mate) and Charles Kigman (seaman) on charge of an assault upon the charterers of the ship."[63] On February 18, 1850, "the English Barque Victoria came in and anchored, hoisted her colours Union down. Sent on board and brought the . . . mutineers from her . . . in double irons."[64] Some crewmembers were arrested for attempted murder, including the ship *Niantic*'s cook in July 1849 and a man from the schooner *Petrel* in June 1850. Deserters were also incarcerated; on March 1, 1850, "Charles Murray was brought on board by one of the Police as a deserter from the ship *Victoria* and put in double irons."[65]

In all, *Warren*'s log indicates that between November 1, 1849, and January 1, 1851, *Warren* received 158 prisoners, among them first and second mates, boatswains, and cooks, from forty vessels, including three naval vessels and ships of British, Norwegian, Portuguese,

Danish, and German registry.[66] *Warren* also rendered assistance to several vessels, including sending "hand and foot irons" to the Chilean brig *Matador* and the English brig *Giraffe,* and helping float the brig *Fawn* in May 1850. At times the mere presence of an armed boat from the ship aided shipmasters. On January 20, 1850, a boat was sent to the English bark *Duke of Roxburg* "to quell a mutiny reported to be on board, and to bring on board any mutineers that the Capt. might see fit to send. The boat returned but did not bring anyone, the men having returned to their duty."[67] Depending on their rank and the severity of the offense, prisoners sent to *Warren* were either confined in irons or were "prisoners-at-large." Prisoners-at-large were put to work on the ship at a variety of tasks. Subject to naval discipline while on board, some prisoners received additional punishment, including being ironed for refusing duty, or receiving twelve lashes of the cat, which was meted out to Patrick Smith of the English ship *Victoria* for "insolence to the officer of the deck."[68]

Although *Warren*'s log provides provocative insights into the ship's activities and prisoners, the journal of *Probus* seaman Adolphus Windeler gives a more detailed picture of *Warren.* Arriving in December 1849 with thirty-two passengers from New York, *Probus* discharged her cargo and complement over the next month. The captain and crew disagreed over wages, and the sailors finally left the ship. Accused of mutiny they were arrested, held in the stationhouse, and finally brought before the alcalde of San Francisco on January 19, 1850. Convicted of desertion, the crew was taken in boats to *Warren* on the twentieth. *Warren*'s log notes the arrival of eight men from *Probus,* including Windeler. Bunking with the crew assigned to the mizzen topmast, Windeler "had to do regular man of wars duty here, sweeping & washing decks, clearing hawse & drying & furling sail, etc. . . . We spent the time here very agreeably, had good living & were kept pretty comfortable. Had fresh beef 3 times a week." Windeler and his mates were released after they hired lawyers who pleaded their case before a judge who declared them "clear of the ship." The men from *Probus* left *Warren* after eleven days of incarceration on January 31.[69]

The amount of time spent by prisoners on board *Warren* varied considerably, with an average stay of two weeks. Some men were released to the care of their captain after three or four days, while others were detained for longer periods, probably at the request of their captain. Crew members accused of mutiny from the ships *Sheffield* and *Robert Pulsford* were actually kept on board for four months. For these men and a few others, release came either from a writ of habeas corpus—which effected the release of *Robert Pulsford*'s

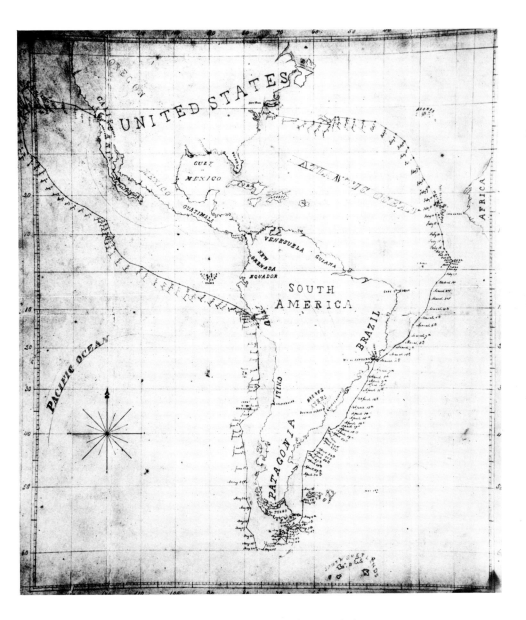

1. Map of the voyage of the Ship *Apollo* of New York, 1849. The original, drawn
by Joseph Perkins Beach, son of the ship's owner and supercargo for the voyage,
depicts the typical route of ships sailing for California by way of Cape Horn or the
Straits of Magellan. San Francisco Maritime National Historical Park.

2. San Francisco in 1851. This two part view, known as the "Forest of Masts Panorama," was taken from the roof of the Union Hotel on Portsmouth Square late in 1850 or early in 1851. Just two blocks away lies open water and the waterfront, crowded with every imaginable type of vessel, including schooners, scows, brigs, barks, ships, and steamers. San Francisco Maritime National Historical Park.

3. Launch of the clipper *Flying Cloud*. The heyday of the clippers came with the need for fast passage with speculative cargoes to Gold Rush markets in California. Gleason's Pictorial Drawing Room Companion.

4. Entrance to the Golden Gate from off Point Lobos, looking east, 1854, by Thomas A. Ayres. In this charcoal and gouache wash, Ayres shows the steamer *Republic* heading for the Golden Gate as a pilot boat and clipper head out. Achenbach Foundation for Graphic Arts, California Palace of the Legion of Honor, the Fine Arts Museums of San Francisco.

Journal of
A
voyage to the
North West Coast
of America.

Ship Niantic receiving her
Passengers at
Panama

In the Ship Niantic
of Warren R.I.
1848. /49.

5. The ship *Niantic* lies off Panama City loading passengers by lighter. This pencil sketch, done by First Mate James Cleaveland, decorated the cover of *Niantic*'s logbook. San Francisco Maritime National Historical Park.

6. The 1291-ton *Tennessee* was the first steamer diverted from eastern seaboard traffic as a result of the gold discovery. Sent to California by the Pacific Mail Steamship Co., *Tennessee* operated between Panama and San Francisco until wrecked on March 6, 1853. San Francisco Maritime National Historical Park.

7. The "steam clipper" *Golden Gate*, built in 1851, was typical of the steamships built by New York shipyards expressly for the Panama route. San Francisco Maritime National Historical Park.

8. Forty-niners pole through the rapids on the Rio Chagres on the overland portion of the Panama route. San Francisco Maritime National Historical Park.

9. View of San Francisco, 1850, showing the crowded waterfront and its forest of masts from the shores of Yerba Buena Island on the bay. This is one of several views that illustrated the first charts and sailing directions prepared by the U.S. Coast and Geodetic Survey for San Francisco Bay and the Sacramento and San Joaquin rivers. San Francisco Maritime National Historical Park.

10. Central or "Long" Wharf, 1850–1851. As its names implies, this wharf was the center of maritime activity in Gold Rush San Francisco. Lighters and scows load or discharge goods, and the offices and stores of commission merchants and steamboat agencies line the waterfront. To the left, with the American flag flying from the roof, is the two-story ship chandlery of W. C. Hoff with the office of the harbormaster on the second floor. San Francisco Maritime National Historical Park.

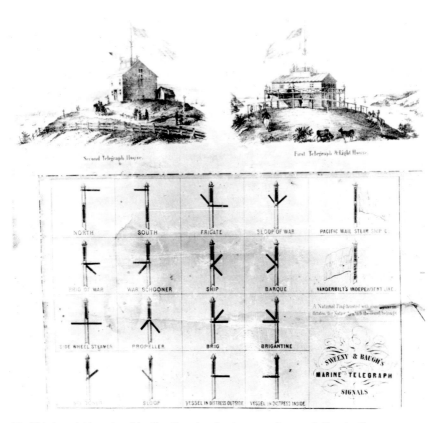

11. This broadside, printed by San Francisco businessmen Sweeny & Baugh, illustrates both signal stations (the first at Point Lobos and the second at Telegraph Hill) and the code for the semaphore signals rigged on the station's wooden mast when a vessel was spotted. San Francisco Maritime National Historical Park.

REGULATIONS

OF THE

HARBOR AND PORT OF SAN FRANCISCO.

Art. 1st. On the arrival of Merchant vessels at the Port of San Francisco, a proper berth will be pointed out to the Masters thereof, by the Harbor Master, when he boards them; and no Master of a Merchant vessel shall shift his berth without permission from the Harbor Master, unless in case of extreme emergency, when he must report his having done so as early as possible at the office of the Harbor Master.

Art. 2d. Should it be the intention of a Master of a vessel to discharge or receive on board any considerable quantity of merchandise, a berth will be pointed out to him as close to the landing places as the safety of the vessel and other circumstances will permit.

Art. 3d. After a proper berth has been pointed out, the master will then moor his vessel with two bower anchors across the tide, with thirty-five fathoms chain cable, in summer, and fifty fathoms from the hawser hole in winter. December, January, February and March to be considered the winter months.

Art. 4th. If any vessel properly moored in the harbor shall have her anchors or cables over-laid by any other vessel in anchoring or mooring, the master or person having the care or direction of such last mentioned vessel, shall immediately, or as soon as may be after application made to him by the party aggrieved, cause the said anchor or cable so overlaying to be taken up and cleared.

Art. 5th. When any merchant vessel may be lying in a berth convenient for discharging, and she shall have completed her unlading or lading, such vessel shall, at the request of the Harbor Master, remove to a place designated, should her berth be required by any other vessel which may desire to load or discharge.

Art. 6th. Merchant vessels arriving with powder on board, must, on arrival, report the same to the Harbor Master, in order that a secure berth may be pointed out.

Art. 7th. No ballast will be allowed to be thrown overboard. Any ballast which may be wanted to discharge, by application to the Harbor Master, a place of discharge will be designated.

Art. 8th. All difficulties arising between ships relative to the foregoing rules, shall be settled before the Harbor Master.

Art. 9th. Disobedience to the orders of the Harbor Master, in the discharge of his duty, will subject the offender to a fine of five hundred dollars, to go towards the Hospital Fund of the Town of San Francisco.

Art. 10th. After mooring, ships must rig in jib and flying jib-booms, and cockbill lower yards.

Art. 11th. The Harbor Master's fees are payble at his office within forty-eight hours after the arrival of the vessel, otherwise double the amount will be exacted, according to law.

JAMES HAGAN,
Harbor Master.

Office Clark's Point

12. Regulations posted in 1850 for the harbor and port of San Francisco by James Hagan, the first elected harbormaster. San Francisco Maritime National Historical Park.

3. Interior of the foundry of the Pacific Mail Steamship Co.'s depot and shops at Benicia, 1855. The Pacific Mail depot was the first major industrial enterprise in California. California State Library, Sacramento.

14. Happy Valley, setting of San Francisco's burgeoning maritime industry, 1851. Foundries, forges and shipyards lined the shores of Yerba Buena Cove's southern extremity. San Francisco Maritime National Historical Park.

16. The sinking of the steamship *Central America* in 1857 killed more than four hundred passengers returning to the eastern seaboard from the California gold fields. Last of the Gold Rush maritime disasters, the wreck of *Central America* inspired vehement reaction and recriminations. From *Frank Leslie's Illustrated Newspaper*, October 3, 1857. San Francisco Maritime National Historical Park.

15. The prison brig *Euphemia*, San Francisco's floating jail during the Gold Rush. Law and order on the waterfront was kept by the U.S. Revenue cutter *Cornelius W. Lawrence*, and prisoners were incarcerated both on *Euphemia* and USS *Warren*, the Navy's guard ship at San Francisco. San Francisco Maritime National Historical Park.

17. "Disasters of 60 Days," depicts five maritime accidents in the short period between February 16 and April 11, 1853—the total loss of three oceangoing steamers, *Independence*, *Tennessee*, and *Samuel S. Lewis*, and the explosions aboard the inland steamers *R.K. Page* and *Jenny Lind*. Reproduced Through the Courtesy of the Bancroft Library, University of California, Berkeley.

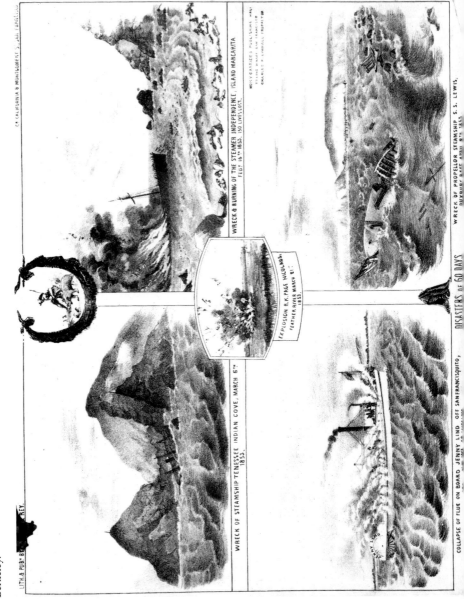

18. "A Few of the First Steamship Pioneers living in 1874, Surrounding the Old Ship," [*California*]. The First Steamship Pioneers were one of many pioneer associations established in California and the New England states that celebrated the great migration by sea and land in response to the gold discovery. The California Historical Society, San Francisco.

19. Ships lying idle on the San Francisco waterfront in the lee of Rincon Point, 1851. One of the most striking maritime images of the Gold Rush, the "abandoned" hulks that clogged the waterfront were cleared by 1857, signalling the rise of a booming, healthy maritime economy that had lasted past the gold-inspired boom of 1849–1850. San Francisco Maritime National Historical Park.

men in mid-June 1850—or escape. In June and July 1850 several escapes occurred. On June 17, John McKinnon, a prisoner from the American ship *Far West,* "deserted from the 2d cutter while ashore watering." Three prisoners from the ship *Sheffield* escaped to shore in a gig on June 29, and on July 4, "Michael Hawks, prisoner from the English barque Eudora, deserted from the fishing party on shore."[70]

The arrival of *Cornelius W. Lawrence* in November 1849 slowly alleviated *Warren*'s responsibilities. The last prisoner was brought on board *Warren* on June 8, 1850. Commodore Jones, then on the eve of his departure for the East, nonetheless urged his successor, Commodore Charles S. McCauley, to continue to use the "indispensible" *Warren* as a guard ship.[71] The establishment of a city jail in San Francisco, albeit a floating facility in the brig *Euphemia,* helped end *Warren*'s two-year career as a prison ship. Moved to Sausalito, *Warren* remained there until 1853, when the sloop of war was moved again, this time to the Mare Island Naval Yard under construction. *Warren* remained at Mare Island for another decade, serving as a storeship. Sold at auction in 1863 at Panama to the Pacific Mail Steamship Company, the former sloop of war ended her days in Panama Bay as a coal hulk.[72]

Mare Island Navy Yard. The Pacific Squadron suffered from the lack of a permanent base and naval shipyard where repairs could be made and new ships laid down for an expanded presence in the Pacific. Vessels in poor repair, such as USS *Warren,* could not be trusted to Cape Horn and had to be left in California. In 1848 it was noted that "at present, ships of war cannot be built or equipped in California, nor can the Pacific trade furnish our ships with seamen. But whenever the latter difficulty will cease, it will be politic to send out a stationary navy to the Pacific."[73] The need had been recognized early by naval officers and government officials alike. In the first months of the Gold Rush, Lieutenant Joseph Warren Revere of the U.S. Navy wrote that "no great time can elapse before our government will perceive the policy of establishing a Pacific navy—a navy built, equipped and maintained from the resources of California and Oregon." Lamenting the fact that it took most naval vessels more than a year to reach the Pacific station from eastern seaboard navy yards, Revere prophesized that "a respectable naval force in the Pacific will be a matter of necessity, and in a few years vessels can be built and equipped at San Francisco and manned from the vast commerce—especially the whaling trade—of the Pacific."[74]

As an avid speculator in Benicia real estate, Thomas Ap Catesby Jones actively lobbied for the town's selection as site of a navy yard and depot. Nonetheless, a joint board of army and naval officers surveying the territory for military installations recommended another site in 1849. The desired location was Mare Island, a 1,500-acre flat island at the mouth of the Carquinez Straits. When President Millard Fillmore set aside large tracts of land in and around San Francisco as government reservations on November 6, 1850, his executive order included Mare Island.[75] The navy did not act to establish a "California dock" until 1852, when Secretary of the Navy Graham instructed Commodore Joseph Smith, chief of the navy's Bureau of Yards and Docks, to appoint a commission of officers who would select a site for a navy yard in California. The officers selected by Smith were Commodore John Drake Sloat, Commander Cadawallader Ringgold (who was immediately replaced by Commander William S. Ogden), Lieutenant Simon Frazer Blunt, and civil engineer William P. S. Sanger of Smith's staff.[76] Sloat was particularly well acquainted with California from his Mexican War service, while Ringgold and Blunt were veterans of the Wilkes expedition that had surveyed the upper reaches of San Francisco Bay. Blunt also served on the 1849 joint board on fortifications in California.

Traveling by way of the Nicaragua route, the naval officers inspected San Francisco Bay, making topographical surveys, charting tides and currents, checking on the availability of labor, supplies, building materials, and provisions, and seeking a site safe from wind, waves, and enemy attack. By July 13 the board had made its decision, and Commodore Sloat wrote Secretary Graham that Mare Island was indeed the best location.[77] With an appropriation in hand of $100,000 to survey and purchase a site for a navy yard on San Francisco Bay, the navy proceeded to negotiate with the owners of Mare Island, securing the island on January 4, 1853, for $83,491. Commander David Glasgow Farragut, then at the Norfolk Navy Yard in Virginia, was selected as the first commander of the new navy yard. He departed on August 19, 1853, and arrived at his new post on September 14 of the same year. His quick passage underscores the vast improvements in isthmian travel by 1853.[78] At Farragut's command, USS *Warren* was towed to Mare Island and anchored, a sectional dry dock shipped around Cape Horn in 1852 was assembled and tested, and construction of the yard's buildings commenced. The dry dock, authorized by Congress in 1850 and built at New York in 1851, was a 1,100-foot-long, 32-foot-wide, $610,000 prefabricated masterpiece of engineering that was shipped around the horn in sections. The dominant feature at Mare Island for many years, the dry dock was used by the navy and leased for a fee to merchant vessels, including the steamers of the Pacific Mail.

Work at the yard progressed quickly, and on September 18, 1854, with an appropriate ceremony, speeches, and the hoisting of the colors, Mare Island Navy Yard was dedicated while army engineers were busily engaged in the construction of harbor defenses closer to the entrance of the bay at Fort Point and on Alcatraz Island.[79] The fortification of the bay's mouth and the establishment of the navy yard firmly backed the Pacific Squadron, providing for the defense of the principal American port and outfitting an essential base for naval operations in the Pacific. Four years later in 1859, USS *Saginaw*, the first ship to be built at Mare Island and the first U.S. warship built on the Pacific, was launched. The pioneer days of the navy in California were at an end.[80]

ESTABLISHING AIDS TO NAVIGATION

The need for aids to navigation along the Pacific coast concerned the U.S. government as the Mexican War ended. The cession of California, combined with the assertion of American hegemony in Oregon, introduced a considerable problem: lighting an isolated, distant, and dangerous coast. In 1848 a lighthouse was proposed at Cape Disappointment, the northern headland marking the entrance to the Columbia River. The proposal was no doubt due to the importance of the river in linking the scattered American settlements in the Willamette Valley to the rest of the nation, along with the need to safely cross the treacherous Columbia River Bar, which had already gained a dangerous reputation after several shipwrecks, notably the U.S. sloops of war *Peacock* in July 1841 and *Shark* in September 1846. The discovery of gold in California, however, focused attention on San Francisco Bay instead. As maritime traffic through the Golden Gate increased in 1849, demands for lighthouses were made. Pierre Charles de Saint-Amant, a French government agent, complained in 1849 that his ship was detained in a thick fog for some time, and he was afraid to enter the harbor because of San Francisco's lack of navigational aids. Americans, said Saint-Amant, were "always less concerned with measures of safety than with taking chances" and hence had neglected to build lighthouses and mark the channel immediately after the war with Mexico had ended.[81]

In 1849 the surveying schooner *Ewing* and her crew were ordered to select the best locations for lighthouses. In 1850 Congress passed the first appropriation for lighthouses on the Pacific coast, but work did not begin on the structures until 1852. Baltimore contractors Francis X. Kelly and Francis A. Gibbons began to ship materials early in the year for eight lights—seven in California and one at Cape Disappointment. The first two lights were to be built on San Francisco Bay, which was given obvious priority due to Gold Rush traffic. The sites selected were Alcatraz Island and Fort Point at the Golden Gate. Like the customhouse of 1850, these first lights were made possible by the importation of construction materials such as brick, wood flooring, hardware, paint, and glass—and the builders' arrival by ship, as was the case with San Francisco's customhouse. Work progressed as soon as the materials arrived by ship in December 1852, with the foundation for Alcatraz Light being laid on December 15.[82] The newly constituted United States Lighthouse Board had meanwhile decided that the Pacific coast lighthouses would have far more superior Fresnel lenses instead of the originally designed Argand lamps. Lieutenant Washington A. Bartlett, U.S. Navy, was dispatched to Paris to buy the lenses. They arrived at New York in April 1853 and were immediately reshipped to San Francisco.

Meanwhile the two lights were completed. Identical in design, the 38-by-20-foot, two-story brick Cape Cod–style buildings were surmounted by short, 8-foot-diameter towers. Alcatraz Light had been finished on June 21, 1853, with Fort Point following a short time later. The lenses, third-order Fresnels, arrived in the summer of 1853, but their installation was delayed because no one skilled in erecting the delicate apparatus could be found. The U.S. Army, then in the process of fortifying Alcatraz, stepped in, and on June 1, 1854, Alcatraz Light was illuminated for the first time, becoming the first American lighthouse to operate on the Pacific coast.[83] Fort Point did not fare as well, since by that time the light, still without a tower, had been torn down by the army to make way for a massive brick-and-granite fortress to guard the Golden Gate. The lens was shipped to Point Pinos, Monterey, instead, and Fort Point did not gain another lighthouse until 1855. Meanwhile other lights were erected, including more around the gate, especially at Point Bonita, whose tower was constructed in 1855 in response to the nearby wreck of the Pacific Mail steamer *Tennessee* in 1853. In time, fifty-nine lighthouses were built on the California coast by the United States.[84]

MARITIME INDUSTRY BEGINS

From 1848 through the 1920s one of the nation's most important steamer lines was the Pacific Mail Steamship Company. As discussed earlier, the Pacific Mail linked the east and west coasts of the United

States during the Gold Rush, later branching out into the transpacific trade. During its first two decades, the Pacific Mail's primary shoreside facility was a large depot and shop complex located at Benicia. The Benicia depot was, next to the Pacific Mail's fleet of steamships, the company's largest investment. It was also the first major industrial enterprise in the infant state of California, a development borne entirely from the maritime commerce of the Gold Rush. The depot was established in 1850 during the excitement and speculative fever of the Gold Rush in a town sired on speculation and reared on great expectations.

Heavy traffic by way of Panama made the routine maintenance, repair, and provisioning of the steamers a vital need. Initially in 1847, the Pacific Mail Steamship Company had planned on making Panama the principal depot for their steamers, but the population flow to California and the growth of the company's traffic to and from San Francisco altered the plans. A depot was needed in or around San Francisco. The site selected for the Pacific Mail depot was Benicia. Established in 1847 as an ostensible rival to San Francisco, Benicia was a small town located in an ideal spot. Built on the shores of Carquinez Straits, a narrow body of water connecting San Francisco and San Pablo bays, Benicia was directly on the route taken by steamers and other vessels sailing into San Pablo Bay and the mouths of the Sacramento and San Joaquin rivers. Benicia was only twenty-seven miles distant from San Francisco, and deep water could be found close to shore. The fresh water of the rivers flowing into Carquinez Straits killed the marine organisms that fouled ships' hulls, another benefit. Considered a town with great expectations, Benicia attracted speculators, including influential friends of Pacific Mail's owners and operators.

The decision to locate in Benicia was agonizingly slow. In December 1848 United States Consul in California Thomas Oliver Larkin noted that "a friend of mine in Valparaiso writes me [that] Alfred Robinson . . . comes here [as] Steam Boat Agent and that Benicia is to be the Depot . . . I hope it is true."[85] As a speculative owner of Benicia town lots, Larkin visualized his property's value increasing should the Pacific Mail locate in the town. While Benicia was obviously being discussed as the site of the Pacific Mail depot in December 1848, by May 1849 the final decision was yet to be made. Pacific Mail president Aspinwall, writing to agent Alfred Robinson on May 25, ordered him to purchase property on Carquinez Straits, authorizing an expenditure of $10,000. Aspinwall's first preference was for land on the south side of the straits (today's Martinez), and if it was not available, his second choice was land on the north side, although he admitted "I have not been able to ascertain where Benicias [sic] is."[86] Meanwhile, Robinson and his partner, George W. P. Bissell, had already approached the Benicia Common Council and several local landowners, including General Mariano Guadalupe Vallejo. A large number of town lots were purchased as a result. In October, Aspinwall advised Robinson to

> close with General Vallejo—looking well to the position of the land & securing all you can—if you can get the peninsula or island as you term it . . . at a moderate price say something like $300 to $500 the square mile—as [we] may make a good thing out of it by selling to [the] government—at any rate get the refusal of it if you can for a length of time sufficient to have me say yes or no.[87]

Property was purchased by Bissell and a variety of associates (including one town council member, H. D. Cooke) for the company, and by spring 1850 the Pacific Mail Steamship Company was the de facto owner of a significant amount of property in Benicia. The real estate placed them in a strong position when G. W. P. Bissell formally approached the town council in May 1850 to seek favorable concessions for the company to locate in town.

The Pacific Mail Steamship Company's proposition to locate the depot in Benicia was discussed by the common council on May 11, 1850; on May 18 the council "resolved unanimously that in consideration of extensive improvements to be made immediately by the Pacific Steamship Company [sic]" the closure of certain streets for a depot was permitted.[88] Immediately a number of town lots were "sold" to the company in consideration of a $1.00 payment. Aspinwall expected this, telling Robinson that Benicia merchants "Stewart & Cooke transfer unconditionally their lots 6, 10, 11 & 12 with all water rights to the Co."[89] With favorable concessions and substantial property holdings in hand, Aspinwall and the Pacific Mail Board of Directors authorized immediate construction of the depot with a strong emphasis on thriftiness:

> If, as I suppose, the dock at the foot of Seventh street alone reverts at the expiration of twenty years to the City, I think that the expenditures thereon should be as light as possible, and I am now inclined to this belief from the large estimate made for decking which you submit. It is but fair to state that the Board was not prepared for such heavy expenditures on property so limited in extent.[90]

Despite Aspinwall's fervent desire for an inexpensive operation, the Benicia depot was a continually costly endeavor.

Work began on the depot in 1850, and by the end of August Pacific Mail steamers began to call at Pacific Mail "hulks" (storeships) moored at Benicia. The depot's establishment at Benicia was a boon to the town:

> . . . Benecia [sic] is going ahead astonishingly—its population has doubled since January [1850]. The agent of Howland & Aspinwall & the Pacific Mail Steamers has absolutely made it their depot, are busily erecting buildings &c, five large ships having already discharged there large cargoes of lumber and stores.[91]

The first structures erected at the depot were woodsheds and a prefabricated iron warehouse shipped around the horn by the Pacific Mail in late 1849.[92] A small wharf was constructed at the foot of Seventh Street for the Pacific Mail steamers.

Throughout 1850 and 1851, a regular pattern developed at the depot. Once a Pacific Mail steamer landed passengers and freight at San Francisco, it cleared for Benicia. At Benicia the crew was put to work readying the steamer for the next trip to Panama. Edward Ely, an officer aboard PMSS *Oregon*, wrote of his steamer's arrival at the depot on September 18, 1851. After "all the paints, oils, riggings, canvas and marine stores for her repair was on board . . . we cast off from the wharf. A three hours' run brought these shores in sight, and before sunset, we had safely moored at our old berth . . . [at Benicia]."[93] At the Pacific Mail depot in Benicia, the steamer's crew joined the depot's workers in making their ship ready for sea, scrubbing her down, painting the hull, cleaning cabins, repairing machinery, coaling, and stocking provisions for the next voyage to Panama.

Damage to a steamer's machinery and hull meant considerable and expensive delays for the Pacific Mail, as the depot was ill-equipped to perform major repairs. In September 1851 Edward Ely, working at the depot, reported the steamer *Northerner*'s arrival with the foremast and a paddlewheel missing along with "much other injury to her immense frame. . . . the *Northerner* will have to lay up at least three months to undergo repairs."[94] Repairs to the Pacific Mail fleet were hampered by the lack of industrial facilities in California. In particular the lack of foundries for iron casting and forging, both necessary to maintain and repair steamship engines, compelled the Pacific Mail to establish its own ironworks at the Benicia depot. A foundry was built and equipped with core ovens, forges, steam hammers, and cranes. Blacksmith, boiler-repair, and machine shops were constructed and equipped in 1851–1852. Two large brick buildings, one housing the foundry, the other shops and offices, rose on the shores of Carquinez Straits; "the site . . . was obtained by an extensive excavation of the hillsides immediately in the rear of their depot, face the Straits. . . . The passer-by is struck by the grandeur and beauty."[95] The depot and shops were aided in 1853 by the construction of a longer wharf served by a small railway. The Pacific Mail Steamship Company facility at Benicia was the first major industrial enterprise of any sort on the Pacific coast and was a direct result of the maritime traffic of the gold rush.[96]

Machinery and boilers of the largest sizes employed on Pacific Mail steamers could be repaired or replaced at Benicia, making the company self-sufficient on the largely undeveloped coast. The San Francisco *Daily Alta California* congratulated the Pacific Mail on the completion of the depot in November 1852:

> The aim has been to furnish not only to the Pacific Mail Company, but to the public, to all who may come, the means of supplying wants in all kinds of machinery, whether for use afloat or on shore; to establish iron and steam works on a scale of magnitude falling little short of the celebrated "Novelty Iron Works," New York, and to accomplish for California and the Pacific, in the application of steam to commercial and all other useful purposes, the same ends that those most famous works have for the Atlantic Ocean, and indeed, for the world at large.[97]

During the pioneer years of the company the Pacific Mail depot kept the company's fleet in good shape and on the sea, despite occasional accidents and breakdowns.

The efficiency of the depot was demonstrated time and again. In 1858, when the Pacific Mail steamer *Golden Gate* was disabled by a broken paddlewheel shaft, company officials in San Francisco wired their superintendent and resident engineer at Benicia to ready the steamer *Sonora*, then repairing, for sea.

> The ship was then dismantled, the greater portion of her machinery disconnected and taken apart for examination. The condensers . . . were in the shop undergoing repairs. In twenty-six hours after receipt of the dispatch, the engine was put together in perfect working order, 400 tons of coal put on board, the specie, mails, freight, and baggage transferred; the vessel fully provisioned and equipped . . . her hull repainted outside throughout, and the steamer got under weigh, to take her berth at San Francisco. . . . We much doubt if this could be excelled, or even equalled, in New York, where extraordinary facilities exist.[98]

Despite the company's wishes, expenditures for the Benicia operation were considerable. The buildings and wharf cost more than $150,000 to build and $100,000 to equip. The annual cost of operation was also large; for the first half of 1854 the payroll amounted to $107,248.02.[99] The depot and ironworks employed a regular staff of forty-eight skilled workmen: boilermakers, mechanics, machinists, ship carpenters, caulkers, moulders, a ship joiner, a patternmaker, and a supervisory "Engineer and Machinist."[100] Nearly half of the staff hailed from Great Britain.

In addition to the permanent staff, the depot and ironworks employed temporary laborers plucked from nearby hiring halls as the need arose. In October 1857 a correspondent writing from Benicia termed the scene at the Pacific Mail works "one of unusual activity":

> . . . the sounds of the various instruments wielded by the sturdy arms of the hundred workmen, together with the noise of the massive machinery of the foundry, were absolutely deafening. The decks of the *Golden Gate* were alive with laborers, repairing and burnishing furniture, and coaling the vessel. . . . In addition to the "Gate" there are now lying at the wharf, the steamers *Oregon, Panama, Northerner* and propeller *Fremont*.[101]

Unfortunately, such scenes were rare. The need for labor was never constant, and payroll costs fluctuated wildly. Business was slow enough in the summer of 1856 to compel the Pacific Mail to suspend work at the depot and shops. "The announcement of this determination is not altogether pleasing to the Benicians, yet they suspect the suspension to be only temporary."[102] By fall 1856 the Benicia operation had just begun to recuperate. Nonetheless, a chart of monthly payroll costs between October 1856 and October 1860 indicates that employment at the depot and shops was anything but stable.

The depot was the most considerable asset the Pacific Mail held on shore; in 1855, $461,142.25 of the company's $597,242.35 in real estate was owned at Benicia. Machinery at Benicia that year totaled $41,907.99 in value and consisted primarily of spare parts for steamer engines.[103] In the 1860 census, the capital invested in the ironworks alone was estimated at $225,000. The list of raw materials used at the works in 1860 is impressive: 200 tons of pig iron, 120 tons of bar iron, 95 tons of boiler iron, 15 tons of copper, 13 tons of brass, and 250 tons of coal, with an aggregate value of $53,500. The average monthly cost for labor was $4,800.[104]

Pacific Mail's operation through the 1850s and 1860s was the economic mainstay of Benicia, employing on some occasions more than 100 workers. Pacific Mail shipwrights built Benicia's Episcopal church, St. Paul's, in 1860, supplied the bell for another church, and donated the first fire engine to the town. Beginning in July 1853, Pacific Mail, by order of the common council, began to pay for additional police to protect the east side of Benicia where the depot and ironworks were located.[105] The arrival of each steamer's crew and officers meant increased revenue for Benicia's saloon and hotel keepers. The presence of the Pacific Mail vessels also enhanced the social scene. William Perkins, visiting Benicia on March 28, 1851, observed that "the time passed slowly enough, enlivened a little by a visit to the palace of a steamer, the "Golden Gate," which is moored here repairing, and an introduction to a pretty American woman, Mrs. Davis, whose name in consequence will be immortalized."[106] William B. Brewer, who passed through town on July 20, 1862, noted in his diary that "the 'City of Benicia' is merely a little, dull, miserable town of not over five hundred inhabitants, and were it not for its United States Arsenal and the shops of the Panama steamers, where they make their repairs, there would be *nothing* here."[107]

Difficulties through the years between the Benicia town council and Pacific Mail officials strained the relationship of town and company. The common council apparently viewed Pacific Mail as a convenient source of revenue for civic improvements. Pacific Mail, on the other hand, felt that an "understanding" existed with the common council that exempted them from certain civic responsibilities, such as paying rent for city property they occupied and taxes of property they owned. The common council requested a $25,000 loan from the company on September 13, 1852. The loan, secured with city stock and redeemable in three years, was to build a new city hall. The council reminded Pacific Mail's agent of "services rendered," authorizing its negotiating committee "to furnish said agent with such statistics as may be requisite for his information and by which to facilitate the negotiation of said loan."[108] The loan was refused. To compound the difficulties, the agent died at sea enroute to the company headquarters in New York with the city's bonds in his possession. Two years passed before the bonds were returned. Meanwhile the common council, in no mood to grant Pacific Mail any favors, had responded to a request for police patrols in their area of the city by requiring Pacific Mail to pay for the officers.

Disagreement between the Pacific Mail Steamship Company and the Benicia Common Council finally erupted into a major dispute at the end of 1852. Pacific Mail's failure to pay delinquent property taxes strained relations to the breaking point. Pacific Mail had complained as early as March 1851 that its property had been overassessed, and in May 1852 had sought "tax relief" from the city. The failure to grant the $25,000 loan ended any thought of tax relief, however, and on April 12, 1853, the common council demanded payment of the delinquent taxes. The demand was backed by a court decision on the tax issue in the city's favor. Pacific Mail refused to pay. Benicia finally brought suit against the company to collect back taxes; in January 1864 the case was settled, with the company paying $9,268.32 for taxes dating to 1851.[109]

The tense relations between the company and the city were only one problem Pacific Mail faced at Benicia. Its facilities, constructed at great expense, initially proved a prudent investment during the pioneer period between 1850 and 1854, but after 1854 industrial development in San Francisco and the numerous shipyards and foundries there offered the company a cheap alternative for repairs and maintenance of its fleet. The outlay for labor and supplies was considerable. In May 1855 the expenditure for the Benicia depot and shops for the previous twelve months was recorded as $71,008.35.[110] To offset the costs, Pacific Mail accepted outside work as early as 1851, greatly aiding steam navigation on San Francisco Bay and the rivers. A variety of vessels, including warships, merchant vessels, and the small steamers running between San Francisco and the inland river ports, began to be serviced and repaired at Benicia. Among those served were the U.S. steamer *Active*, overhauled at the depot on June 1858; the California Steam Navigation Company's steamer *Yosemite*, which received a new cylinder in December 1864; and the former Pacific Mail steamers *Cortes, Republic, Panama,* and *Oregon*, then operating coastwise for Holliday and Flint, all four of which were regularly overhauled, provisioned, and repaired at Benicia through the 1860s.[111] The revenue from the outside work never made the Benicia operation profitable, however. In July 1861, for example, the receipts for sundry outside jobs for the previous twelve months totaled a mere $3,593.76, as compared to the same year's payroll costs of $13,867.36.[112]

Economic difficulties in 1854–1855 and the failure of the company to pay a dividend to stockholders led to an effort to cut costs through the sale of the Benicia depot and shops. In the Pacific Mail's first annual report, President William Henry Aspinwall noted that "arrangements which were thought indispensable in the earlier history of California can now be provided cheaper by others than by ourselves," and even though "the establishment at Benicia has enabled us to keep our steamers in repair, at a cost comparatively low, and has saved us a very large amount in storage of coal . . . I think the time has come when the disposal of these works would be desirable; so also with the hulks at Benicia, which are not only expensive, but constantly depreciating."[113]

Aspinwall was pressured to sell everything at Benicia by a committee of disgruntled stockholders, who felt that "these works are a source of serious direct and indirect loss. . . . the sooner a fair sale can be made, and this Company cease to act as manufacturers of engines, the better."[114] The recommendation was not acted upon, Aspinwall stating that it "would be wise" for the Pacific Mail to sell everything at Benicia at some future time. For the immediate future, though, the works were directed toward more efficiency and profit, because "our steamers are repaired there at an average of expense less than is usual in New York and these repairs at any other foundry in California would cost double."[115] The decision to abandon the Benicia depot and shops, though postponed, had been made. Rumors of closure at Benicia were rife in San Francisco in 1856; "The Pacific Mail Steamship Company intend suspending operations at their machine shop and foundry at Benicia. The announcement of this determination is not altogether pleasing to the Benicians."[116]

The abandonment of the Pacific Mail Steamship Company depot and shops at Benicia was finally announced in 1868, when the company stated its determination to repair its steamers by contract in the future. The property was sold in 1869 just as the transcontinental railroad finally linked the eastern and western shores of the continent. The decision to close the depot was unfavorably viewed in Benicia, which had "greatly benefitted by the location of the company's works, and its liberal disbursements."[117] The reason behind the closure was, according to some Benicians, due to the company's disposition to branch out, to water the stock and provide for the friends of the new management. All this was not so conveniently managed while the works were located at Benicia, so it was determined to move everything to the city."[118] The actual reasons were the depreciating real estate values in Benicia, the decline of the Panama route, the increased availability of shipyards and large ironworks to provide competitive service, and a consolidation of Pacific Mail operations in San Francisco to capitalize on its transpacific service from that port. Simply stated, "the day had passed when the company needed to provide all the equipment necessary for the operation of its ships."[119]

The closure of the Benicia depot was largely propelled by industrial development in San Francisco. By the summer of 1849, urbanization reached south of Market Street, pushing the sand dunes into a small depression on the bay shore in the lee of Rincon Point, an area that became known as "Happy Valley."[120] By the spring of 1850 Happy Valley was fast becoming San Francisco's first industrial district, and numerous foundries were erected there. These included the Union Iron Works (which later would boom into the state's major ironworks and iron and steel shipbuilding firm), the Vulcan Iron

Works, the Sutter Iron Works, the Alta Foundry, and the Pacific Iron Works. The various foundries and ironworks comprised San Francisco's principal industries, and their business came primarily from steamers. The Happy Valley foundries repaired numerous small river and bay steamers plying the inland waters of the state, and provided machinery for small steamers building at San Francisco.

The construction of steamers and vessels at San Francisco reportedly started in 1849–1850 with the construction of dismantled steamers on the beach near Rincon Point at a spot thereafter hailed as "steamboat point." The construction of steamers from scratch was underway by 1850–1851. One early example was the seventy-one-ton sidewheel steamer *Boston*, built by G. M. Burnham in 1850.[121] Other vessels were being built as well; in July 1851, for instance, an "iron scow, 65 ft. long, 15 ft. wide, and 6 ft. deep" capable of carrying 100 tons, was built at Egery and Hinckley's foundry at Happy Valley and offered for sale.[122] The shipbuilding and ship-repair business was small in 1850 (the city directory listed only four individuals: a shipwright, a ship carpenter, a caulker, and a boilermaker) but boomed after 1851; by 1852 the city directory listed fifty-six individuals involved in shipbuilding or ship repair, including one "ship builder," a marine surveyor, six shipwrights, twenty-two ship carpenters, nine caulkers, nine ship joiners, six ship smiths, and two blockmakers, all located in the vicinity of Happy Valley, Rincon Point, and South Beach.[123] The presence of these industries, which ultimately overshadowed Pacific Mail's Benicia depot, and the expansion of federal agencies with maritime responsibilities into California, provide clear evidence of the harbor and state's maturation and are another long-lasting impact of the Gold Rush migration by sea.

Chapter Five

MARITIME DISASTER ON THE ARGONAUT MIND

The tragedy of shipwreck, fear of being stranded, and other perils of the ocean weighed heavily on the minds of most argonauts. Forty-niners traveling overland, guidebooks in hand, shuddered at the thought of Indian attack, or the possibility of being trapped in a snowbound pass or dying of thirst in the desert. Those who went by sea had their own litany of fear. And just as surely as there was death on the plains, and the decimation of one desert-stranded party forever gave a name to California's Death Valley, so were maritime disasters associated with the Gold Rush migration by sea.

Early in 1849 the California-bound bark *Express* with twenty-five passengers on board foundered four days out of New York with the loss of all hands except the second mate, who clung to a spar until rescued. The event shocked seafaring gold-seekers who heard the tale. In April, C. H. Ellis on the brig *North Bend* was told of the wreck of *Express* by the passengers of the New York schooner *Sea Witch* while his ship was lying to in the Straits of Magellan to avoid stormy seas. "This is melancholy news and causes us to reflect seriously on the dangers of our present situation. Had we been at sea last night I know not but we should have shared the same fate."[1] The drama, tragedy, and pathos of shipwreck were already a popular theme during the Gold Rush period. Thus the anxieties of sailors and passengers were aroused by wrecks like *Express*, and maritime disaster weighed heavily on the argonaut mind.

Close calls, stormy weather, and the terrifying experience of rounding Cape Horn inspired many fears. In 1833, upon sighting Cape Horn, Charles Darwin wrote in his diary that "the sight . . . is enough to make a landsman dream for a week about death, peril, and shipwreck."[2] In 1849, many gold-seekers echoed Darwin as ships were battered by Cape Horn's "graybeards," huge waves eighty to ninety feet tall that travel at thirty knots. Swept by seas, and weighted down with ice that coated decks and rigging, most Gold Rush ships were mauled as they sailed past Cape Horn. Spars snapped in gale-force winds, bulwarks stove in, and men were lost. On the ship *Apollo* of New York, while off the Falkland Islands, yards crashed to the deck, the rudder unshipped, and the third mate was thrown in the sea on a dark night.[3]

The waters off Cape Horn were littered with debris swept by high seas from the ships fighting for westing, fueling images of disaster in many minds. Joseph Lamson, on board the bark *James W. Paige,* wrote after seeing a broken spar trailing rigging in the water:

> What a history of suffering and disaster may there be connected with that spar! Perhaps it belonged to our acquaintance at Rio, the *North America.* She may have been wrecked on this coast, and her five hundred souls have been sunk in the waves and dashed on the rocks. In their efforts to save themselves, may not some of them been lashed to this very yard? . . . Oh! what an hour of horror must that have been to them! What thoughts of deep and bitter anguish did they send to the homes they had seen for the last time. . . . And may we not, even now . . . be reserved for the same or a worse fate?[4]

Nelson Kingsley, aboard the bark *Anna Reynolds,* lamented: "I have heard many stories about the terrors of Cape Horn, but it is more interesting to hear stories about it, than enjoy the realities."[5] Many others agreed, and as a result more than a hundred masters heading to California in 1849 sought to avoid the weather, storms, and difficult passage by Cape Horn. They opted instead for the Straits of Magellan.

Yet storms and shipwreck fears plagued passengers in the straits. One mariner noted that "the most difficult and dangerous feature of navigation in the straits is the encountering of sudden and violent squalls, which strike the vessel without the least warning." In support of this contention, he mentioned going ashore at St. Nicholas Bay in the straits. "On a branch of a tree overhanging a little stream, we found a bottle, suspended, containing papers. . . . Three or four vessels, passing through the straits, had left memoranda of their experience— such as snowstorms, loss of spars, anchors, chains & c."[6]

Among the most telling evidence of the difficulty of the straits was the wreck of a California-bound vessel, the schooner *John A. Sutter,* which lay at Tamer Harbor in the straits where the vessel had drifted after going aground in a thick fog. Benjamin F. Bourne, passing by the wreck late in 1849, described the melancholy scene at the desolate, isolated tip of South America:

> . . . we noticed the wreck of a new vessel, lying well up on the shore, her bottom badly shattered by the rocks on which she had been driven, and both masts gone; it proved to be the "John A. Sutter" of Rhode Island. On the opposite shore were parts of iron-mills, and other machinery, probably designed for use in California. The shore was strewed with trunks and chests, from the wreck; she had been stripped of everything valuable. The cabin on deck had been cut, and partially burned, by those touching at the harbor. We fished up a bundle of steel rods from the hold, which was partly filled with sand and water.[7]

Several other vessels met with serious accidents off the horn or in the straits, forcing them either to turn back to Rio or to limp into the ports of Stanley, Talcahuano, Callao, or Port Famine. However, very few ships were actually lost in those rough waters during the Gold Rush, probably due to skilled seamanship and sturdy ships.

Gold Rush shipwrecks and other maritime disasters were confined mostly to the Pacific. A few notable disasters, such as the sinking of the Pacific Mail steamer *San Francisco* and the United States Mail steamer *Central America,* both beaten and broken by hurricanes, did occur in the Atlantic, and a few vessels, including the steamer *Lafayette,* were lost in the Caribbean off Panama's shores. But the majority of vessels engaged in Gold Rush trade and commerce was lost between Timm's Point in southern California and Trinidad in northern California. Hinton Helper, writing in 1854, tabulated that $5,060,000 had been lost in twenty-four shipwrecks, along with "sundry sailers and steamers, the names of which have been misplaced," on the California coast or on the state's inland waters.[8] Most Gold Rush–era wrecks on the Pacific coast were lost on repeat voyages and numbered approximately fifty vessels, including eleven oceangoing steamships, seven steamers plying the waters of San Francisco Bay or the Sacramento, San Joaquin, or Feather rivers, and a variety of sailing craft.

Predictably, many of these vessels wrecked at the busy entrance to San Francisco Bay. One, the ship *Arkansas,* went aground on Alcatraz Island. Pounding on the rocks and losing her mizzenmast, *Arkansas* escaped disaster when she drifted free. Twelve vessels, however, were total losses at the Golden Gate, one of the earliest being the ship *Tonquin* of Boston. Arriving at San Francisco on November 23, 1849, with five passengers, the ship ran aground on a sandbar off Black Point opposite Alcatraz Island. Stranded and bilged, the ship could not be saved, but some of the cargo of lumber, bricks, and stoves was salvaged. *Tonquin* remained visible for some time, and the scene of the wreck became known as "Tonquin Shoal."⁹ Adolphus Windeler, arriving at San Francisco on December 6, 1849, saw *Tonquin* "amongst the rocks . . . 12 months ago I saw her coming down the Boca Tigris as proud as any ship of her size, now she lays low."¹⁰

Since many of the Gold Rush wrecks near the Golden Gate were not accompanied by the death of passengers and crew, and for the most part were confined to occasional loss of valuable cargoes, the reaction in San Francisco was quite different than it might have been on the high sea. The regret on land was not for lives lost and opportunities that would never be achieved; nor was the fear of imminent death at sea. Rather the regret was for destroyed cargoes, fortunes quashed, and mercantile opportunity gone by the boards. The fear was that of not seeing the cargo invested in safely arrive.

The accounts of many Gold Rush wrecks, particularly those at the harbor entrance, lose the romantic flair found in seafaring forty-niner journals. Newspaper accounts did not dwell on most of the "disasters." When the Boston ship *Tagus*, with a large cargo and only a handful of passengers, missed the harbor and ran aground four miles north of Golden Gate on February 3, 1851, the mention of the wreck was brief and to the point, focusing on the cargo and chances for its survival. On February 4, the steamer *California* was sent to try and pull her off but could not. *Tagus* was declared a total loss, but "most of the cargo will probably be saved. . . . Several schooners and lighters are engaged in getting out her cargo."¹¹ On August 8 the ship had been written off, but a notice in the *Alta California* informed "consignees by the ship *Tagus*" that "a considerable portion of her cargo has been landed here by the Salvors, which is ready for delivery upon securing the freight, salvage charges, and expenses."¹²

Salvage of ship and cargo commanded public attention in California. When the 718-ton ship *Aberdeen* of Warren, Maine, was lost on the rocks at Fort Point at the end of 1852, no lives were lost. The revenue marine cutter *Frolic* was dispatched to the wreck on January 8, 1852, and found the ship broken in two. The next day a boat crew was landed to "save property" for the owners, saving thirteen hams, five pieces of pork, a keg of butter, and a box of soap for their trouble.¹³ When the ship refused to break up, remaining on the rocks for more than a year, no romantic illusions were entertained for her. On February 16, 1854, the California legislature passed a joint resolution urging the state's Congressional delegation to "obtain an appropriation from Congress, if possible, sufficient to procure the removal of the wreck of the ship . . . which now lies at the entrance to the Bay of San Francisco, and presents a serious obstruction to commerce."

One of the most protracted shipwreck salvage attempts near the Golden Gate sought to rescue the 752-ton former Black Ball Line packet *Oxford*. The sixteen-year-old ship ran between New York and Liverpool for fourteen years, surviving storms and a hurricane that drove her ashore on the west coast of Britain in 1839.[14] Sold in 1850 to Henry A. Heiser of New York, *Oxford* sailed from Boston in late 1851 for San Francisco, carrying a speculative cargo for the city's gold-inflated market. Heiser and his partners hoped to double their investment on the ship's $100,000 cargo. Arriving off California at the end of June 1852, *Oxford* drifted in heavy fog about 500 miles off the Golden Gate for two weeks, the master unable to ascertain the ship's position. On July 12 the fog cleared. Captain McLane, spotting the promontory of land at Tomales Head, mistook it for the Golden Gate many miles to the south. He sailed her in "slowly until close under the land, when the ship brought up suddenly upon a reef making out into the [Bodega] bay."[15] News of the wreck reached San Francisco the following day.

The steamer *Sea Bird*, carrying the owner's and underwriter's agents, reached *Oxford* on the evening of July 15. They found her "hard and fast head on, with all her spars standing and in easy condition." Some fifty tons of cargo were taken aboard *Sea Bird* from the ship, but *Oxford* could not be pulled free. The masts were then cut away, but the vessel was still stuck. "The force of the wind and heavy sea rolling in under her stern, works her every moment farther on, while the quicksand piles up about her, forming an embankment or bed in which she lies comparatively easy, though we think without the slightest prospect of getting out."[16]

Over the next week much of the ship's cargo of dry goods, liquor, provisions, and 475 tons of ice was landed with the assistance of the bark *Sulla*, the revenue cutter *Frolic*, the steamer *Sea Bird*, and the schooners *John W. Brown* and *Wm. A. Tarlton*. The crew of *Frolic* succeeded in pulling *Oxford* free of the beach on the evening of July 18, but as "the ship on being hauled into deeper water commenced leaking badly," *Frolic*'s crew let up on the hawser and she went "farther up on the bar."[17] On July 20 *Sea Bird* attempted to tow off *Oxford* after she was lightened of more cargo, but failed. According to *Frolic*'s officers, who witnessed the attempt, the failure was due to "gross mismanagement" on the part of *Sea Bird*'s officers, who let *Oxford* ground twice after pulling her free of the beach.[18]

Meanwhile, the cargo landed in San Francisco from the various salvage vessels was sold. The *Alta California* noted on July 18 that an "assortment of liquors, provisions, dry goods, boots and shoes, just received from the wreck, per steamer Sea Bird and schooner J. W. Brown [were being offered] for sale" by the ship's agents. The attempts to pull the ship free having failed, *Oxford* was abandoned, "the chief object of the efforts to get her down, viz., the saving of the ice, having been accomplished."[19] Work to salvage the last of the cargo and strip the vessel of usable materials continued through the end of July. The last mention of salvage was reported by *Frolic*'s officers, who noted that when they left the wreck on July 25, *Oxford* was nearly discharged, "having about 90 bbls. of whiskey, and 100 tons of ice on board."[20] The stripped hulk of *Oxford* remained aground at Tomales Point for decades, mute testimony to a master who mistook an obscure point for the Golden Gate.

The wrecks of two clippers at the Golden Gate three months apart were among the more remarkable salvage efforts of the Gold Rush. The first was the 1307-ton clipper ship *San Francisco*, built at New York in 1853 by Abraham C. Bell and owned by Rich and Elam, and Thomas Wardle of New York. Clearing for San Francisco on October 25, 1853, the ship made an uneventful 106-day passage on her maiden voyage by way of the Straits of LeMaire and Cape Horn, arriving on the California coast on January 29, 1854. Becalmed for three days, *San Francisco* was enshrouded by fog. The captain, feeling his way through the thick mists, found himself off the Farallon Islands on February 6.[21] Picking up a bar pilot, *San Francisco* sailed toward the Golden Gate. Passing close to Point Bonita, the clipper was caught by the current and swept toward the rocks. Missing stays as it came about, the ship struck the rocks near the point, losing the jibboom, bowsprit, head, and cutwater. The ship drifted off the rocks and into Bonita Cove, where Captain Sitzer anchored his badly damaged and sinking vessel. The steam tugs *Abby Holmes* and *Resolute* took off the passengers and tried to pump out the ship, but the water rose too fast. Slipping her anchor, *San Francisco* was towed "close inshore," where she sank on her port beam, awash in the surf. The sea was calm, though, and it was hoped that "if the weather continues fine, most of the cargo will be saved in a damaged condition," although "the vessel will probably become a total loss, and a bad loss it is."[22]

Captain Robert H. Waterman, former captain of the clipper *Challenge*, bought the wreck for $12,000 from the underwriters. The value of the new ship was close to $125,000, and it carried an assorted cargo of merchandise valued between $150,000 and $400,000. Waterman's investment was diminished, however, by the immediate plundering of the wreck by looters who took to the scene in a variety of small craft. Resisting attempts to drive them off, they commenced stripping the ship. A storm on February 9 and 10, however, dispersed the looters. "Several boats were stove alongside or destroyed trying to land in the surf." The sloop *Midnight City,* with a drunken crew of eight looters, was swept out to the sea and swamped, killing all on board. A whitehall boat with two wreckers was also swamped, drowning the men as "lighters, tugboats and steamers" fled the cove to seek shelter in more protected waters.[23] The storm finished *San Francisco.* When the waves subsided, she was a "complete and total wreck. Her foremast has gone by the board, and in falling it carried away the main yard. . . . Her upper deck is cut open fore and aft as far as it could be to enable the persons employed to remove the cargo. Hundreds of boats are on the scene saving what they can."[24] Captain Waterman recouped only $20,000 on his investment before the ship disintegrated.

The second clipper wreck was the 968-ton ship *Golden Fleece.* Like the ill-fated *San Francisco, Golden Fleece's* maiden voyage was to California. Clearing Boston on August 16, 1852, with eleven passengers and a cargo of lumber, provisions, liquor, tools and machinery, grindstones, and assorted general goods, *Golden Fleece* had a storm-plagued passage to San Francisco, arriving on January 4, 1853.[25] The ship made a return voyage to Boston by way of Manila, then sailed from New York for San Francisco, arriving on April 10, 1854, after a 128-day passage.[26] On April 22, 1854, *Golden Fleece* departed San Francisco for Manila, only to be lost while beating out of the Golden Gate. Caught in an eddy, the ship missed stays and drifted ashore at Fort Point. The next day she was observed "lying broadside on to the rocks . . . bilged and full of water, her mainmast is gone, also the fore and main top mast."[27] The tugs *Resolute* and *Hercules* attempted to pull *Golden Fleece* from the rocks but failed, and on April 24 the salvage of the ship was underway. *Resolute* took away "two loads of sails and rigging" from the ship, lying stern on and dismasted.[28]

The remains of *Golden Fleece* were sold at public auction on April 24, 1854, by Messieurs Bokee and Thromb of San Francisco for $2,600.[29] During the next week they worked to strip and lighten the ship, sending 300 men to the wreck. "The purchasers of the wreck are busily engaged stripping her of everything moveable, at the same time preparations are being made to raise her. . . . The sails, riggings, guns, etc. saved by the consignees of the ship, were sold at auction yesterday, the two brass pieces bringing $580."[30] The salvage of *Golden Fleece,* just like that of the *San Francisco,* claimed lives. Four men were drowned on May 1 when their boat capsized in the surf as they headed from ship to shore.[31] Six days later all efforts to get the ship off the rocks had ceased, since "the parties who purchased her have stripped her of everything moveable, and now await the time she may break up for further gain."[32] No further mention was made of the wreck.

Some vessels were not salvageable. On March 19, 1850, the Danish bark *Caroline Amelia* was wrecked on the Mile Rocks outside the Golden Gate. Clearing San Francisco on the sixteenth, the vessel was bound for Costa Rica, perhaps to pick up passengers crossing the isthmus. Becalmed on the way, an ebb tide set in and the vessel drifted toward shore. The anchors were dropped but the cables parted, and *Caroline Amelia* struck a submerged rock, staving a hole in her bottom. "Being an old ship, her timbers soon gave way, and filling steadily she went down in about ten fathoms of water, entirely out of sight." The captain and crew were able to save their personal effects, which were the only items saved.[33] The ten-year-old Canadian bark *Mersey* was another unsalvageable wreck. On December 16, 1850, the vessel, inbound with a cargo consigned to Starkey Brothers and Company of San Francisco, encountered stormy weather and went ashore near Point Bonita. All hands were saved "with the greatest difficulty," but the ship was a total loss. The ship was boarded after the wreck in calm weather by the mate, who saved some of the crew's effects, but the ship and cargo were not recovered.[34]

One largely unsalvageable wreck recouped a greater fortune for California. Built in Baltimore for the Chinese opium trade, the 210-ton brig *Frolic* operated as a heavily armed opium clipper for the Boston-based firm of Russell and Company beginning in May 1845 when she cleared Bombay, India, with a cargo of opium.[35] For the next five years *Frolic* was an active participant in the opium trade, sailing between Bombay, Canton, Shanghai, Hong Kong, and Macao. Then in 1850, when steamers were beginning to replace sailing vessels in the trade, *Frolic* was sent to California in response to the increased opportunities for trade. On May 25, 1850, *Frolic* arrived at Canton from Bombay, off-loaded her cargo of opium, and took on a cargo of merchandise. On May 30 she cleared for Hong Kong, seventy-eight miles distant, where she loaded more cargo, identified as sundries. Sailing from Hong Kong on June 7, 1850, the brig made an extremely fast fifty-day passage across the Pacific under the command of Captain Edward H. Faucon, a veteran of the California hide-and-tallow trade.[36]

On July 26, 1850, while beating down the California coast to San Francisco, *Frolic* struck a reef off Point Cabrillo. Filling rapidly, the brig was driven toward shore by the waves, going aground in a small cove where she quickly broke up and sank, killing six of her crew. Captain Faucon, the mates, and three crew members reached Fort Ross in one of the ship's boats while the remainder of the crew hiked overland to Bodega and thence to San Francisco. The news of *Frolic's* rich cargo quickly spread when the *Daily Alta California* reported the loss on August 5, 1850. The *Alta's* editors noted that *Frolic* "was bound for this port with a valuable cargo of Chinese goods. The loss is estimated to be about $150,000." Since the cargo included jewelry, tea, and other expensive Chinese trade goods and lay in only 20 feet of water some 150 feet from shore, it was easy prey for looters. As the brig disintegrated in 1850 and 1851, local Indians and Americans salvaged goods from the wreck. By August 1851 a number of salvaged items had reached the interior valleys of California. George Gibbs, an interpreter with an expedition seeking treaties with northern coastal ranges Indians, described his visit to the house of George Parker Armstrong on the Russian River. Noting the rough and crude thatch-and-clay hut, Gibbs found the furnishings "somewhat incongruous, for upon the earthen floor and beside a bull's hide partition, stood huge china jars, camphor trunks, and lacquered ware in abundance, the relics of some vessel [*Frolic*] that had been wrecked on the coast last spring."[37]

The only documented attempt to salvage *Frolic's* cargo was made by Jerome B. Ford in 1851. Visiting the sawmill of Stephen Smith and Harry Meiggs at Bodega in 1851, Ford heard of the wreck and laid plans to salvage what he could of the cargo with Meiggs. Making his way of the coast early in 1851, Ford contacted a survivor of the wreck, William Kasten. Directed to the cove where the wrecked brig lay, Ford found the local Indian women wearing silk shawls that they had salvaged from *Frolic*, but he was too late to save anything.[38] The trip was not a loss for Ford and Meiggs, however. The need for lumber to build up San Francisco and other settlements in California had inspired the importation of timber and the logging of the San Francisco Bay area and environs as far north as Bodega. Searching for the wrecked *Frolic*, Ford was the first American known to visit the thick groves of redwoods on the Mendocino coast. He reported his discovery to Harry Meiggs upon his return to San Francisco. Meiggs, realizing the profit to be made from the untouched forests, purchased additional sawmill equipment, chartered a vessel, and sailed north, where he established in July 1852 a small logging settlement initially known as Meiggsville, later as Big River, and finally as Mendocino City. Meiggsville was the first town on the Mendocino coast and was the genesis for dozens of similar lumber camps and sawmills in the redwoods. The settlement engendered the beginning of the Pacific coast lumber trade, which introduced a coastal trade between San Francisco and the various "doghole" ports north that by 1889 had surpassed (by number of voyages) maritime trade on the Atlantic coast.

The impact of shipwreck was felt more strongly in San Francisco and elsewhere in California whenever passengers' lives were lost and scores of people were injured. Explosions of river and bay steamers frequently caused death and dismemberment. One of the worst early disasters was the explosion of the steamer *Sagamore* at San Francisco on October 29, 1850. Packed with hundreds of passengers, the steamer was ready to depart Central Wharf for Stockton at 5:00 P.M. Suddenly the boilers exploded, blowing steam, splinters, and shrapnel through the crowded decks. One survivor, James Kirker, recounted that he

> . . . had just gone on board and was going aft to pay my passage, when the explosion took place, and was thrown some 10 or 15 feet in the air and lit on the bodies of 2 persons (dead). When I recovered my presence of mind and the steam cleared away, I saw as many as 25 persons on the deck who were apparently not hurt, and a great many who were killed or wounded. I saw 2 hanging on the side of the wreck badly wounded and crying for help. I caught hold and pulled them in. By this time several boats had got alongside and were busy picking up people who were thrown into the water. As I was late getting on board, I should think there was as many as 130 people on the upper deck when the explosion took place.[39]

The disaster was compounded the next day when the city hospital, where the survivors had been taken, caught fire and burned to the ground, severely burning a number of already badly scalded passengers.

Another tremendous loss of life occurred on April 10, 1853, when the steamer *Jenny Lind*'s boiler flue collapsed while enroute from Alviso in Santa Clara County to San Francisco. The dinner bell having just rung, many passengers had taken seats when a large cloud of scalding steam blew through the dining saloon. A number of passengers were killed, many lingering for days and dying a horrible death as their skin slipped from scalded limbs and infection set in. Among the dead were some prominent citizens of San Jose, including Postmaster Jacob D. Hoppe, a signer of the California Constitution in 1849.[40] The disaster was strongly felt. The editors of the San Francisco *Daily Alta California*, writing on April 12, observed, "The disaster on the bay has smote with appalling suddenness the hearts of our community. The distressing circumstances of the accident, the terrible effects, and the familiarity with most of the names in the list of sufferers, have caused a deep impression among our citizens."

Most steamboat disasters on California's inland waters were the result of negligence, mainly in the form of neglected safety precautions with boilers and the overtaxing of engines and steam plants during reckless races between steamers on the bay and rivers. In February 1851 the Marysville *Herald* explained the current definition of two terms: "unlucky" meant a passenger had missed the steamer, while "lucky" meant the passenger was safe at home when the steamer exploded.[41] Among the lucky were those at home when the steamer *Fawn*, bound from Sacramento to Marysville, exploded while racing the steamer *Gabriel Winter* on August 16, 1851, killing several passengers and maiming others. An investigation failed to pinpoint the cause of the boiler explosion, but two likely theories emerged. Either the engineer had tied down the safety valve to gain extra steam, or the boilers were made of brittle iron.[42] Faulty equipment was certainly the cause of the *Jenny Lind* disaster of 1853 and also the explosion of the steam chimney of *New World* as she pulled away from her moorings at Marysville in June 1851. The *New World* explosion killed one man instantly. Two others drowned, and fourteen men were scalded.[43] When the steamer *Pearl* exploded in February 1856, the editors of the Marysville *Herald* specifically blamed the boilers, stating that most on the various riverboats were "refuse stuff . . . fit only for old iron," but nonetheless sent to California on speculation.[44]

The presence of maritime disaster was intensified in 1853, when in the space of sixty days five separate wrecks and accidents occurred. The events were described in a lithographed broadsheet, "Disasters of 60 Days," issued by the firm Britton and Rey of San Francisco. The broadsheet showed panels of the wrecks *Tennessee, Independence,* and *Samuel S. Lewis,* the accident aboard *Jenny Lind,* and in a centrally located inset depicted the explosion of the boilers on the riverboat *R. K. Page.*

The active maritime traffic between New York, Panama, Nicaragua, and San Francisco resulted in the loss of ten steamers. The steamer *Lafayette* burned off Chagres, Panama, on September 11, 1851. The steamer *Union* wrecked on the Mexican coast on July 5, 1851, followed by the loss of the steamer *North America* in Mexico on February 27, 1852. The steamer *Pioneer* went ashore and was lost near San Luis Obispo, California, on August 17, 1852. A spate of disasters then followed, beginning with the destruction by fire of the steamer *Independence* on February 16, 1853, with a tremendous loss of life and great suffering by the survivors. *Tennessee* went ashore on March 6,

1853, *Samuel S. Lewis* was wrecked on April 9, 1853, and the two inland steamers met with accidents. The year ended on a bad note when the steamer *Winfield Scott* was wrecked on December 2, 1853, and the new steamship *San Francisco*, enroute to California, was battered by a hurricane in the Atlantic, killing more than a hundred passengers and forcing the abandonment of the slowly sinking hulk.

The loss of SS *Independence* was the first major maritime disaster of the California Gold Rush. The 613-ton wooden sidewheel steamer had been built at New York in 1850 by William H. Brown for California service on Cornelius Vanderbilt's Nicaragua line.[45] Clearing New York on January 13, 1850, the steamer headed to the Pacific, stopping to pick up passengers at San Juan del Sur, Nicaragua, before arriving at San Francisco for the first time on July 12, 1851. The steamer then commenced a regular run in conjunction with the steamer *North America* to San Juan and back. The bad reputation of Vanderbilt's steamers was reinforced by *Independence*. In July 1852, passengers landing at San Francisco from *Independence* paraded through the streets with an effigy of Cornelius Vanderbilt. A placard inscribed "Vanderbilt's Death Line" was hung from the figure's neck.[46]

The epithet proved true on February 16, 1853, when *Independence* was lost off the coast of Baja California while enroute to San Francisco from San Juan. Early in the morning while the crew washed down the decks and the steamer passed near Isla Margarita, a number of passengers called the captain's attention to a group of rocks lying directly in the path of the steamer. Captain Sampson "curtly replied, 'mind your own business,' at the same time declaring that what they took to be rocks *were nothing but whales.*"[47] A few minutes later, *Independence* struck the rocks. The engines were reversed and the steamer backed off. Down in the engine room, Chief Engineer Collins was accosted by a fireman who reported the fireroom was flooding. The blower channels were flooded, the blowers useless, and water was nearing the fireboxes, threatening to extinguish the boilers and render the vessel helpless. As the captain turned the ship toward the beach of nearby Isla Margarita, Engineer Collins and his men waged a desperate battle in the flooding fireroom to keep up steam and drive the vessel ashore. When the coal bunkers flooded, slats from the berths in the staterooms were tossed into the furnaces. Unfortunately, the loss of the blowers and the lack of a draft forced the flames out of the furnaces and into the fireroom, setting the ship on fire. The ladders to the fireroom were blocked by the flames, and the engineroom "black gang" had to cut their way into the room with axes. Water thrown on the flames put out the blaze in the fireroom, but by this time fire had erupted from the chimneys. Engineer Collins and his men fought the fire with hoses pumping water from the sea, but as Collins later noted, he was soon "satisfied that it was useless to do more, as the flames were bursting out from the kitchen, engine room, dead lights fore and aft, and spreading rapidly throughout the ship."[48]

As the ship burned panic swept the decks. Order broke down and the exodus from the vessel was haphazard. A few boats were lowered and headed for the island, while those passengers still on deck made split-second decisions as to whether they would burn to death or drown. The scene was described as "agonizing":

> Females could be seen clambering down the sides of the ship, clinging with deathlike tenacity to the ropes, rigging, and larboard wheel. Some were hanging by their skirts, which unfortunately in their efforts to jump overboard, were caught, and thus swung, crying piteously and horridly, until the flames relieved them from their awful position by disengaging their clothes, causing them to drop and sink in the briny deep. Mothers, going to meet their husbands [in death], threw their tender offspring into the waves, rather than see them devoured by the fury of the flames, and trusted to fortune and chance to take their bodies to shore.[49]

Passenger John Greenbank dove over the side. Swimming around the burning wreck, he saw Mrs. Ayers, wife of the proprieter of the Commercial Hotel of San Francisco, standing at the rail with her six-year-old daughter. "She threw me the child, but when she sprang the steel frame of her skirt caught in some projection on the side of the ship, and unable to free herself, she hung there and burned to death before my eyes, I being powerless to aid her."[50]

The steamer finally beached on the island and continued to burn. Engineer Collins, lying exhausted on the sand, looked seaward: ". . . what a sight! The ship completely enveloped in flames, on the beach some two hundred people, many in the water, and some drowned ones on shore, still others floating off seaward on coops and what they could get that would hold them from sinking, spars, etc. and hundreds crying for help."[51] A heavy surf crashed on the beach, hampering efforts to land the boats that had gotten away and forcing many passengers to swim for land. Without assistance, many passengers still in the water outside the surf stayed close to the ship. Passenger Ezra Drown remarked:

> As I passed through the surf, how horribly sounded the piteous moans for help! All around me were the sinking bodies of the passengers and crew. . . . O God! What a situation to be in!

Planks, spars, trunks and coops, covered with human beings struggling energetically for life, some wafted to shore, others out to sea, some sinking, others being miraculously preserved. Here I saw females and children providentially rescued—then lost! Here was a kind husband who had sworn before God to protect her whom his soul loved, struggling for her safety; there was a father bearing his affectionate son to safety on the shore, looking around but to see the wife of his love dashed from the position in which he had left her, by mad and unthinking men jumping upon her and driving her into the bottomless deep.[52]

The death toll from the disaster was variously estimated between 125 and 174 passengers and crew.

Scores of bodies were thrown on the beach by the waves, where "could be seen the sacrilegious pillaging and plundering the dead—old men and young men stripping the bodies of clothing, securing the contents of their pockets, and actually quarreling, yea fighting over a corpse for the plunder!"[53] When a woman's body washed ashore, "two men immediately stepped up, each claiming her as his wife, and seemed determined to take possession of her gold ornaments, and money. But while these were quarreling for the plunder over the corpse, the real partner of the deceased lady appeared, and proved, by the testimony of the passengers, the priority of his claim."[54] When the flames subsided a few boats pulled the last survivors from the water and the sides of the wreck, including Captain Sampson, who had clung to the bows as the flames swept aft. Spars were laid across a steep ravine and sails erected on them to form a tent for the women and children while the captain and some passengers set out in a boat for help, hoping to find some of the whalers who frequented the Baja coast. By nightfall the steamer had burned down to the water's edge and lay broadside to the shore, allowing the mates and some of the crew to reach her in a boat and take off some salt beef and pork with canned meats and fruit, since the desolate volcanic island had no fresh water or available food.

The next morning the bodies were buried, more food was salvaged from the ship, and Engineer Collins, using salvaged lead steam pipe, a copper pot from the kitchen, and wooden kegs, rigged up a distillery to render the seawater drinkable. The series of devices generated a gallon and a half of water per hour, enough to keep the survivors alive.[55] Meanwhile, parties trekking across the island discovered a fleet of four whalers anchored nearby and managed to signal them. Late in the afternoon on February 18, the passengers and crew were taken aboard the whaleships, cleaned, and fed. The ships did not immediately depart, however, and remained anchored off Isla Margarita for almost two more weeks. The bodies of the dead, covered only by a thin layer of sand on the beach, had to be constantly reburied while sufficient water was desalinated and provisions salvaged for the trip to San Francisco. Captain Sampson arranged to charter the 325-ton ship *Meteor* of Mystic to carry the survivors to San Francisco. *Meteor* cleared Isla Margarita on March 1, 1853, arriving in San Francisco on March 31, 1853. The *Independence*'s failure to arrive on time had caused the city considerable anxiety. Early reports stated up to 300 passengers and crew lost, but the numbers were later revised to a more correct figure.[56]

San Franciscans were appalled by the disaster. The San Francisco *Daily Alta California* stated, "We have never recorded a more distressing calamity upon our shores, our columns have never depicted a more fearful scene of horror than has been shown in the destruction of the steamer *Independence*."[57] Outrage over the disaster prevailed throughout San Francisco. Captain Sampson's "carelessness, mismanagement or willingfulness" were blamed by 150 of the survivors who signed a testimonial. Ezra Drown publicly damned Captain Sampson:

> With these rocks laid down upon the chart, with warnings in the books to keep away from the entrances into Magdalena Bay, on account of the strong currents there; or without this knowledge previous to coming near the Island, when the breakers could be seen, and the rocks themselves for a considerable space—and sufficient at least to have averted the accident, as good men will swear—does it not come irresistably home to the mind of everyone, that the Captain, who would stand upon the wheelhouse of his ship, and permit her to be stove in upon rocks, plainly to be seen, is either insane or one of the earth's most heartless creatures? That he was insane no one will say, would to God we could. That the act was deliberate and intentional, can and we believe, will be successfully established.[58]

The sentiments were not quickly forgotten, though most focused instead on the horror of the "acts performed." The next steamship wreck was not attended by the tragedy and public indignation associated with the wreck of *Independence*.

The Pacific Mail Steamship Company's steamer *Tennessee* was the second steamship wreck of 1853. Unlike *Independence*, *Tennessee* was lost close to San Francisco. The morning of Sunday, March 6, 1853, found *Tennessee* at anchor near the Farallon Islands, twenty-six miles west of the Golden Gate. Fog shrouded the harbor entrance and was so dense that passengers could see no farther than sixty feet ahead.[59] Captain Mellus was confident of his position, though, and navigated the steamer slowly ahead, occasionally stopping to take soundings with the lead. Soon a rock loomed out of the fog, and Mellus, supposed it to be Mile Rock near the Golden Gate, ordered the steam to be "let on a little more." On the open bridge atop one of *Tennessee's* paddlewheels, Mellus suddenly heard breakers. The lookout at the bow spotted surf ahead, and then someone at the stern spotted a ledge of rocks in the water just astern, which the ship had just missed. There was not enough room to back *Tennessee* out, so Mellus ordered the ship ahead slowly to acquire enough room to maneuver back out to sea. As she steamed ahead, *Tennessee* struck the rocks aft and began to swing broadside toward the rockbound shoreline. The fog lifted enough for Mellus to see a narrow opening in the cliffs leading to a small sand beach. If *Tennessee* struck the rocks, the loss of life would be considerable, so Mellus ordered her full ahead, aiming for the beach. At about 9:00 A.M., *Tennessee* struck the beach and went ashore, swinging broadside onto the sand. "It seemed a great shudder went through the ship, and the hull, and the masts, and the engines, and all things that were on her trembled." Below decks, many passengers had just sat down to breakfast.[60] Passenger Fred Stocking had just taken his seat when "suddenly there came an awful crash of the steamer. Everybody knew instantly we'd struck. Everything went off the table in a heap."[61]

The passengers screamed and ran up on deck. *Tennessee* lay with her bow on shore, listing to starboard with the port side broadside to the surf. The seas were heavy, and the hull was pounded by the waves. The decks were packed with screaming and crying men and women, some of them praying as the ship rocked in the trough of the waves. The ship's bell was constantly ringing, "tolling a terrible toll, sounding the Tennessee's doom. It sounded awfully, scared . . . people. . . . The women took it for the toll of doom."[62] In the midst of the confusion a few of the passengers and crew sprang into action. Chief Mate Richard Dowling tied a line to his waist and leapt overboard into the surf. He was thrown up on the rocks and managed to hang on, securing the rope to a rock. A heavy hawser was pulled ashore to guide boats ashore.[63] Following Dowling's lead, steerage passenger Johann Hein threw himself over the side and swam through the surf to the beach and safety.[64] Meanwhile, Adams and Company agent Thomas Gihon began gathering women and children. With a steward's help he lowered a boat and began to ferry his charges ashore. Using his pistol to keep back an anxious crowd of men who attempted to rush the boat, Gihon made several trips through the surf until all the women and children were safely landed on the beach.[65]

The male passengers and crew were followed by the mail and baggage. "Awnings and sails were sent on shore for tents, also provisions and cooks, and in a few hours, a desolate and sandy beach presented the appearance of a busy and cheerful encampment."[66] Landing baggage was a long and difficult task. Fred Stocking remarked, "I worked like the devil all day, and the last piece of baggage I got ashore was a friend's side-saddle that was in a locker in her cabin, way down aft, and I dug it out for her just as the water was filling the cabin."[67] The passengers built fires along the beach—using wreckage that washed ashore from *Tennessee*—to dry off and keep warm as night fell. The ship had come ashore four miles north of the Golden Gate in a small inlet known locally as Indian Cove. The cove was also called Potato Cove, due to its proximity to Potato Patch Shoal off the Golden Gate. The land was owned by William A. Richardson and was part of his Rancho Sausalito. Richardson's home, in the small town of Sausalito, was just a few miles over the coastal hills from the wreck site. One of Richardson's employees had been riding by when *Tennessee* came ashore and had raced back to Sausalito for help, which arrived early the next morning.

There was not enough space in the tents for all the passengers, and a number of them decided to hike over the hills to Sausalito once they determined where they were. The passengers who left the wreck hiked for hours "over a dark rough road, but finally saw the light from the top of the hill." In Sausalito many were able to hire small boats to take them to San Francisco for twenty-five or thirty dollars.[68] Hence news of the wreck reached San Francisco on the afternoon of March 6: "The excitement throughout the city . . . was very great, until the facts of the case became better known." As passengers arrived in San Francisco from Sausalito, the news that all were safe was met with relief. "Any of our citizens that have friends or their family on board may rest assured that they are well provided for, and that every thing in this casualty will be managed with the well known energy of the P.M.S.S. Co."[69]

On the morning of March 7, help arrived from San Francisco. The steamer *Confidence* was dispatched to Sausalito to pick up passengers from *Tennessee*, who continued to arrive from the wreck site. The previous evening the steamboat *Goliah* had steamed to Sausalito for passengers and to ask for help from the USS *Warren*, which was anchored off the town. *Warren* sent forty-five fathoms of cable and a spare anchor with *Goliah*, and also sent her gig to help pick up passengers on shore.[70] On the morning of March 7 *Goliah* was at Indian Cove with the Pacific Mail agent, Captain E. Knight, Captain Totten, and *Tennessee*'s underwriter, Joshua P. Haven, aboard.[71] *Ten-*

nessee lay heeled offshore. "She is perfectly tight, and although her copper is much chafed and rubbed off there is every reason to suppose no serious injury has thus far been sustained by her. Her engines and all the apparatus are in perfect order, nothing as yet being displaced."[72]

At that time everyone supposed *Tennessee* could be pulled free of the beach. The vessel was embedded in only two feet of sand, and the surf had died down. *Goliah* had been dispatched for this purpose. Her crew loaded passengers and baggage, making more than forty-three trips to the beach. To assist in the operation, USS *Warren* sent her boats over to the wreck to "bring the 'Tennessee' passengers from off the shore."[73] *Confidence* returned to San Francisco with a hundred passengers on March 7. Later that afternoon *Goliah* arrived, "having on board all the passengers that were left, with their baggage and trappings. The mail and all the express matter were brought up."[74] *Goliah* came close to being wrecked on the return trip to San Francisco, steaming too close to shore at the Golden Gate and striking the submerged wreck of the ship *Aberdeen*, lost at that spot in 1852.[75] Since *Goliah* had not been able to attempt to pull *Tennessee* off, she returned the next morning, March 8, with the steamer *Thomas Hunt*. With passengers, baggage, mail, and specie safe in San Francisco, work to save the steamer could now begin in earnest.

Goliah and *Thomas Hunt* were not able to pull *Tennessee* off. Pumping freed *Tennessee* of the water, but

> during the night the rollers came in heavily on the beach, lifting the ship up from four to five feet and thumping her heavily on the sand as they ran back. When the morning dawned it was soon discovered that she was much out of shape, her back broken, butt ends started and bottom probably bilged; she was then making a great deal of water; her connecting pipes were all broken, rendering the engines entirely useless. The sea did not fall, and at 9 A.M., the tide flowed and ebbed into her.[76]

After a careful examination of the interior of the ship by captains Knight, Mellus, and Totten, she was pronounced a total loss. All hands were put to work landing "the goods, stores, &c., most of which were landed by 2 P.M." The *Alta California* reported:

> The hope of saving the ship seems abandoned. . . . Her officers and crew feel as if they were attending the funeral obsequies of a dear and valued friend. She was a favorite craft and one of the best sea boats that plowed the Pacific Ocean. She was the home, the pride and refuge of her officers and crew, and many a tear as salt as the brine that surrounds her shattered hulk has coursed unbidden from manly eyes, and sprung up involuntarily from the bold

and courageous hearts of those whose pride and delight she was, as they have gazed upon the last resting place of the gallant Tennessee.[77]

As workers frantically stripped the steamer, it began to go to pieces in the surf. Around noon on March 8 the hull split, and "all that heavy machinery went right down through the bottom" as the engine tore free of its timber mounts and broke apart.[78] The hull, now breached in several locations, filled with water and began to disintegrate. A visit to the wreck on March 10 "revealed her condition to be perfectly helpless. . . . She is fast going to pieces. Every joist appeared started. The sea was thumping heavily against her side, and the surf flying wildly over her. She cannot hold together another week."[79]

Tennessee, with an estimated value of $200,000, was insured at only $150,000.[80] In addition to the $50,000 loss on the ship and the revenue she would have made, the Pacific Mail Steamship Company expended a total of $28,892.62 on rescue and salvage efforts. The SS *Tennessee* was the first casualty Pacific Mail suffered on the Pacific coast. Generally favored by the public, unlike the Vanderbilt Line, the company received an outpouring of sympathy (no doubt encouraged by the rescue of all passengers, cargo, mail, and baggage). At the same time, the passengers were quick to absolve Captain Mellus and his officers of any blame for the wreck. "The passengers are desirous that justice shall be done, in placing Capt. E. Mellus and his officers in a proper position. . . . Resolved, that in our opinion the disaster is in no way attributable to any want of skill, or prudence in seamanship, or vigilant foresight, which could have averted so sad a result."[81] Passenger Alfred DeWitt may well have commented on the consensus when he wrote home about the wreck of *Tennessee*: "I experienced some of the risk that occurs sometimes with those who trust themselves in ships on the deep water."[82] The abiding emotion of the passengers, their families, and their friends was relief, for "had she gone on to the rocks near by probably very few if any would have got safely ashore."[83]

There was no absolution of blame for the next two steamer disasters. Two weeks after *Tennessee* crashed ashore, the tiny riverboat *R. K. Page* exploded on the Feather River near the town of Nicolaus. Leaving Marysville on the morning of March 21, 1853, along with the steamer *Governor Dana*, *R. K. Page* raced the other steamer along the river. As they approached Nicolaus, *Governor Dana* edged into the lead. Her boilers already approaching a dangerous pressure, *R. K. Page* dropped back. The engineer, not wanting to lose, grabbed a keg of oil lying on the deck, threw open the firebox door, and tossed the keg in. The resulting explosion tore through the steamer, instantly killing many and injuring everyone else on board with the exception of one man. The bodies of four victims were never found. [84]

The next wreck was another Vanderbilt liner, the screw steamer *Samuel S. Lewis,* which was lost on April 9, 1853, under the same conditions as the recently wrecked *Tennessee,* in a thick fog but several miles north of the former on Duxbury Reef. The reef was named, ironically, for an 1849 arrival, *Duxbury,* that had grounded but not wrecked there.

Lewis struck early in the morning hours. William Tecumseh Sherman, a passenger, was awakened by "a bump and sort of grating of the vessel." Then, "instantly the ship struck heavily; the engines stopped, and the running to and fro on deck showed that something was wrong." The sea was smooth and the night calm. The vessel, however, "would rise with the swell, and come down with a bump and quiver that was decidedly unpleasant. Soon the passengers were out of their rooms, undressed, calling for help, and praying as though the ship was going to sink immediately." [85] The officers maintained order, stopping passengers attempting to lower the boats. Everyone dressed and got ready to abandon ship, waiting three hours for daylight. Instead of breaking up, the steamer gradually filled with water "to a level with the sea outside, the ship swung broadside to the swell, and all her keel seemed to rest on rock or sand." [86] A boat was launched to find help while the passengers and crew remained behind. Gradually *Samuel S. Lewis* broke up, "wriggling with every swell like a willow basket—the sea all around us full of the floating fragments of her sheeting, twisted and torn into a spongy condition." [87]

The steamer's 385 passengers were all safely landed on the beach, where bonfires had been lighted to dry their clothes and warm them in the foggy morning hours. The next day the U.S. surveying steamer *Active* and the revenue cutter *Frolic* arrived at the scene, having first passed through a field of "drift,"

> consisting of mattresses, benches, spars, and loose timber, which had floated down from the wreck; and what was the surprise of all on board to find that of the wreck itself, barely the hull remained! The *S.S. Lewis,* in one night, had completely gone to pieces! At the point on which she struck was to be seen a fragment of her hull—the lower portion—and even this remnant was being fast washed apart. Her timbers are strewn along the beach. [88]

All that was saved from the ship was passenger baggage, the specie carried aboard, and other valuables. The steamer *Goliah* returned from the wreck site on the afternoon of April 10 with "the balance of the passengers and the baggage of the vessel. Nothing now remains of the wreck together, as she has broken up, and fragments can be seen strewn all along the beach."[89] The loss of *Lewis* was a terrible blow to the line, costing more than $125,000 and following embarrassingly close on the heels of the wreck of *Independence*. While the Vanderbilt Line was again criticized, the *Alta California* ascertained "no charge of negligence or incapacity" toward the captain, who had acted responsibly in assuring the safety of his passengers after the wreck. "As there were no lives lost and no distress occasioned by this disaster, other than the temporary inconvenience to the passengers and the anxiety of their friends, this loss may be considered as rather beneficial to the traveling public than otherwise, as the *S.S. Lewis* could not be considered wholly seaworthy."[90]

The collapse of the chimneys on *Jenny Lind* the day after the wreck of *Samuel S. Lewis* culminated the "disasters of 60 days," but there was one more steamship loss on the Pacific in 1853. This was the total loss of *Winfield Scott*, recently purchased to replace the wrecked *Tennessee*. Departing San Francisco on December 1, 1853, *Winfield Scott* steamed down the coast, arriving off the Channel Islands by nightfall. During dinner a heavy fog set in, but Captain Blunt, confident of the ship's position, ordered the vessel to stay on course and at full speed. About eleven o'clock *Winfield Scott* struck an outcropping of rock off the shore of east Anacapa Island. Down below, passenger Asa Cyrus Call had fallen asleep. Jarred awake and only partly dressed, Call rushed on deck to find a mass of milling passengers. Officers were running about in the darkness, attempting to calm the crowd, insisting that everything was all right. The steamer backed off. Call headed back to his cabin, little believing the persistent claims of the officers that the ship was not in danger. He finished dressing and, grabbing the saddlebags that contained his gold, headed up to the next deck and took a seat in the saloon. Below him in the darkness, water was pouring in through two gaping holes in the bow. Almost immediately after Call sat down, the ship struck again, this time tearing her rudder away.[91] The stern settled beneath the water, and the steamer lurched to one side.

Captain Blunt gave the order to abandon ship. Life preservers were handed out and a boat was lowered to search for a safe landing place. A group of men rushed the bow but were held off at gunpoint by the captain and his officers. Meanwhile passengers began to fill the remaining lifeboats. In the darkness the crew spied a ledge surrounded by crashing surf. The boats made for it and were able to land on a pinnacle. Gradually the sinking steamer was emptied. When daylight came, the ship's company found themselves on a small rock about 200 yards off Anacapa Island. Using the boats, everyone was ferried over to the main island. Provisions were secured from the now partially submerged ship, and camp was set up on the desolate island. Food was a problem, but fortunately a passing boat was hailed and pioneer George Nidever, resident of a nearby island, was able to loan the castaways some fishhooks and line. Passenger Edward Bosqui spoke to Captain Blunt, "who readily complied with my request to let me have one of the ship's boats and go fishing off the island. I got three or four to accompany me, and in a very short time we caught a fine mess of fish. After this, relays of crews were engaged fishing from morning till night while we remained on the island."[92] Other meals came from the sea as well. Asa Cyrus Call shot a seal with his pistol and noted "we shall have a luscious dinner." Despite the harvests from the sea, it was still necessary to ration the food. The establishment of order on the island followed the provisioning activities. Call noted on December 5 that "robbery and plunder has been the order of the day since the wreck," forcing the passengers to form a "committee of investigation" and search baggage. "A good deal of property has come to light," he added, "and two thieves have been flogged. I have recovered a pair of revolvers, a bowie knife and some clothing but I am a good deal out of pocket yet."

On the morning of December 5, Captain Blunt sent a boat to the mainland, twelve miles distant, for help. Arriving in Santa Barbara, the boat carried a dispatch for the Pacific Mail's San Francisco agent. Former Pacific Mail agent Alfred Robinson of Santa Barbara earned $1,000 for riding to San Francisco with the dispatch. Rescue for some came sooner, though. On December 3 the Pacific Mail steamer *California* had passed the island and taken off some passengers. Too full to take many, *California*, enroute to San Francisco, promised to send help. The news created an uproar in San Francisco, and the steam tug *Goliah*, the steamer *Republic*, and the *California* were sent to the wreck.[93] The day *Scott*'s boat was sent to Santa Barbara, *Goliah* arrived at Anacapa Island and stood by; she was too small to carry passengers and had been sent only to try to pull *Winfield Scott* free. Some provisions were landed before *Goliah* returned to San Francisco, where her crew reported that "the passengers are all well, and as comfortable as could be under the circumstances. The ship lies in a small cove, head on shore. The tide ebbs and flows in her. Should the weather continue favorable, it is supposed that a great portion of her machinery may be saved. Should a blow come on, however, it is feared that the ship would break in two, and sink."[94]

The passengers soon depleted the meager resources of the island, and the situation became desperate. Passenger Charles Holden noted that all of the food and water was exhausted on December 9. But on the morning of the tenth, "the report of a cannon was heard on the island. Instantaneous as it seemed, the crowd hurrahed, screamed and yelled for joy. Assistance was close at hand. . . . As it was quite dark, large piles of seagrass were lighted, and the gun which had been taken from the wreck made to answer in tones of thunder."[95] *California* was soon in view, "feeling her way towards us," through the early morning fog. Anchoring a mile and a half offshore, *California* sent her boats to pick up the passengers. By 2:00 P.M. most people were on board with whatever luggage they had saved, and bound once again for Panama. Salvage of the ship was then attempted for the mail, the remaining baggage, and the ship's machinery and furnishings still on board. As late as December 10 the steamer "resisted the action of the breakers," but within a few days *Winfield Scott* was reported "on the rocks and bilged, her midship section much sunk."[96] Abandoning all hope of saving the ship, the crew turned to stripping what they could from the shattered hulk.

According to the San Francisco *Daily Alta California*, "considerable mails and baggage" were saved from the wreck. Some twenty-four mailbags were salvaged from the submerged strongroom. Frank Key Henderson, a postal clerk sent to the island to rescue the mails, paid one of *Winfield Scott's* sailors ten dollars a bag to dive into the wreck and pull them out. The recovered mailbags were brought back to San Francisco where the postal department dried them out. "These letters were brought to this city, a room taken, a hot fire built, frames with network[s] of strings formed, upon which the letters were laid, one by one, to dry, and although they lay for days beneath the waves, they will be dry enough to forward to their destination by the next mail."[97]

In addition to the mail, the ship's furniture and "small portions of the machinery" were also saved. On December 12 the wreck was abandoned. Captain Blunt and his crew embarked on *Republic* and left *Winfield Scott* for the last time. As they pulled away, *Scott* was "heaving with the swell," and it was thought she would "go to pieces" in a short time.[98] Again Pacific Mail was held blameless in San Francisco. Captain Blunt's navigation had been faultless and his seamanship "masterful." The passengers in a signed statement declared in the *Alta California*, "In consequence of the dense fog prevailing at the time, and it is the opinion and firm conviction of *all*, that no other than a Divine hand caused the calamity which has befallen us all."[99]

The last Gold Rush steamship disaster on the Pacific was the wreck of the 1767-ton sidewheel steamer *Yankee Blade* in 1854. Built in 1853 for Edward Mills of New York for his Independent Opposition Line, *Yankee Blade* operated between New York and Panama in competition with both the Pacific Mail Steamship Company and the Vanderbilt Line. Departing New York in December 1854 for the first time, *Yankee Blade* headed for the Caribbean port of Chagres on the Panama route. News of the steamer reached San Francisco in the aftermath of 1853's many maritime disasters. The *Alta California* welcomed the new ship. "It will be hard to keep Edward Mills down, even if his wealthy and powerful competitors unite for the purpose."[100] *Yankee Blade*, however, was fated to join Vanderbilt's depleted fleet, for in January 1854 Edward Mills merged his line with Vanderbilt to form a new line, the Nicaragua Steamship Company.[101] *Yankee Blade* was sent to the Pacific coast to operate between Nicaragua, Panama, and San Francisco. Departing New York on February 2, 1854, *Yankee Blade* steamed under the command of Captain Henry Randall to San Francisco, arriving on May 5, 1854. No trace of the previous animosity toward Vanderbilt's steamers was apparent in the welcome by the local press; "This splendid steamship was the center of attraction yesterday for parties walking in the neighborhood of the city front. The *Yankee Blade* since her arrival in this port has been thoroughly overhauled and extensive alterations made to suit the trade she is engaged in."[102]

Yankee Blade departed for San Juan del Sur on June 1, 1854. Entering into service on the Pacific, the steamer was immediately embroiled in the bitter rivalry between Vanderbilt and the Pacific Mail. In August 1854, *Yankee Blade* ran out of coal off Coiba Island near Panama. The Pacific Mail steamer *Sonora* passed but did not stop in response to *Yankee Blade*'s guns and distress rockets. Some of *Sonora*'s passengers reported the steamer's plight on arriving at Panama. As the rescue steamer was about to sail, *Yankee Blade* steamed into harbor, the passengers and crew having cut enough firewood on Coiba Island to reach port.[103] *Yankee Blade* did not remain long in Vanderbilt's hands. In the summer of 1854 a deal was negotiated in which *Yankee Blade* and her running mate *Uncle Sam* were sold to the Nicaragua Transit Company for $500,000, while the steamer *North Star* on the Atlantic side was sold to the United States Mail Steamship Company for $300,000. In addition, Vanderbilt received another $100,000 for promising to stay out of the opposition steamship business.[104]

Operating still for Vanderbilt and Mills but now in the hands of her new owners, Cornelius Garrison and Charles Morgan, *Yankee Blade* cleared San Francisco on September 30, 1854, for San Juan de Sur with 800 passengers. Like many other steamship wrecks, *Yankee Blade* was the victim of poor navigation and thick fog. Running close to the coast, the steamer struck the rocks near Point Arguello just past three o'clock in the afternoon on October 1, 1854. The bow and about sixty feet of the ship's forward section were firmly wedged into a rock reef that ran offshore, while the stern settled in twenty-four feet of water. The boats were manned and a number of women and children reached shore. The boat commanded by the mate, however, capsized in the surf with twenty-one passengers, killing many. As darkness fell, numerous passengers were left on board clustered on the bow, the promenade deck and various deckhouses having washed away. Those left on the stranded, half-sunk steamer included many crewmen, while the captain and officers camped on the beach with the rescued passengers.

Through the night bodies washed ashore from the wreck and were buried on the beach. Among them were "a female with a child clasped in her arms, the wife of Mr. Brennan, who, as an instance of devoted love, went on shore, spade in hand, dug up his wife and child, kissed them, and then reburied them."[105] The worse scene, however, was on board. Without anyone of authority present, stranded passengers were left to the mercies of ruffians in the crew and among their own ranks, who pillaged baggage and took control of the ship:

> They burst into the state-rooms, ripped open carpet-bags and trunks, plundered them of all the money and valuables they found, and cast the rest aside or overboard. They displayed knives and revolvers, and threatened the lives of all who attempted to interfere. . . . They got hold of the liquors—many of them drank themselves furiously drunk—ransacked all the luggage . . . attacked, beat, cut and shot all who got in their way, and became, indeed, a band of infuriate fiends. . . . Some of the passengers . . . were dreadfully cut with knives and bottles. . . . Our informant saw one man stagger out with his head dreadfully cut and streaming with blood. He saw the ruffians throw a cloth over the head of another, who appeared badly wounded, and force him into a dark recess of the steerage.[106]

The night of terror on board *Yankee Blade* subsided around dawn while the wind and sea rose. The foremast fell through the keel, the sponson decks broke, and the stern tore free of the still tightly wedged forward section. When daylight came, boats were again dispatched from shore, landing the remaining passengers and crew on the beach.

At 9:00 A.M. the steam tug *Goliah* reached the scene, having been alerted to the wreck, and took several passengers off. The steamer *Brother Jonathan* came up from San Diego and rescued the remaining passengers. In all, between fifteen and thirty lives were lost, and the steamer was a total loss with her furnishings and the majority of the passengers' baggage. By October 3 "most of the steamer had disappeared, excepting some floating fragments, such as pilot house, part of the deck, etc."[107]

An angry reaction by both passengers and crew damned Captain Randall. A public meeting held at Portsmouth Square in San Francisco by the survivors resolved: "We have come to a firm conclusion that sheer negligence on the part of the managers of the *Yankee Blade*, in directing her course, and in running so near a coast well known to be dangerous, was the cause of the disastrous wreck. . . . duty compels us to censure Capt. Randall, in so quickly deserting the wreck, and leaving the boat without a leading officer on board to quiet the passengers and prevent the plundering. Had the captain remained on board, it is our candid opinion this could have been done."[108] Thus the pioneer period of Gold Rush navigation and maritime trade and commerce ended with another round of fierce condemnation.

The last Gold Rush wreck, however, came in the aftermath of the gold excitement. The final burst of outrage and anger followed the sinking of the United States Mail steamer *Central America*, which foundered off Cape Hatteras on September 12, 1857, in the midst of a wild Atlantic storm. The steamer carried 423 persons, $1,230,000 in gold, and tons of freight, baggage, and mail to the bottom.[109] When news of the disaster reached New York and the rest of the country, howls of rage and indignation arose, for it was disclosed that the vessel had been unseaworthy, with rotten frames, leaky planking, and a sprung bottom. Her culpable owners had sent her out rather than incur the costs of repair. In San Francisco, where most of the passengers had hailed, the cold fury of the press was matched only by that of the populace, who saw in this wreck the culmination of nearly a decade of unsafe steamers and a host of maritime disasters:

> Wherever we went, at every turn, we heard the query put, "Who is responsible for the murder of four hundred of California's worthy citizens?" Ay, who is responsible for their murder? For murder it is, most foul. . . . We answer, unhesitatingly, the United States Mail Company . . . and their coadjutors, the Pacific Mail Steamship Company. To the cupidity and heartless inhumanity of these unchristian companies is to be attributed the recent disaster. What care they for the many children made

fatherless, or for the wives suddenly thrown upon the cold, heartless world, and the poor, unprotected widows, by the foundering of their rickety, filthy old hulk?[110]

Controversy over the wreck raged in San Francisco for over a month. The press published lurid accounts of the disaster and survivor tales that hinted of the crew's cowardice, a lack of tools to repair damage to *Central America* done by the storm, and an unseaworthy, rotten vessel, conditions that had combined to send four hundred innocent citizens to a watery grave. Old complaints and old wrecks were recalled. Editorials demanding action, angry public meetings, sermons, and other proddings resulted in cries for retribution.[111]

On October 30, 1857, a mass meeting held in San Francisco passed resolutions indicating California's feelings about the disaster. It was not a circumspect group. "This meeting attributes the loss of the *Central America* to the negligence and indifference of the U.S. Mail Steamship Company to the safety of those whose money it had received. . . . we view such negligence as falling little short of crime."[112]

Perhaps the most telling response to the disaster, though, was a song penned by a longtime critic of the steamer companies, songster John A. Stone. Stone, an 1850 arrival, wrote many songs about life in Gold Rush California, always striving to hold "the mirror up to nature," and "if the *reflections* to some may seem harsh, I have only to say that . . . recognition of their truthfulness has incited me."[113] Many of Stone's songs were parodies exploding the myths of that time and place, illustrating the "humor and drudgery of mining, the hopes and disillusionments of the miners, the hardships and humbugs of life in California."[114] This attitude, when turned to the subject of the Gold Rush steamers, resulted in "humbug" songs such as Stone's "A Ripping Trip":

> You go aboard of a leaky boat,
>   And sail for San Francisco;
> You've got to pump to keep her afloat,
>   You have *That*, by jingo.
> The engine soon begins to sqeak,
>   but nary a thing to oil her;
> Impossible to stop the leak—
>   *Rip* goes the boiler![115]

Stone also wrote "Steam Navigation Thieves" and "Humbug Steamship Companies," clearly reflecting California's prevalent attitude after years of indifferent service, poor maintenance, high fares, and disasters. His "Humbug Steamship Companies" even contained a reference to the ill-fated *Yankee Blade,* which sank just months before he wrote the song in 1855:

> The greatest imposition
>   that the public ever saw,
> Are the California steamships
>   that run to Panama;
> They're a perfect set of robbers
>   and accomplish their designs,
> By a general invitation
>   of the people to the mines.
> Then come along, come along,
>   You that want to go,
> The best accommodations,
>   and the passage very low;
> Our boats they are large enough,
>   don't be afraid,
> The *Golden Gate* is going down
>   to beat the *Yankee Blade.*[116]

Stone's predisposition to write unflattering songs about the steamship companies and the widespread anger felt in San Francisco culminated in the angry ditty about the loss of *Central America.* Stone's "Loss of the *Central America*" was not a standard parlor offering of romantic views of shipwreck replete with pathos, heroics, and fatalism. It was a symbol of California's arousal from complacent acceptance of the helpless terror of maritime disaster. The song called for action and the need to protect innocent humanity from human error while vividly reflecting an integral part of a reaction to disasters that should have not happened:

> The *Central America,* painted so fine
>   Went down like a thousand of brick,
> And all the old tubs that are now on the line
>   Will follow her, two at a lick.
> 'Twould be very fine were the owners aboard,
>   And sink where they never would rise;
> 'Twould any amount of amusement afford,
>   And cancel a million of lies.
> These murdering villains will ne'er be forgot,
>   As long as America stands;
> Their bones should be left in the ocean to rot,
>   And their souls be at Satan's commands.
> They've murdered and swindled the people for years,
>   And never will be satisfied

Till death puts an end to their earthly career,
Then may they with demons reside.

The last Gold Rush maritime disaster starkly realized the fears of gold-seeking landlubbers. Sailing shipwrecks were few and nearly all resulted in a loss of profits, not lives. However, steamer disasters, which reached an alarming frequency by 1853, reinforced poor opinions of captains and companies fostered by sailing to the state in 1849. The outrage over these maritime disasters of the Gold Rush provided the impetus for aids to navigation, steamship inspection, and despite the continued primacy of shipping, stronger support for the transcontinental railroad that firmly linked California to the rest of the nation.

Conclusion
AFTER THE GOLD RUSH

The disappearance of the hundreds of ships caught up in the Gold Rush captured the attention of contemporary observers not long after the excitement died away in the mid-1850s. Responding to an editorial inquiry of the Boston *Transcript*, a Nantucket correspondent to the paper wrote to answer "What Becomes of the Old Ships?" Recounting the fate of numerous ships, he noted that most were gone, "thrown aside, the rage for the pursuit of gold being so great, everything else was deemed and became worthless."[1] His requiem, while only partly correct, was solemnly agreed to and repeated through the years without argument.

What was the fate of the California fleet of 1848–1849 and the ships that followed in 1850–1851? A fair number were converted to other uses—mostly storeships—but in time many of the more recently built vessels were refitted, rigged, and sent to sea, trading on the Pacific coast, whaling, or in a few cases returning home to the eastern seaboard. Numerous vessels sitting idle at San Francisco were cleared from the harbor in the early 1850s. The ships broken up in California were old, cranky maritime relics that had been pressed into service in 1849.

As early as 1850 the crowded San Francisco waterfront was plagued by hulks blocking incoming steamers and clippers seeking to discharge passengers and cargoes. Most hulks were in poor shape or of little value. The only solution to the problem was to break them up, and between 1854 and 1859, more than 200 vessels disappeared be-

171

neath the sledges, axes, and torches of ship breakers Charles Hare, Nicholas Bichard, George Howgate, and scores of Chinese laborers.

Of all of San Francisco's ship breakers, the career of Charles Hare best exemplifies the role and practice of the trade. Born in Buckingham, England, in 1819, Hare arrived in Baltimore around 1840, where he entered the ship-breaking trade, married, started a family, and applied for American citizenship. In 1851 he sailed with his family to California, arriving on board the ship *Atalanta* on September 3, 1852.[2] Hare began to break up ships in San Francisco not long after he arrived, although the first mention of his activities was not until 1856, when his name appeared in the San Francisco City Directory as a "dealer in ship gear, Rincon Point." Establishing his business near Rincon Point, the southern extremity of San Francisco's Gold Rush waterfront, and nearby South Beach, a narrow strip of sand a few hundred yards wide, Hare located in an ideal location. South Beach was covered by a few feet of water at high tide; at low tide the beach lay exposed. Ships could be floated in at high tide and be left high and dry at low tide for easy salvage and dismantling. Labor was readily available at a Chinese fishing village on the shore. Established around 1851, "by January of 1852 this village boasted 150 fishermen, and had twenty-five fishing craft."[3]

With the help of the Chinese fishermen, Hare purchased hulks. Some were towed to Rincon Point and South Beach, where they were knocked apart or burned for their metal fastenings. Others were broken up at the spot, including several storeships that had outlived their usefulness but lay trapped by encroaching piers and landfill. Some of Hare's men were observed hard at work in 1856 by Prentice Mulford, a recent arrival:

> Rows of old hulks were moored off Market street wharf, maritime relics of " '49." That was "Rotten Row." One by one they fell victims to Hare. Hare purchased them, set Chinamen to picking their bones, broke them up, put the shattered timbers in one pile, the iron bolts in another, the copper in another, the cordage in another, and so in a short time all that remained of these bluff-bowed, old-fashioned ships and brigs . . . was so many ghastly piles of marine debris.[4]

An account in the San Francisco *Daily Evening Bulletin* of February 11, 1857, also described Hare's workers:

> The beach at the Rincon exhibits a scene which recalls the past in a most affecting manner. In almost every portion are to be seen

the relics of old ships that once braved the storms and dangers of a hundred seas, being broken up for their old iron and fire wood. This work is chiefly being carried on by Chinamen, who hammer and saw and chop, day after day, week after week, with the most exemplary patience and perseverance. Under the continued blows the old vessels fall to pieces. One after the other for a few days the yawning wrecks and then the bare skeletons of keel and ribs are seen; but in a short time the skeletons themselves fall to pieces; the iron and copper are stored, the wood piled up and carried away, and not a vestige of the once mighty masters of the deep remains.

Hare was probably the first ship breaker in San Francisco. He quickly gained competition, including some of the Chinese who had previously worked for him. One competitor was George Howgate, who may have started in Hare's employ; the 1856 city directory lists him as "Howlgate, George, laborer, Rincon Point." Another was Nicholas Bichard, a pioneer dealer in coal, lumber and junk who became a ship-owning millionaire. But of the various ship breakers, Charles Hare reigned supreme. Newspaper accounts indicate that he broke up seventy-eight vessels; Howgate is credited with twelve and Bichard with five. Miscellaneous wreckers, including the Chinese, broke up seventeen ships.[5] The actual figures varied somewhat, because record keeping was poor, and some of the vessels listed as being broken up by Hare were not broken up at all—a tribute to his impact on the waterfront.

By the end of the 1850s most of the derelict vessels left afloat in the harbor were cleared, refitted, or broken up. Once the floating hulks were gone, Hare and the other ship-breakers turned their attention to sunken vessels along the waterfront that were raised for demolition, and landlocked storeships that were demolished where they lay. By 1857 the business of dismantling Gold Rush hulks was nearly over. Hare himself noted in an interview that year that "the business must soon all but stop, for want of material, as the old stock of vessels is almost used up, and the decreased importing shipping will not afford old tubs enough to keep any great number of workmen busy."[6] The passing of the idle hulks on the waterfront and the end of Charles Hare's business comprised the last act in the maritime drama of the Gold Rush.

Whatever their fate, the hundreds of ships that sailed to California and did not return to Boston, New York, Nantucket, Savannah, Norfolk, Salem, or Bath did a great service by not coming home. The deadwood of America's merchant marine was in large part cleaned out in 1849–1850, paving the way for new vessels of better design, including many new steamers.

The removal of older vessels, the impetus given to clippers and their progeny, the boost to steam at sea, the firm linking of the two coasts and the California trade were all major boosts to American maritime trade and commerce. The establishment of San Francisco as the principal American port on the Pacific and the continued growth of the port in the later years of the nineteenth century were perhaps the greatest gifts of the Gold Rush, in time surpassing in value the gold shipped from California's shores to the East. San Francisco became a hub of coastal and intercoastal trade. Lumber logged on the coast was shipped to San Francisco and from there to national and international markets. Agricultural produce harvested in California's fertile soil was also sent to the world via San Francisco. The reaping of tons of wheat from the heartland—California's Central Valley—inspired a new "gold rush" in the 1880s and 1890s as hundreds of vessels again cleared for the Golden Gate, this time for golden grain.

San Francisco also evolved into the world's principal whaling port. The importance of San Francisco Bay to the nation's whaling fleet was well established before the Gold Rush. After the initial disruption to whaling occasioned by the rush, business boomed. A number of former whalers and a few ships not previously engaged in the trade commenced whaling out of San Francisco in the early 1850s. Whalers from the city, notably Captain Charles Melville Scammon, discovered and harvested the rich grounds off Baja California and in the Sea of Cortez. San Francisco became an active home port for hundreds of eastern seaboard whalers as the Atlantic grounds were fished out. The decline of New Bedford, a rise in the price of whale oil, and the active harvest of Arctic whaling grounds in the 1870s helped San Francisco's status as a whaling port. By the late 1880s a few old sailing ships and the new steam whalers operating annually from San Francisco commenced a new era in American whaling.

San Francisco also achieved a significant destiny as the nation's gateway to the Orient. In the 1860s the Pacific Mail Steamship Company reached beyond its Gold Rush origins on the Panama route and out into the Pacific. Pacific Mail steamers—at first huge wooden sidewheelers, later iron and steel screw steamers and finally liners—were the pipeline of the Far East and the Orient into the United States. Immigrant Chinese, Japanese, and other Asians, and the commodities and luxuries of their homelands, poured in on the Pacific Mail's ships by way of San Francisco.

Coastal steamers running to and from San Francisco (including some Gold Rush veterans) boosted the population of more remote regions of the Pacific coast. Steamers following in the wake of the pioneer Gold Rush riverboats linked the Delta and the heartland of California with San Francisco. Ferries and other craft, particularly scow schooners plying San Francisco Bay with passengers, produce, and freight, continued a tradition begun in the 1850s when argonauts strove to link San Jose, Marin, and the "Contra Costa" with San Francisco via the bay.

By the close of the nineteenth century San Francisco had matured into a major port and maritime center. Where wooden piers once crisscrossed the shallows of Yerba Buena Cove and ships converted into warehouses floated, a city of brick and stone now stood. On what had originally been the deep-water anchorage for the "forest of masts" in 1849–1850 a booming waterfront now thrust out several blocks from the old shoreline. Every day the harbor was the scene of lumber schooners arriving from the northern coast, scows discharging coal or hay, South Seas traders disgorging copra, coconuts, and oranges, ferries packed with hundreds of commuters, British deepwatermen and Yankee Down-easters unloading cobbles, bricks, cement, and other bulk cargoes for grain, and coastal and transpacific steamers landing passengers and freight.

REMEMBERING THE EVENT

Numerous contemporary observers and later historians felt that the Gold Rush resembled a military campaign. A major portion of the nation's young male population left home for the first time, armed and provisioned for an extended stay in a strange and hostile land. They met with danger and came home changed by the experience. As a result the adventure was endowed with an almost mythic significance. Romance and legend wove their stories through the various events of the Gold Rush, including the voyages by sea and the maritime experience in California. Like veterans of foreign wars, the argonauts banded together in fraternal orders based on having participated in the adventure. The two principal organizations were located on either coast. The Society of California Pioneers, organized in 1850, was (and is today) headquartered in San Francisco. Members were required to have arrived in California prior to 1850.[7] While a number of pre–Gold Rush pioneers joined, the majority were Gold Rush arrivals, and among the cherished records and archives of the society are journals, diaries, letters, and reminiscences of voyages via the Horn and the Isthmus. The *Quarterly* of the Society of California Pioneers published several accounts of seafaring experiences of members and the harbormaster's list of vessel arrivals in 1849.[8] The Society of California Pioneers, now composed of the descendants of the pioneers, continues as an active and important historical organization.

On the eastern seaboard, another pioneer organization was created in the nostalgic afterglow of the event. In 1883 the surviving passengers of the bark *LaGrange*'s 1849 voyage to San Francisco and Sacramento organized the LaGrange and Pioneer Association in Salem, Massachusetts. Five years later the forty-member group expanded to include all New England residents or their descendants who had participated in the Gold Rush. The LaGrange and Pioneer Association members renamed themselves the Society of the California Pioneers of New England. The society boomed in the declining decade of the century with more than 400 members, in 1896 taking a triumphant tour to the scenes of their youth. By 1908 most of the members were dead. In 1914 the last four survivors held the association's final meeting. The papers, scrapbooks, and personal memorabilia of members associated with the now-defunct organization are preserved at the Essex Institute in Salem.[9] Several other short-lived pioneer organizations sprang up, including the First Steamship Pioneers, composed of the first passengers to arrive at San Francisco in 1849 on board the Pacific Mail steamers *California, Oregon,* and *Panama.* The First Steamship Pioneers had banquets and published a nostalgic look at their participation in the great adventure in 1874.

The nostalgia and romanticism of the Gold Rush inspired a spate of reminiscences. Contemporary narratives of the Gold Rush experience were published beginning in 1849, though the first true retrospective was not released until 1860, when L. M. Schaeffer published his *Sketches of Travel in South America, Mexico and California.* Schaeffer's adventures included a Cape Horn voyage and a return trip home via Panama. By the close of the 1860s Edwin Dunbar struck at the heart of the matter in this title: *The Romance of the Age; Or, The Discovery of Gold in California.* In the 1870s a number of books followed, many discussing the maritime experience. Among those was Dr. Jacob D. B. Stillman's book, *Seeking the Golden Fleece.* Stillman claimed that the Gold Rush was the greatest mass migration of humanity since the Crusades. The 1880s and 1890s saw a new round of publications, including one of the most significant, C. W. Haskins's *The Argonauts of California.* . . . Haskins attempted to name "the first to venture forth," including a list of vessels, ports of departure, and arrivals at California. About the time the last of the pioneers were dying out, a number of posthumous reminiscences were published. The trend continues to this day, although the number of Cape Horn journals has a long way to to go to surpass the number of published overland narratives.[10] Ironically, while nostalgia inspired the publication of these accounts, discord and discontent aboard ship is as prevalent in the reminiscences as it was during the voyage under recollection. The romanticism of Gold Rush voyages to California was an appeal to "the good old days—they were terrible!"

Appendix

Resolution of Shipmasters and Owners Protesting Conditions at the Port of San Francisco, 1850

The jurisdiction of state and municipal authorities over all aspects of shipping on San Francisco Bay, except customs and regulating the law afloat, led to serious conflict and angry discussion by shipmasters and owners who felt extorted and ill-used. The crowded condition of the port and the seeming inability of the harbormaster to rectify the situation, along with high pilot fees and extralegal maritime courts, led to a protest meeting and the drafting of the following resolutions and petition to the secretary of state. This document, and the reports of Collector of the Port James Collier, were instrumental in the passage of federal and state legislation to better administer the port, notably in the establishment of a United States admiralty court.

San Francisco, August 21, 1850

Sirs—At a large and highly respectable meeting of Ship Masters and Owners, held in this city on the 20th inst., for the purpose for taking into consideration the many peculiar difficulties to which they are subjected here, after a very general expression of the opinions and grievances of which complaint is made, the following Preamble and Resolutions prepared by a committee appointed for the purpose, were reported and unanimously passed; and in accordance with one of them, we forward you the following copy, to which we respectfully solicit your attention and consideration.

After the passage of the Resolutions, remarks were made by Col.

COLLIER, Collector of the Port, Dr. ROGERS, Health Officer, and several other gentlemen; and a Memorial, to be signed and forwarded to U.S. Secretary of State, was read and accepted by the meeting.

Capt. N. S. MAURAN, President

Capt. O. R. Mumford

Vice Presidents

Capt. Frank Smith

PREAMBLE

Whereas we, the masters and owners of ships trading at the Port of San Francisco, in meeting assembled, do honestly and sincerely believe that we are subject to many and great obstacles in the pursuit and transaction of our business here, to many unnecessary and unjust expenses which are very onerous to bear, and which we believe are working to the injury of the commercial prosperity of the port, we have now met together deliberately to discuss and to endeavor to point out the grievances of which we complain—to give a calm expression of our opinions upon them in order that the public, and more particularly the mercantile part of this community, and our employers and friends at home may be made aware of them. In the hope that some remedy for them or some course of action on our part by which we may avoid them may be suggested, that the more unjust and onerous charges upon us may be removed, or at all events that some regulations may be enforced by which it may be possible for us to calculate with some degree of confidence upon the course we ought to pursue, with a probability of being, if right supported by the laws and by an enlightened and unprejudiced public opinion in the maintenance of our rights.

Therefore—

Resolved. That being in almost every instance deserted by our crews immediately upon our arrival here, and finding our contracts with them, however binding, and however fully certified, set at naught, or only made available against us by the legal decisions that are daily made here, and considering that these decisions are not only at variance with the spirit but with the letter of the laws of the United States, to which we are bound to conform, we feel it our duty herein to assert and hereafter maintain our rights, and to use our earnest and strenuous exertions to procure a just legal decision upon a proper *pro forma* case, by a court exercising competent jurisdiction as in such case made and provided.

Resolved. That while we view with regret the desertion of crews from our ships, it is with unqualified disapprobation that we see the officers in many instances pursuing the same course—men occupying responsible situations under us now, and probably some time to take rank among and of us, in whom we have placed confidence, and who it is not to be supposed signed the contracts and entered on the voyage under any misapprehension of its objects, become so lost to all sense of honor and to all the moral obligations of their positions as to desert from their duty or refuse to fulfill their agreement, we cannot look upon as in any way worthy of our further confidence; and we feel it our duty to withhold from all such our countenance or support. (To comply with the published request of the insurance Companies of the Atlantic ports, and to report to them directly, or through their agents here, the name, place of residence, and such other particulars as we may possess of all officers so deserting) and if called upon hereafter for our opinions as to their capabilities as officers, we should feel bound to qualify that opinion by making known the fact of such desertion in California, where more than in any other port of the world the cause is of itself evident—pecuniary gain.

Resolved. That it is with sorrow that we look upon the sad neglect of the many natural advantages possessed by this spacious harbor for a safe and convenient arrangement of the vast fleet now floating in its waters, it matters little to us, whether the dangers of inconveniences we see and hear of every day arise through the incompetency of officials, or their neglect of their proper duties. We know that we are compelled by law to pay a harbor or anchorage fee within forty-eight hours after arrival, of such an amount as should entitle our ships to some care and protection receiving it; we never receive any such attention from them, except in the one instance of pointing out to us a berth, which we could ourselves, as we often are obliged to do as well. We think that any ordinary accidental arrangement of the fleet could scarcely be more dangerous or inconvenient than the one now existing; and we hold that any intelligent man at all conversant with such matters, could readily and would willingly suggest a better, a more convenient, and safer arrangement; and further, that if the harbor regulations, so called, were properly enforced in all cases, it would vastly benefit all parties interested.

Resolved. That we consider the present existing regulations in regard to Harbor Pilots, as unlawful, and the policy of exacting their fee of $50 for each ship, as onerous and unjust to the last degree. It may be true so far as the laws of this port are concerned it is optional with us whether to employ these pilots or not; but we should, as a punishment for not employing them, be subjected to more trouble and annoyance than the saving of the fee would warrant, and incur a great risk of receiving decisions against us, if unfortunately necessitated to submit a question in dispute to the Harbor Master; and also, it is a well understood requirement of the policies of insurance on our ships, that we should, wherever we are strangers, employ pilots, if any are provided. It is also well known that the sea pilots are willing, and consider it part of their duty here, as well as in almost every port in christendom, to place ships at their proper moorings or in dock before leaving them, and it seems to us unjust that at this most easily entered port in the world, we should be obliged to employ two pilots at exorbitant fees, to take our ships in, when one is enough, and more than one necessary. This is one of the cases of thorough, unqualified extortion, of which we have a right to complain.

Resolved. That we hail with pleasure the organization of a Chamber of Commerce in this city, as it must tend to rectify many of the abuses which are practised upon us here, and promote the establishment of such regulations and customs as shall go far to assist us in the settlement of differences with freighters and others, to which we are unfortunately liable from the variance in commercial usages in different ports. That we extend our sincere thanks to that body for the notice already taken of our complaints. And we hereby invite and solicit its co-operation with us in our attempts to bring about a reform. That we recommend all parties having mercantile differences upon which they cannot arrive at a satisfactory settlement themselves to submit them to a committee of arbitration of that body, with full confidence in the obtaining of a just and equitable decision according to facts, and mercantile usages, rather than trust to the distant and uncertain contingence of obtaining justice by suit at law.

Resolved. That as we are at present situated, we consider the property entrusted to our care as unsafe and almost beyond our control.

Resolved. That we recommend for the consideration of the proper authorities, the following propositions:

1st. That no sea pilot for the harbor of San Francisco should be entitled to his fee for sea pilotage until he has moored the ship safely at the berth designated by the Harbor Master. And also that no sea pilot should be entitled to fees for outward pilotage, until he has taken the ship from her moorings safely to sea, as is usual in other ports.

2nd. That no ship is bound to pay the demands of the Harbor Master, unless furnished with the harbor regulations within twenty-four hours after arrival.

3rd. That the Harbor Master should receive his nomination from those most interested in the faithful performance of his duties, as represented by the Chamber of Commerce, the Pilot Commissioners, or other mercantile bodies, for the support of the community.

4th. That the Board of Health have no right to charge, sue for, or collect from any ship, either American or foreign, entering the harbor of San Francisco, anything more than a simple visit fee, as in nearly all other ports in the world; and that in the future we shall pay such demands only under protest.

5th. That no hospital money should be paid by the ship or master except that chargeable by the United States.

6th. That no one has any right, in California or elsewhere, to occupy public highways to the injury of navigation, for private purposes.

Resolved. That our thanks as shipmasters are due to the mercantile communities of Liverpool and New York for so ably supporting the proceedings of the meeting of shipmasters in Liverpool. In regard to some alterations in the dock arrangements of their port, in which they not only co-operated, but through their perseverance, the important suggestions there made were followed up until such alterations are about to be made in the said regulations as will vastly conduce to the comfort and convenience of those of our profession who visit their port.

Resolved. That we hereby pledge ourselves to exert our influence and to use our best endeavours to interest others to exert themselves to procure a remedy for the above-mentioned just and well founded complaints, to endeavour to procure the enactment of proper laws and regulations by the authorities having jurisdiction, to advocate the appointment of competent officers, to enforce the regulations when enacted, and to procure a just and equal administration of the existing laws. That we feel that, as orderly, law-abiding citizens, which we have ever been, we are bound to submit to the laws as we find them, though with very little voice or influence in their enactment; and we cannot but regret that the laws in regard to our interests, as now enforced in this State, are but little conducive to the advancement of that respect to which it has ever been our pride to consider the laws of our country to be pre-eminently entitled.

That while we look with pride upon the evidences everywhere surrounding us in this infant offshoot of our common country, of the indomitable energy of the Anglo-American race, and its peculiar adaptiveness to every soil, to every clime, and to every source of remunerative labor, that pride is sadly reduced by the evidences constantly coming before us, of the existence of a short-sighted policy on the part of those in power, placing unjust restrictions upon all branches of commerce, that branch of the body politic which more than any other has conduced to place our country in the proud position she now occupies among the nations of the world, which it has been the constant object, mistaken though the course may sometimes have been of legislative enactments, of judicial decisions, and of enormous outlays by the general government to cherish and protect; that as Americans we deeply regret the necessities which have called from us this public complaint of an American port, but with full confidence in the honesty of the intentions, and in the justice-loving spirit of our fellow-citizens here, we have full faith in the speedy and just correction of the abuses of which we complain.

On motion, the following memorial was adopted:

To the Honorable, the Secretary of State of the United States:

We, the undersigned, masters and owners of ships trading at the port of San Francisco respectfully represent that under the now existing regulations and customs at this port, we suffer many grievous and unjust burdens in the pursuit and transaction of our business here, and are denied or prohibited, by the existing authorities, the use and benefit of many of the advantages of this fine harbor, to which, as the property of the United States, and as a reserve for a common highway of nations, we are justly and legally entitled; that the present administration of the laws of the United States by which we are governed and under which we have a right to claim protection, is such as is not customary, so far as we your petitioners have ever known, in the Atlantic States, and which operate very much to our prejudice and injury, all of which are more fully detailed in a report &c. of a committee of ship masters and owners appointed to draft such report herewith appended.

To all of which your petitioners would respectfully solicit your attention, and that of the other honorable members of the Government of the United States, to the end that some course may be adopted by your honorable body for the establishment of courts of maritime jurisdiction here, for the preservation and appropriate use of the rights vested in the United States to this, one of the finest of its many fine harbors, and that the protecting arm of the General Government may be extended over us here, as we have been accustomed to know it to be in other parts of our country, for the just administration and execution of the laws and statutes enacted, and the secure enjoyment of our own just rights under them; and your petitioners will ever pray.

President, N. S. MAURAN

Vice Presidents, O. R. MUMFORD
"   "   FRANK SMITH
"   "   JAMES W. GOODRICH

NOTES

PROLOGUE

1. Robert Greenhalgh Albion, *The Rise of New York Port, 1815–1860* (Boston: Northeastern University Press, 1984), pp. 354–355.
2. John Lyman, "The Intercoastal Trade Before 1850," *Log Chips* 4, no. 4 (August 1957), pp. 37–39, passim.
3. See Adele Ogden, *The California Sea Otter Trade, 1784–1848* (Berkeley and Los Angeles: University of California Press, 1941) and Robin W. Doughty, "The Farallones and the Boston Men," *California Historical Quarterly* 53, no. 4 (Winter 1974), pp. 309–316.
4. Samuel Eliot Morrison, *The Maritime History of Massachusetts, 1783–1860* (Boston: Houghton Mifflin Co., 1961), p. 261.
5. William Robert Garner, *Letters from California, 1846–1847*, ed. Donald Munro Craig (Berkeley and Los Angeles: University of California Press, 1970), p. 205.
6. Ibid., p. 88.
7. Doyce B. Nunis, Jr., ed., *Josiah Belden, 1841 California Overland Pioneer: His Memoir and Early Letters* (Georgetown, Calif.: Talisman Press, 1962), p. 49.
8. William Heath Davis, *Seventy-Five Years in California* reprint (San Francisco: John Howell Books, 1967), p. 281.
9. Hubert Howe Bancroft, *The History of California* (San Francisco: A. L. Bancroft and Co., 1888), vol. 5, p. 578. Also see William Heath Davis, "Accounts, 1846–1847," Bancroft Library Manuscript C-B 105-50.
10. Richard Henry Dana, *Two Years Before the Mast* (New York: Modern Library, 1936), p. 58.
11. Alexander Starbuck, *History of the American Whale Fishery from Its Earliest Inception to the Year 1876.* (Washington, D.C.: Government Printing Office, 1878; reprint, 2 vols. New York: Argosy-Antiquarian, 1964), vol. 2, p. 90.
12. John G. B. Hutchins, *The American Maritime Industry and Public Policy, 1789–1914* (Cambridge: Harvard University Press, 1941), p. 269.
13. Davis, *Seventy-Five Years in California*, p. 117.

14. As cited in Robert J. Parker, "Larkin, Anglo-American Businessman in Mexican California," in *Greater America: Essays in Honor of Herbert Eugene Bolton*, ed. Adele Ogden (Berkeley and Los Angeles: University of California Press, 1945), p. 419.

15. See Boyd Francis Huff, *El Puerto de los Balleneros: Annals of the Sausalito Whaling Anchorage* (Los Angeles: Dawson's Book Shop, 1972).

16. Thomas Oliver Larkin to John C. Calhoun, Monterey, December 9, 1844, *The Larkin Papers: Personal, Business, and Official Correspondence of Thomas Oliver Larkin, Merchant and United States Consul in California*, ed. George P. Hammond (Berkeley and Los Angeles: University of California Press, 1952), vol. 3, pp. 330–331.

17. Larkin to Henry Lindsey, Editor, *Whalemen's Shipping List*, New Bedford, Monterey, December 11, 1844, in Hammond, *Larkin Papers*, vol. 2, p. 320.

18. Consul Hooper to John C. Calhoun, Honolulu, June 30, 1846, Department of State, Consular Despatches, Honolulu, RG 59 M-144, National Archives, Washington, D.C.

19. Davis, *Seventy-Five Years in California*, pp. 6–12.

20. Nunis, *Josiah Belden*, pp. 75–76.

21. Garner, *Letters from California*, p. 190.

22. *Boundary, United States and Mexico; Message from the President . . . Transmitting the Information Required by a Resolution of the House*, Supt. of Docs. no. 311-42, pp. 18–19.

23. Juan Crespi to Juan Andres, San Diego, February 8, 1770, quoted in Theodore E. Treutlein, *San Francisco Bay: Discovery and Colonization, 1769–1776* (San Francisco: California Historical Society, 1968), p. 30.

24. William Frederick Beechey, *Narrative of a Voyage to the Pacific and Beering's Strait, to Cooperate with the Polar Expeditions, Performed in His Majesty's Ship Blossom, under the Command of Capt. F. W. Beechey, R.N., F.R.S., etc., in the Years 1825 . . . 1828* (London: Colburn and Bentley, 1831) 2 vols., pp. 66–67. In 1832, American and German editions were published.

25. Neal Harlow, *California Conquered: War and Peace on the Pacific, 1846–1850* (Berkeley and Los Angeles: University of California Press, 1982), pp. 34–35.

26. Alpheus B. Thompson to Abel Stearns, February 25, 1834, *China Trade Days in California: Selected Letters from the Thompson Collection, 1832–1863*, ed. D. McKenzie Brown (Berkeley and Los Angeles: University of California Press, 1947), p. 24. Also see George Tays, ed., "Commodore Edmund B. Kennedy, U.S.N., vs. Governor Nicolas Gutierrez—An Incident of 1836," *California Historical Society Quarterly* 12, no. 2 (June 1933): 137–146.

27. Harlow, *California Conquered*, p. 38; and Bancroft, *History of California*, vol. 4, pp. 33–37.

28. Charles Wilkes, *Narrative of the United States Exploring Expedition, during the Years 1838, 1839, 1840, 1841, 1842* (Philadelphia: Lea and Blanchard, 1845), 5 vols.

29. Harlow, *California Conquered*, p. xv.

30. As cited in Bancroft, *History of California*, vol. 4, p. 259.

31. See Harlow, *California Conquered*, pp. 3–13.

32. George Bancroft to Jonathan Drake Sloat, Washington, D.C., June 24,

1845, National Archives Record Group (NARG) 45, M89, R32, Washington, D.C.

33. See K. Jack Bauer, *Surfboats and Horse Marines: U.S. Naval Operations in the Mexican War, 1846–48* (Annapolis: United States Naval Institute, 1969), pp. 135–233 passim.

34. Thomas Oliver Larkin to William A. Leisdesdorff, Monterey, September 21, 1846, *First and Last Consul: Thomas Oliver Larkin and the Americanization of California*, ed. John A. Hawgood (Palo Alto, Calif.: Pacific Books, 1970), p. 87.

35. Bauer, *Surfboats and Horse Marines*, pp. 246–252 passim.

36. New Bedford *Whalemen's Shipping List*, March 9, 1847.

37. Monterey *Californian*, November 28, 1846.

38. San Francisco *California Star*, January 30, 1847.

39. As cited in Oscar Lewis, *San Francisco: Mission to Metropolis* (Berkeley: Howell-North Books, 1966), p. 43.

40. Donald C. Biggs, *Conquer and Colonize: Stevenson's Regiment and California* (San Rafael: Presidio Press, 1977), pp. 93–98 passim.

41. As cited in Lewis, *San Francisco*, p. 45.

42. Philadelphia *North American*, September 14, 1848.

43. San Francisco *Californian*, May 29, 1848.

44. *Message from the President of the United States to the Two Houses of Congress. . . . December 5, 1848*, 30th Cong., 2d sess., H.Ex. Doc. 1, p. 10.

45. New York *Herald*, January 11, 1849.

46. James M. Morris, *Our Maritime Heritage: Maritime Developments and Their Impact on American Life* (Washington, D.C.: University Press of America, 1979), pp. 125–142, passim; and Robert G. Albion, William A. Baker, and Benjamin W. Labaree, *New England and the Sea* (Mystic, Conn.: Mystic Seaport Museum, 1972), pp. 97–140 passim.

CHAPTER 1.

1. John B. Goodman III, *The California Gold Rush Encyclopedia*, 11 vols., n.d., collection of John B. Goodman III, Beverly Hills, California. This massive tome is the most comprehensive history yet assembled of the individual vessels of the California fleet of 1848. Mr. Goodman has made provisions to donate the manuscript to the Huntington Library.

2. Boston *Daily Transcript*, October 31, 1849.

3. San Francisco *Daily Alta California*, January 31, 1850.

4. Sacramento *Transcript*, October 18, 1850.

5. Lyman, "Intercoastal Trade," p. 39.

6. Ibid.

7. Registration No. 350, Port of New York, issued October 4, 1831, NARG 41, Records of the Bureau of Marine Inspection and Navigation, "Records Relating to Merchant Vessel Documentation, 1774–1958," Washington, D.C. (Hereafter vessels will be cited by registration number, name of port, and date of issue.) Also see Carl C. Cutler, *Queens of the Western Ocean: The Story of America's Mail and Passenger Sailing Lines* (Annapolis: United States Naval Institute, 1961), pp. 403, 491.

8. San Francisco *Daily Alta California*, March 12, 1849.

9. Lyman, "Intercoastal Trade," p. 40.
10. Katherine Wood Richardson, "The Gold Seekers: The Story of the *LaGrange* and the California Pioneers of New England," *Essex Institute Historical Collections* 115, no. 2 (April 1979), p. 74.
11. Lyman, "Intercoastal Trade," p. 40.
12. New Beford *Mercury,* January 3, 1849.
13. Richardson, "Gold Seekers," p. 74.
14. Jethro C. Brock, comp., *A List of Persons from Nantucket Now in California, Or On Their Way Thither; Including the Names of the Vessels in Which They Sailed, the Time of Sailing, and of Their Arrival There; Also, Persons Returned, &c* (Nantucket: Jethro C. Brock, 1850).
15. Richardson, "Gold Seekers," p. 75.
16. Salem [Mass.] *Gazette,* October 6, 1849.
17. Wilmington [N.C.] *Weekly Commercial,* December 28,1848.
18. Ibid., February 9, 1849.
19. Ibid., November 9, 1849.
20. Ibid.
21. Wilmington *Weekly Commercial,* August 31, 1849.
22. Ibid., March 2 and May 4, 1849.
23. Ibid., January 9 and February 8, 1950.
24. San Francisco *Daily Alta California,* August 2, 1849.
25. Brian H. Smalley, "Some Aspects of the Maine to San Francisco Trade, 1849–1852" Unpublished manuscript, J. Porter Shaw Library, National Maritime Museum, San Francisco, 1967. Smalley based much of his research on the shipping information in the San Francisco *Daily Alta California.*
26. Boston *Daily Transcript,* October 31, 1850.
27. Ibid.
28. See Gilbert Chinard, *When the French Came to California . . .* (San Francisco: California Historical Society, 1944).
29. Saint Malo *La Verite,* July 11, 1850.
30. Valeska Bari, ed., *The Course of Empire: First Hand Accounts of California in the Days of the Gold Rush of '49* (New York: Coward-McCann, 1931), p. 13.
31. Lyman, "Intercoastal Trade," p. 39.
32. John B. Goodman III, ed., *The Gold Rush: Voyage of the Ship Loo Choo Around the Horn in 1849* (Mount Pleasant, Mich.: Cummings Press, 1977), p. iii.
33. Robert Greenhalgh Albion, *Square-Riggers on Schedule: The New York Sailing Packets to England, France, and the Cotton Ports* (Princeton: Princeton University Press, 1938), p. 104.
34. Registration no. 97, Port of Norfolk and Portsmouth, Virginia, issued December 9, 1847; Registration no. 148, Port of Norfolk and Portsmouth, issued December 12, 1848; Registration no. 5, Port of Norfolk and Portsmouth, issued January 16, 1849; and Cutler, *Queens of the Western Ocean,* p. 452.
35. Goodman, *Gold Rush,* p. iii.
36. Goodman, *The California Gold Rush Encyclopedia* s.v. "Zoroaster;" and San Francisco *Daily Alta California,* April 9, 1849.
37. See Gordon Newell, *Paddlewheel Pirate: The Life and Adventures of*

Captain Ned Wakeman (New York: E. P. Dutton & Co., 1959), pp. 65–90 passim for a recounting of *New World's* adventurous "hijacking" and voyage to California.

38. Richardson, "Gold Seekers," pp. 104–105.
39. San Francisco *Daily Alta California*, July 15, 1852.
40. Oscar Lewis, *Sea Routes to the Gold Fields: The Migration by Water to California in 1849–1852* (New York: Alfred A. Knopf, 1949), pp. vi–vii.
41. I have relied on the discussion of shipboard society in Larry Murphy's excellent and well-stated essay, "Shipwrecks as Data Base for Human Behavioral Studies," and Daniel Lenihan's cogently stated "Rethinking Shipwreck Archaeology: A History of Ideas and Considerations," in Richard A. Gould, ed., *Shipwreck Anthropology* (Albuquerque: School of American Research and the University of New Mexico Press, 1983), pp. 37–89, passim.
42. San Francisco *Daily Alta California*, March 1, 1849.
43. Hamden and Co. to Henry L. Dodge, New York, N.Y., December 23, 1848, in Henry L. Dodge Papers, MS 593, California Historical Society, San Francisco. The letter has the appearance of being a form letter.
44. Octavius Thorndike Howe, *Argonauts of '49: History and Adventures of the Emigrant Companies from Massachusetts, 1849–1850* (Cambridge: Harvard University Press, 1923), pp. 187–213, passim; and Lewis, *Sea Routes to the Gold Fields*, p. 22.
45. Willard B. Farwell, "Cape Horn and Cooperative Mining in '49," *The Century Magazine* 42, no. 75 (1896), p. 592.
46. George G. Webster and Linville J. Hall, *The Journal of a Trip Around the Horn, as Written and Printed on the Ship Henry Lee. . . . 1849* (Ashland, Oreg.: Lewis Osborne, 1970), p. 17.
47. Richardson, "Gold Seekers," p. 76.
48. Webster and Hall, *Journal of a Trip Around the Horn*, p. 9.
49. Howe, *Argonauts of '49*, pp. 214–216, passim.
50. San Francisco *Daily Alta California*, March 1, 1849.
51. Farwell, "Cooperative Mining," pp. 592–593.
52. Ibid., p. 593.
53. Goodman, *Gold Rush*, p. v.
54. George Coffin, *A Pioneer Voyage to California and Round the World, 1849 to 1852* (Chicago: Gorham B. Coffin, 1908), p. 10.
55. Ibid.
56. Edwin Ayer, "Reminiscence," Typescript, J. Porter Shaw Library, National Maritime Museum, San Francisco, 1877, p. 12.
57. Samuel C. Upham, *Notes of a Voyage to California Via Cape Horn, Together With Scenes in El Dorado, in the Years 1849–50 . . .* (Philadelphia: Published by the author, 1878), p. 32.
58. J. Lamson, *Round Cape Horn: Voyage of the Passenger-Ship James W. Paige, from Maine to California in the Year 1852* (Bangor, Maine: O. F. and W. H. Knowles, 1878), pp. 13–14.
59. New York *Sun*, January 1, 1849.
60. New York *Sun*, January 16, 1849.
61. Robert Gordon, "Journal of a Voyage from Baltimore to San Francisco Via Cape Horn," ed. Reginald R. and Grace D. Stuart, *The Pacific Historian* 6, no. 3 (August 1962), p. 98.

62. Richardson, "Gold Seekers," p. 80.
63. New York *Sun*, January 17, 1849.
64. James P. Delgado, ed., *The Log of Apollo: Joseph Perkins Beach's Journal of the Voyage of the Ship Apollo from New York to San Francisco, 1849* (San Francisco: Book Club of California, 1987), p. 30.
65. Upham, *Notes of a Voyage to California*, p. 26.
66. Edwin Franklin Morse, "The Story of a Gold Miner: Reminiscences of Edwin Franklin Morse," *California Historical Society Quarterly* 6, no. 3 (September 1927), p. 206.
67. Lamson, *Round Cape Horn*, p. 15.
68. Delgado, *Log of Apollo*, p. 35.
69. Alexander McFarlan, "Log Book from Boston to San Francisco via Cape Horn, 1849, Ship California Packet," Unpublished manuscript, J. Porter Shaw Library, National Maritime Museum, San Francisco, California, 1849–1850. Entry for March 7, 1850.
70. Webster and Hall, *Journal of a Trip Around the Horn*, p. 12.
71. Delgado, *Log of Apollo*, pp. 30–31.
72. Gordon, "Journal of a Voyage from Baltimore to San Francisco," p. 99; and Cyrus W. Pease to "My Dear Friend," on board ship *Walter Scott*, June 9, 1849, Photostat, J. Porter Shaw Library, National Maritime Museum, San Francisco. (Hereafter cited as Pease Letter.)
73. Delgado, *Log of Apollo*, p. 73.
74. John N. Stone, "Brief Notes of a Cape Horn Voyage in 1849," in John E. Pomfret, ed., *California Gold Rush Voyages, 1848–1849: Three Original Narratives* (San Marino, Calif.: Huntington Library, 1954), pp. 117–118.
75. June Allen Reading, ed., *Consignments to El Dorado: A Record of The Voyage of the Sutton by Thomas Whaley* (New York: Exposition Press, 1972), p. 125.
76. Carolyn Hale Russ, ed., *The Log of a Forty-Niner* (Boston: B. J. Brimmer Co., 1923), p. 26.
77. Jacob D. B. Stillman, *Around the Horn to California in 1849* (Palo Alto, Calif.: Lewis Osborne, 1967), p. 26.
78. Howard C. Gardiner, *In Pursuit of the Golden Dream: Reminiscences of San Francisco and the Northern and Southern Mines, 1849–1857*, ed. Dale L. Morgan (Stoughton, Mass.: Western Hemisphere, 1970), pp. 46–47.
79. Charles L. Camp, ed., "An Irishman in the Gold Rush: The Journal of Thomas Kerr," *California Historical Society Quarterly* 7, no. 3 (September 1928), pp. 209–210.
80. Coffin, *Pioneer Voyage to California*, pp. 18–19.
81. Delgado, *Log of Apollo*, p. 39.
82. Webster and Hall, *Journal of a Trip Around the Horn*, pp. 55–56.
83. Garrett W. Low, *Gold Rush by Sea*, ed. Kenneth Haney (Philadelphia: University of Pennsylvania Press, 1941), p. 152.
84. Reading, *Consignments to El Dorado*, p. 115.
85. Lamson, *Round Cape Horn*, p. 17.
86. Ibid., p. 51.
87. Ibid., pp. 102–103.
88. Delgado, *Log of Apollo*, p. 38.
89. Ibid., p. 81.
90. Stone, as cited in Pomfret, *California Gold Rush Voyages*, p. 149.

91. Seth Draper, "Journal," as cited in Robert W. Weinpahl, ed., *A Gold Rush Voyage on the Bark Orion: From Boston Around Cape Horn to San Francisco, 1849–1850* (Glendale, Calif.: Arthur H. Clark Co., 1978), p. 189.
92. Morse, "Story of a Gold Miner," p. 208.
93. Pease Letter, June 9, 1849.
94. As cited in Howe, *Argonauts of '49*, p. 92.
95. Camp, "Irishman in the Gold Rush," p. 210.
96. Delgado, *Log of Apollo*, p. 34.
97. Howe, *Argonauts of '49*, pp. 67–68.
98. Charles R. Schultz, "A Forty-Niner Fourth of July," *The Log of Mystic Seaport* 38, no. 1 (Spring 1986), p. 3.
99. Stone, as cited in Pomfret, *California Gold Rush Voyages*, pp. 100–101.
100. Reading, *Consignments to El Dorado*, p. 101.
101. Camp, "Irishman in the Gold Rush," p. 224.
102. Webster and Hall, *Journal of a Trip Around the Horn*, p. 29.
103. Stillman, *Around the Horn to California*, p. 15.
104. Ibid., p. 28.
105. Lamson, *Round Cape Horn*, p. 73.
106. "A Tribute to Those Life-Lasting Feelings of Disgust, Contempt, and Scorn Unanimously Entertain'd, By the Passengers, Officers, and Crews of the Bark JOHN G. COLLEY; For Captn. William Smith of N.Y., Who Commanded Her on Her Voyage from Norfolk, to San Francisco Upper California. . . ," Unpublished manuscript, J. Porter Shaw Library, National Maritime Museum, San Francisco, 1948. (Hereafter cited as J. G. Colley Tribute).
107. Upham, *Notes of a Voyage to California*, p. 204.
108. Weinpahl, *A Gold Rush Voyage on the Bark Orion*, p. 92.
109. Webster and Hall, *Journal of a Trip Around the Horn*, p. 54.
110. Weinpahl, *A Gold Rush Voyage on the Bark Orion*, p. 94.
111. Richardson, "Gold Seekers," p. 98.
112. New York *Sun*, January 17, 1849.
113. Howe, *Argonauts of '49*, p. 100.
114. Bancroft, *History of California* 6, p. 198.
115. Thomas Senior Barry, *Early California: Gold, Prices, Trade* (Richmond, Va.: Bostwick Press, 1984), pp. 111–114.
116. David R. MacGregor, *Clipper Ships* (Watford, Herts, England: Argus Books, 1979), p. 3.
117. Ibid., p. 50.
118. MacGregor, *Clipper Ships*, p. 50.
119. Louis J. Rasmussen, comp., *San Francisco Ship Passenger Lists* (Colma, Calif.: San Francisco Historic Records, 1979), vol. 4, passim.
120. Ibid., p. 55.
121. Ibid., p. 148.
122. Frank Marryat, *Mountains to Molehills; Or, Recollections of a Burnt Journal* (London: Green, Longmans, and Green, 1855), pp. 169–170.

CHAPTER 2.

1. See Gerstle Mack, *The Land Divided: A History of the Panama Canal and Other Isthmian Canal Projects* (New York: Alfred A. Knopf, 1944);

and Alejandro Perez-Venero, *Before the Five Frontiers: Panama from 1821–1903* (New York: AMS Press, 1978).

2. See John Haskell Kemble, "The Genesis of the Pacific Mail Steamship Company," *California Historical Society Quarterly* 13, nos. 3–4, which was reprinted by the California Historical Society as a special publication in 1934.

3. John Haskell Kemble, *The Panama Route, 1848–1869* (Berkeley and Los Angeles: University of California Press, 1943), pp. 17–22; and Col. Duncan S. Somerville, *The Aspinwall Empire* (Mystic, Conn.: Mystic Seaport Museum, 1983), p. 8.

4. *Charter of the Pacific Mail Steamship Company, With Its Amendments Inclusive of May 1st, 1867* (New York: Pacific Mail Steamship Company, 1867).

5. Victor M. Berthold, *The Pioneer Steamer California, 1848–1849* (Boston and New York: Houghton Mifflin Co., 1932); and Kemble, *Panama Route*, pp. 218, 239–240, 242.

6. William Henry Aspinwall to Jonathan Meredith, New York, January 10, 1849, Jonathan Meredith Papers, Manuscript Division, Library of Congress, Washington, D.C.

7. John M. Cushing, "Memoirs," Typescript, Society of California Pioneers, San Francisco, 1925, pp. 14–15.

8. Joseph Crackbon, "Narrative of a Voyage from New York to California via Chagres, Gorgona & Panama; Journey Across the Isthmus &c.," Manuscript, Huntington Library, San Marino, California, 1849.

9. *Niantic* Logbook, 1848–1849, Manuscript, J. Porter Shaw Library, National Maritime Museum, San Francisco.

10. H. Philip Spratt, *Transatlantic Paddle Steamers,* (Glasgow, Scotland: Brown, Son and Ferguson), pp. 36–37. For a description of the vessel, see the London *Artizan*, September 1849, p. 202.

11. New York *Herald*, March 17, 1849; Enrollment no. 8, Port of New York, March 20, 1849, NARG 41, Records of Merchant Vessel Documentation, Washington, D.C.; and Charles B. Stuart, *The Naval and Mail Steamers of the United States* (New York: Charles B. Morton, 1853), p. 148.

12. New York *Herald,* November 22, 1849.

13. New York *Herald,* December 5, 1849.

14. Daniel Cosad to "Dear Sister," Valparaíso, Chile, February 23, 1850, Manuscript, California Historical Society, San Francisco.

15. San Francisco *Daily Alta California*, April 16, 1850.

16. Panama *Echo*, March 16, 1850.

17. Broadsheet advertising the Pacific Mail Steamship Company, 1852, Elwin Eldredge Collection, Mariner's Museum, Newport News, Virginia.

18. Charles F. Winslow to "Dear Lydia," Panama, May 6, 1849, Winslow Papers, California Historical Society, San Francisco.

19. Marryat, *Mountains and Molehills*, p. 18.

20. James P. Jones and William Warren Rogers, eds., "Across the Isthmus in 1850: The Journal of Daniel A. Horn," *Hispanic American Historical Review* 41 (November 1961), p. 541.

21. Diary, David Knapp Pangborn, entry for June 25, 1850, as reproduced in "A Journey from New York to San Francisco in 1850," *American Historical Review* 9 (October 1903), pp. 108–109.

22. Gardiner, *Pursuit of the Golden Dream*, p. 39.
23. Edward Hotchkiss to "Dear Mother," Panama, March 9, 1850, Manuscript, California Historical Society, San Francisco.
24. Fessenden Nott Otis, *Illustrated History of the Panama Railroad, Together with a Traveler's Guide and Business Man's Handbook for the Panama Railroad and Its Connections* (New York: Harper and Brothers, 1861), pp. 16–46, passim; and Robert Tomes, "A Trip on the Panama Railroad," *Harper's New Monthly Magazine* 11, no. 65, (October 1855), pp. 616–622.
25. James Rogers to "Dear Parents," Panama, March 20, 1850, as cited in Marie Rogers Vail, ed., "Gold Rush Letters of the Reverend James Rogers," *New York Historical Society Quarterly* 44, (July 1960), p. 274.
26. John B. Peirce to his wife as quoted in Philip P. Chase, "On the Panama Route to California During the Gold Rush to California," *Transactions of the Colonial Society of Massachusetts* 27, no. 3 (1932), p. 253. Peirce's original letters are at Harvard University but access to them at this time is denied to all scholars.
27. Peirce to his wife, p. 253.
28. Diary, Henry H. Peters, entry for March 25, 1850, Manuscript, Special Collections, New York Public Library.
29. Edward Hotchkiss to "Dear Mother," at Sea, March 31, 1850, Manuscript, California Historical Society, San Francisco.
30. Peters diary, March 24, 1850.
31. As cited in Kemble, *Panama Route*, p. 159.
32. Peirce to his wife, p. 255.
33. John Walton Caughey, ed., *Seeing the Elephant: Letters of R. R. Taylor, Forty-Niner* (Pasadena, Calif.: Ward Ritchie Press, 1951),   34. Peters diary, March 28, 1850.
35. Peirce to his wife, p. 254.
36. Hotchkiss to mother, March 31, 1850.
37. Ibid.
38. Ibid.
39. Peters diary, April 5, 1850.
40. Peirce to his wife, p. 255.
41. Vail, "Gold Rush Letters of the Reverend James Rogers," pp. 276–77.
42. Peters diary, April 14, 1850.
43. Pacific Mail Steamship Company Journal, 1851–1852, Bound manuscript, Pacific Mail Steamship Company Collection, Henry E. Huntington Library, San Marino, California. Also see James M. Parker, comp., *The San Francisco Directory for the Year 1852–'53 . . .* (San Francisco: James M. Parker, 1852); and A. W. Morgan and Co., *San Francisco City Directory* (San Francisco: F. A. Bonnard, 1852) passim.
44. Kemble, *Panama Route*, p. 46.
45. Ibid., p. 51.
46. New York *Herald*, June 20, 1851.
47. John A. Stone, *Put's Original California Songster, Giving in a Few Words What Would Occupy Volumes, Detailing the Hopes, Trials and Joys of a Miner's Life* (San Francisco: John A. Stone, 1856), pp. 43–44.
48. For the best discussion of the Nicaragua route, see David I. Folkman, Jr., *The Nicaragua Route* (Salt Lake City: University of Utah Press, 1973); and Kemble, *Panama Route*, pp. 58–77, passim.

49. Folkman, *Nicaragua Route*, p. 163.
50. Ibid.
51. Enrollment no. 45, Port of New York, May 21, 1851, Certificates of Enrollment for American Flag Vessels, NARG 41, Records of Merchant Vessel Documentation, Washington, D.C.; and [Boston] *Gleason's Pictorial Drawing Room Companion*, July 15, 1851.
52. Broadside advertising the New York and San Francisco Steamship Company, 1851, Printed manuscript, Bancroft Library, University of California, Berkeley.
53. Kemble, *Panama Route*, p. 64.
54. L. M. Schaeffer, *Sketches of Travel in South America, Mexico, and California* (New York: James Egbert, 1860), p. 227.
55. Kemble, *Panama Route*, p. 65. For a more detailed history of the vessel, see James P. Delgado, "Water Soaked and Covered with Barnacles: The Wreck of the S. S. *Winfield Scott*," *Pacific Historian* 27, no. 2 (Summer 1982).
56. Cedric Ridgely-Nevitt, *American Steamships on the Atlantic* (Newark: University of Delaware Press, 1981), p. 189; also see Register no. 269, Port of Boston, Massachusetts, October 1, 1851; and "Steamers Building in Philadelphia, August 1, 1851," *Journal of the Franklin Institute* 3d ser., vol. 22, no. 3 (September 1851), pp. 212–213.
57. [Boston] *Gleason's Pictorial Drawing Room Companion*, October 25, 1851.
58. Ridgley-Nevitt, *American Steamships*, p. 190.
59. Register no. 6, Port of New York, March 1, 1852; and San Francisco *Daily Alta California*, July 8, 1852.
60. San Francisco *Daily Alta California*, July 8, 1852.
61. Ibid., January 5, 1853.
62. Ibid.
63. San Francisco *Daily Alta California*, January 13, 1853.
64. Kemble, *Panama Route*, p. 51.
65. Ibid., p. 40.
66. William H. Webb, Certificate Book, 1848–1851, Bound manuscript, Webb Institute of Naval Architecture, Glen Cove, New York, Certificate no. 56.
67. San Francisco *Daily Alta California*, November 20, 1851.
68. San Francisco *Daily Herald*, November 20, 1851; see also San Francisco *Daily Alta California*, December 2, 1851.
69. Kemble, *Panama Route*, pp. 88, 124; and San Francisco *Daily Alta California*, July 19, 1853.
70. San Francisco *Daily Alta California*, April 16, 1853.
71. John Y. Simon, ed., *The Papers of Ulysses S. Grant, Volume I: 1837–1861* (Carbondale and Edwardsville: Southern Illinois University Press, 1967), pp. 247–256; see also San Francisco *Daily Alta California*, August 20, 1852.
72. San Francisco *Daily Alta California*, July 19, 1853.
73. San Francisco *Daily Alta California*, January 4, 1854; see also Helen Rocca Goss, "An Ill-Starred Voyage: The S.S. *Golden Gate*, January 1854," *California Historical Society Quarterly* 32, no. 4 (December 1953), pp. 349–361.
74. Andre Chavanne, "The Burning of the *Golden Gate* in July 1862," trans.

and ed. Desire Fricot, *California Historical Society Quarterly* 19, no. 1 (March 1940) p. 32.

75. Ibid.; see also *Report of the Secretary of the Treasury on the State of the Finances for the Year Ending June 30, 1862*, 37th Cong., 3d sess., S. Ex. Doc. 1 (Washington, D.C.: Government Printing Office, 1863), pp. 159–162; and the San Francisco *Daily Alta California*, August 7, 1862.
76. Kemble, *Panama Route*, p. 254.
77. Berry, *Early California*, p. 72.
78. Kemble, *Panama Route*, p. 207.
79. San Francisco *Daily Alta California*, July 3, 1850.
80. Gardiner, *In Pursuit of the Golden Dream*, p. 71.
81. Broadside advertising, United States and Pacific Mail Steamship Company steamers and policies, 1852, Elwin Eldredge Collection, Mariner's Museum, Newport News, Virginia.
82. The manifests of the Panama steamers cited, as well as of many sailing vessels for the period, can be found in the San Francisco Customhouse Collection at the Bancroft Library, University of California, Berkeley. Newspaper accounts of arrivals also list cargo and consignees. Joseph B. Gregory, *Gregory's Guide for California Travellers Via the Isthmus of Panama . . .* , reprint (San Francisco: Book Club of California, 1949), p. 12.
83. Receipt, Anne Brown Papers, Miscellaneous manuscripts, California Historical Society, San Francisco.
84. San Francisco *Daily Alta California*, January 20, 1851.
85. Letter, Lucius Fairchild, as cited in J. S. Holliday, *The World Rushed In: The California Gold Rush Experience* (New York: Simon and Schuster, 1981), p. 310.
86. San Francisco *Daily Alta California*, July 21, 1851.
87. San Francisco *Daily Alta California*, January 9, 1851.
88. Diary, Augustus Burbank Ripley, entry for April 1, 1851, Manuscripts Division, Library of Congress.
89. San Francisco *Daily Alta California*, June 21, 1850.
90. United States Congress, *An Act Providing for the Building and Equipment of Four Naval Steamships*, 28th Cong. 2d sess., ch. 62, March 3, 1847.
91. David Dixon Porter to Secretary of the Navy William A. Graham, United States Mail Steamer *Georgia*, New York, June 1850, as reproduced in *Mail Contracts by Steamships Between New York and California, Letter from the Postmaster General Transmitting Information in Relation to Contracts for Transportation of the Mails Between New York and California*, 32d Cong., 1st sess, August 31, 1852, H. Ex. Doc. 124, p. 99.
92. San Francisco *Daily Alta California*, December 10, 1849.
93. San Francisco *Daily Alta California*, May 1, 1862.
94. William A. Graham, Secretary of the Navy, to E. J. Phelps, 2nd Comptroller, Treasury Department, Washington, D.C., November 10, 1851, NARG 45, Naval Records Collection of the Office of Naval Records and Library, entry 464, subject files DM, "Mail Steamers," Washington, D.C.
95. "Z" File, James Findlay Schenck, Naval Historical Center, Washington Navy Yard, Washington, D.C.; and Edward W. Callaghan, ed., *List of*

Officers of the Navy of the United States and of the Marine Corps from 1775 to 1900: Comprising a Complete Register of all Present and Former Commissioned, Warranted and Appointed Officers of the United States Navy, and of the Marine Corps, Regular and Volunteer, reprint (New York: Haskell House, 1901).

96. "Z" File, William Lewis Herndon, Naval Historical Center; and Callaghan, *List of Officers.*
97. "Z" File, Thomas A. Budd, Naval Historical Center; and Callaghan, *List of Officers.*
98. George P. Hammond, ed., *Digging for Gold Without a Shovel: The Letters of Daniel Wadsworth Coit from Mexico City to San Francisco, 1848–1851* (Old West Publishing Co., 1967), pp. 94–95.
99. Diary, Robert Beck, entry for November 1, 1850, Manuscript, Bancroft Library.
100. Ulla Staley Fawkes, ed., *The Journal of Walter Griffith Pigman* (Mexico, Mo.: Walter G. Staley, 1942), p. 57.
101. John Phoenix [Lt. George H. Derby], *Phoenixiana; Or, Sketches and Burlesques* (New York: D. Appleton and Co., 1856), pp. 190–191.
102. Shirley H. Weber, ed., *Schleimann's First Visit to America, 1850–1851* (Cambridge: Harvard University Press, 1942), p. 76.

CHAPTER 3.

1. J. M. Letts, *California Illustrated; Including a Description of the Panama and Nicaragua Routes by a Returned Californian* (New York: William Holdredge, 1852), p. 47.
2. Berry, *Early California,* p. 21.
3. San Francisco *Daily Alta California,* February 8, 1849.
4. Ibid., February 1, 1849.
5. Bayard Taylor, *Eldorado; Or, Adventures in the Path of Empire,* reprint (New York: Alfred A. Knopf, 1949), p. 90.
6. San Francisco *Daily Evening Picayune,* September 6, 1850. The marine lookout station was apparently patterned after a similar system built on the Thames River in the eighteenth century and used to signal impending vessel arrivals to London.
7. *Daily Evening Picayune,* March 7, 1851.
8. T. A. Barry and B. A. Patten, *Men and Memories of San Francisco, In the "Spring of '50."* (San Francisco: A. L. Bancroft and Co., 1873), pp. 126–128.
9. James M. Parker, *The San Francisco Directory for the Year 1852–53 . . .* (San Francisco: James M. Parker, 1852), p. 97.
10. San Francisco *Daily Alta California,* September 23, 1853.
11. San Francisco *Morning Call,* September 19, 1909; and San Francisco *Chronicle,* November 14, 1961. Also see Robert O'Brien, *The Beginnings of the Marine Exchange* (San Francisco: Marine Exchange, 1959). The last Point Lobos lookout station is now administered by the National Park Service as part of Golden Gate National Recreation Area. The site of the previous stations and the present structure, which dates to 1926, was listed on the National Register of Historic Places in 1980. See James P. Delgado, "Inventory/Nomination Form, National Register of Historic Places: Point Lobos Marine Lookout Stations," (April 1980)

Unpublished manuscript, National Register of Historic Places, National Park Service, Washington, D.C.

12. San Francisco *Daily Alta California*, June 21, 1849.
13. Ibid., October 30, 1849.
14. Ibid., November 1, 1851.
15. "List of Passenger Ships Arriving From March to December, 1849," *Quarterly of the Society of California Pioneers* 1, no. 4 (December 1924), pp. 35–45. This article is a publication of a manuscript record kept by Harbormaster Edward A. King in 1849.
16. San Francisco *Daily Alta California*, January 31, 1850.
17. Ibid., October 30, 1849.
18. Ibid., December 26, 1850.
19. Ibid.
20. Sacramento *Transcript*, October 18, 1850.
21. San Francisco *Daily Herald*, August 19, 1851.
22. Ibid., September 2 and 26, 1851.
23. Ibid.
24. San Francisco *Daily Herald*, January 1854; see also *Daily Alta California*, July 26, 1851.
25. Frank Soule, John H. Gihon, and James Nisbet, *The Annals of San Francisco . . . Containing . . . A Complete History of All Important Events Connected with Its Great City . . .* (New York: D. Appleton and Co., 1850), p. 427.
26. William Shaw, *Golden Dreams and Waking Realities; Being the Adventures of a Gold-Seeker in California and the Pacific Islands* (London: Smith, Elder and Co., 1851), p. 46.
27. Monterey *Californian*, April 17, 1847.
28. Ibid.
29. Alfred Wheeler, *Land Titles in San Francisco, and the Laws Affecting the Same, with a Synopsis of All Grants and Sales of Land Within the Limits Claimed by the City* (San Francisco: Alta California Steam Printing Establishment, 1852), p. 20.
30. Ibid., p. 96; and San Francisco *Daily Evening Picayune*, September 19, 1851.
31. Wheeler, *Land Titles in San Francisco*, p. 105.
32. San Francisco *Daily Alta California*, August 31, 1890.
33. Ibid.
34. Ibid.
35. Ibid.
36. Benjamin Vicuna y MacKenna, "Pages from the Diary of My Travels," as quoted in Edwin Beilharz and Carlos U. Lopez, *We Were '49ers! Chilean Accounts of the California Gold Rush.* (Pasadena, Calif.: Ward Ritchie Press, 1976), p. 146.
37. San Francisco *Daily Alta California*, November 12, 1850.
38. Hubert Howe Bancroft, *History of California*, vol. 6, p. 178.
39. John S. Hittell, *A History of San Francisco and Incidentally of the State of California* (San Francisco: A. L. Bancroft and Co., 1878), pp. 164–165.
40. San Francisco *Daily Alta California*, October 10, 1850.
41. Ibid., August 31, 1849.
42. Davis, *Seventy-Five Years in California*, p. 178.
43. Barry and Patten, *Men and Memories of San Francisco*, p. 107.

44. San Francisco *Daily Herald,* May 8, 1851.
45. Gerald Robert Dow, "Bay Fill in San Francisco: A History of Change" (Master's thesis, San Francisco State University, (1973), pp. 47–48.
46. Charles P. Kimball, *The San Francisco City Directory* (San Francisco: Journal of Commerce Press, 1850), passim.
47. Barry and Patten, *Men and Memories of San Francisco,* p. 107.
48. San Francisco *Daily Evening Picayune,* October 23, 1850.
49. Ibid.
50. San Francisco *Daily Alta California,* May 4, 1851.
51. San Francisco *Daily Herald,* May 8, 1851.
52. Bancroft, *History of California,* vol. 6, p. 198.
53. As quoted in James A. B. Scherer, *The Lion of the Vigilantes: William T. Coleman and the Life of Old San Francisco* (Indianapolis and New York: Bobbs-Merrill Co., 1939), p. 81.
54. Ibid., p. 80.
55. San Francisco *Daily Alta California,* February 4, 1850.
56. Kimball, *San Francisco Directory,* p. 131.
57. San Francisco *Daily Alta California,* June 25, 1850.
58. Davis, *Seventy-Five Years in California,* p. 10.
59. John Morland Cushing, "From New York to San Francisco in 1849 Via the Isthmus of Panama, Including the Voyage from Panama to San Francisco on the Ship *Niantic,*" *Quarterly of the Society of California Pioneers* 6, no. 3 (October 1929), p. 132.
60. San Francisco *Daily Alta California,* May 15, 1882.
61. Ibid., December 21, 1849.
62. San Francisco *Daily Herald,* August 26, 1850.
63. "An Act in Relation to the Appointment of Pilots for the Ports and Harbors of California," *Laws of the State of California, Passed at the First Session of the Legislature . . . ,* ch. 3.
64. San Francisco *Daily Alta California,* January 22, 1850.
65. "An Act to Establish Pilots and Pilot Regulations for the Port of San Francisco," in *Compiled Laws of California,* ch. 8, pp. 88–95.
66. Kimball, *San Francisco Directory,* pp. 128–129.
67. San Francisco *Daily Alta California,* August 21, 1850.
68. Ibid., July 4, 1851.
69. Parker, *San Francisco Directory,* pp. 16–17.
70. San Francisco *Daily Alta California,* October 27, 1853.
71. Adolphus Windeler, *The California Gold Rush Diary of a German Sailor,* ed. W. Turrentine Jackson (Berkeley: Howell-North Books, 1969), pp. 38–39.
72. Ibid., p. 46.
73. Ibid., p. 47.
74. Taylor, *Eldorado,* p. 90.
75. Barry and Patten, *Men and Memories of San Francisco,* p. 106.
76. San Francisco *Daily Alta California,* June 3, 1882.
77. Kimball, *San Francisco Directory,* p. 133.
78. San Francisco *Daily Alta California,* June 3, 1882.
79. Ibid.
80. Ibid.
81. San Francisco Daily *Alta California,* December 18, 1850.
82. Ibid., May 8, 1882.

83. Cushing, "From New York to San Francisco," p. 132.
84. Howard I. Chapelle, *American Small Sailing Craft: Their Design, Development, and Construction* (New York: W. W. Norton and Co., 1951), pp. 195, 198.
85. New London [Conn.] *Daily Chronicle*, November 29, 1848.
86. San Francisco *Daily Herald*, September 21, 1851.
87. Ibid., September 26, 1851.
88. San Francisco *Daily Alta California*, January 7, 1852.
89. William Taylor, *Seven Years' Street Preaching in San Francisco* . . . (New York: Published for the author, 1856), p. 236.
90. Ibid., pp. 231–232.
91. Bill for the ship *Charles Crooker*, Crosby, Crooker and Company, shipchandlers, New York, November 11, 1850, Unpublished manuscript, G. W. Blunt White Library, Mystic Seaport Museum, Mystic, Connecticut.
92. Kimball, *San Francisco Directory*, p. 132.
93. Barry and Patten, *Men and Memories of San Francisco*, p. 58.
94. Ibid., p. 169.
95. Catalog, Folger and Tubbs, ship chandlers, circa 1851, Unaccessioned document, Tubbs Cordage Company, J. Porter Shaw Library, National Maritime Museum, San Francisco; and David Warren Ryder, *Men of Rope; Being the History of the Tubbs Cordage Company* . . . (San Francisco: Historical Publications, 1954), p. 20.
96. Ryder, *Men of Rope*, p. 18.
97. Roger Lotchin, *San Francisco, 1846–1856: From Hamlet to City* (New York: Oxford University Press, 1974), p. 173.
98. *Minutes of the Legislative Assembly of the District of San Francisco* . . . (San Francisco: Towne and Bacon, 1860), pp. 12–69, passim.
99. Ernest de Massey, "A Frenchman in the Gold Rush," ed. Marguerite Wilbur, *California Historical Society Quarterly* 5, no. 1 (March 1926), p. 11.
100. *Act of Incorporation and Ordinances of the City of San Francisco* (San Francisco: *Daily Evening Picayune*, 1850).
101. San Francisco *Daily Alta California*, November 7, 1849.
102. Kimball, *San Francisco Directory*, p. 129.
103. Ibid., p. 128.
104. Sacramento *Transcript*, November 22, 1850.
105. Ibid.
106. San Francisco *Daily Evening Picayune*, December 6, 1850.
107. *Ordinances and Joint Resolutions of the City of San Francisco* . . . (San Francisco: Monson and Valentine, 1851), pp. 262–263.
108. San Francisco *Daily Herald*, June 20, 1851.
109. San Francisco *Daily Alta California*, June 25, 1851.
110. San Francisco *Daily Herald*, August 8, 1851.
111. San Francisco *Daily Alta California*, January 5, 1852.

CHAPTER 4.

1. As cited in William M. Meredith to James Collier, Washington, D.C., April 3, 1849, *Message from the President of the United States, Transmitting Information in Answer to a Resolution of the House of the 31 of*

December, 1849, on the Subject of California and New Mexico 31st Cong., 1st sess., 1850, H. Ex. Doc. 17, p. 13. (Hereafter cited as *Message from President*, H. Ex. Doc 17.

2. Ibid., pp. 13–15. See also Grant Foreman, *The Adventures of James Collier, First Collector of the Port of San Francisco* (Chicago: Black Cat Press, 1937).
3. J. D. Carr and Abraham Kentzing, Jr., to William M. Meredith, San Francisco, October 30, 1849, *Message from President*, H. Ex. Doc 17, p. 24.
4. James Collier to William M. Meredith, San Francisco, November 13, 1849, *Message from President*, H. Ex. Doc. 17, p. 25.
5. Ibid.
6. Ibid., p. 27.
7. James Collier to William M. Meredith, San Francisco, November 29, 1849, *Message from President*, H. Ex. Doc. 17, p. 31.
8. San Francisco *Daily Alta California*, July 16, 1850.
9. Charles F. H. Menges, "The *Gold Hunter* and the U.S. Custom House, San Francisco," *Nautical Research Guild Secretary's Monthly Letter* 2, no. 11 (November 1949), pp. 139–143.
10. Thomas Ap Catesby Jones to James Collier, Flag-ship *Savannah*, Bay of San Francisco, November 12, 1849, *Message from President*, H. Ex. Doc., 17, p. 34.
11. James Collier to Thomas Ap Catesby Jones, San Francisco, November 15, 1849, *Message from President*, H. Ex. Doc. 17, p. 35.
12. James Collier to William M. Meredith, San Francisco, February 28, 1850, NARG 26, Records of the United States Revenue Marine, Correspondence from Collectors of the Port to the Secretary of the Treasury, Washington, D.C. (Henceforth all National Archives correspondence, which includes Financial Correspondence, Correspondence from Revenue Marine Officers to the Secretary of the Treasury, Correspondence from Collectors of the Port to the Secretary of the Treasury, and the muster rolls for *Cornelius W. Lawrence*, will be referenced as NARG 26, Correspondence, with the date of the cited correspondence.)
13. See Christian G. Fritz, "Judicial Style in California's First Admiralty Court: Ogden Hoffman and the First Ten Years, 1851–1861," *Southern California Quarterly* 64, no. 3 (Fall 1982).
14. *Report of the Secretary of the Treasury, Communicating, in Compliance with a Resolution of the Senate, the Report of Gilbert Rodman, esq. Upon the Subject of the Custom-House at San Francisco, Cal.* Special sess., 1853, S. Ex. Doc. 5.
15. Foreman, *Adventures of James Collier*, p. 46.
16. An excellent account can be found in Stephen H. Evans, *The United States Coast Guard, 1790–1915* (Annapolis: The United States Naval Institute, 1949).
17. Ibid., pp. 31–37, 63.
18. Wilhelmine Easby-Smith, *Personal Recollections of Early Washington and a Sketch of the Life of Captain William Easby* (Washington, D.C.: Association of the Oldest Inhabitants of the District of Columbia, 1913).
19. NARG 26, Correspondence, December 14, 1847.
20. NARG 26, Records of the United States Coast Guard, "Records of the Revenue Cutter Service, 1790–1915," Logbook, U.S. Revenue Cutter

Cornelius W. Lawrence, October 1848–November 1851," entry for December 22, 1848. (Henceforth all logbook entries will be referenced as NARG 26, Logbook, with the date of the entry.)

21. NARG 26, Logbook, August 9, 1849; and Richardson, "Gold Seekers," vol. 115, no. 2 (April 1979), pp. 94–95.
22. NARG 26, Logbook, August 9, 1849.
23. Ibid., October 20, 1849.
24. Alexander V. Fraser to William M. Meredith, San Francisco, November 1, 1849, NARG 26, Correspondence.
25. Ibid., November 25, 1849.
26. Ibid., November 26, 1849.
27. James Collier to William A. Meredith, San Francisco, December 13, 1849, NARG 26, Correspondence.
28. Ibid.
29. NARG 26, Logbook, March 25, 1850.
30. Ibid., October 18, 1850.
31. Ibid., October 29, 1850.
32. Ibid., November 19, 1850.
33. Alexander V. Fraser to Thomas Corwin, San Francisco, October 31, 1850, NARG 26, Correspondence.
34. James Collier to Alexander V. Fraser, San Francisco, November 21, 1850, NARG 26, Correspondence.
35. Ibid.
36. NARG 26 Logbook, June 10, 1851.
37. Ibid., October 10, 1851.
38. Ibid., October 29, 1851.
39. Alsop and Company to Douglass Ottinger, San Francisco, October 31, 1851, NARG 26, Correspondence.
40. For a more detailed discussion of the *Challenge* affair, see A. B. C. Whipple, *The Challenge* (New York: William Morrow and Co., 1987).
41. Douglas Ottinger to Thomas Butler King, San Francisco, October 27, 1851, NARG 26, Correspondence.
42. Ibid., October 30, 1851.
43. NARG 26 Logbook, November 10, 1851.
44. Ibid., November 25, 1851. The wreck was reported by the local newspapers, notable articles appearing in the San Francisco *Daily Alta California* and the San Francisco *Daily Herald* of November 26, 27, and 28.
45. Douglass Ottinger to Thomas Butler King, San Francisco, November 26, 1851, NARG 26, Correspondence. The wreck is marked on a manuscript survey chart done in early 1852 by the United States Coast and Geodetic Survey entitled, "A Map of Part of the Coast of California From Point Lobos Southward . . . 1852".
46. San Francisco *Daily Alta California,* November 26, 1851.
47. San Francisco *Daily Alta California,* November 28, 1851.
48. Douglass Ottinger to Thomas Butler King, San Francisco, November 28, 1851, NARG 26, Correspondence.
49. Thomas Butler King to Collector Gallaer of Benicia, San Francisco, December 1, 1851, NARG 26, Correspondence.
50. Bauer, *Surfboats and Horse Marines,* p. 239.
51. As cited in Thomas Ap Catesby Jones to J. Y. Mason, Monterey, Califor-

nia, November 2, 1848, NARG 45, "Letters from Captains to the Secretary of the Navy," Washington, D.C.

52. Monterey *California Star and Californian*, November 18, 1848.

53. J. Y. Mason to Thomas Ap Catesby Jones, Washington, D.C., March 1, 1849, NARG 45, M625, roll 286.

54. Robert Erwin Johnson, *Thence Round Cape Horn: The Story of United States Naval Forces on Pacific Station, 1818–1923* (Annapolis: United States Naval Institute, 1963), pp. 95–97.

55. A. D. Bache to Lieutenant Commander W. P. McArthur, Norfolk, Virginia, October 27, 1848, *Message from President*, H. Ex. Doc. 17, p. 47.

56. William Gibson's account in *Army and Navy Journal*, March 9, 1878, was reprinted twice, first in the San Jose (California) *Pioneer* of February 26, 1881, and then along with official dispatches in Erwin G. Gudde, "Mutiny on the *Ewing*," *California Historical Society Quarterly* 30, no. 1 (March 1951), pp. 40–41.

57. Gudde, "Mutiny on the *Ewing*," p. 42.

58. As cited in Gudde, "Mutiny on the *Ewing*," pp. 43–46.

59. Thomas Ap Catesby Jones to J. Y. Mason, San Francisco, October 25, 1849, NARG 45, "Squadron Letters."

60. See Johnson, *Thence Round Cape Horn*, p. 100. Jones's court-martial, case no. 1187, is in RG125, Records of the Office of the Judge Advocate General (Navy), "Records of Courts-Martial and Courts of Inquiry," M273. Jones openly called Benicia his "darling" and "pet" in private correspondence. See C. Norman Guice, ed., "The 'Contentious Commodore' and San Francisco: Two 1850 Letters from Thomas ap Catesby Jones," *Pacific Historical Review* 34, no. 3, pp. 337–342.

61. Charles S. McCauley to Charles Gaunt, San Francisco, October 7, 1850, NARG45, M625, Roll 286.

62. *Dictionary of American Fighting Ships*, volume 8 (Washington, D.C.: U.S. Naval Historical Center, 19—), pp. 106–107.

63. Logbook, USS *Warren*, NARG 24, Records of the Bureau of Naval Personnel, "Logs, 1801–1946," entry for November 29, 1849. (Hereafter cited as NARG 24, *Warren* Logbook with entry date.)

64. Ibid., February 18, 1850.

65. Ibid., March 1, 1850.

66. The logbooks for *Warren* were read for the period November 1849 (the earliest surviving gold rush log) through January 1851. The vessels specifically listed as sending prisoners were recorded in the log as USS *Savannah*, USS *St. Mary's*, USS *Vandalia*, the English bark *Helen Stewart*, ship *Flavius*, Chilean brig *Matador*, American bark *Clarissa*, American ship *Golconda*, ship *Jacob Perkins*, Hamburg bark *America*, American ship *Mariposa*, American ship *Far West*, American ship *Boston*, American bark *Connecticut*, American ship *Louis Philippe*, American ship *Queen Victoria* of New York, English bark *Zealand*, American ship *Manilla*, English ship *Chasely*, Hamburg ship *Probus*, English bark *Victoria*, American ship *Robert Pulsford*, American ship *Sheffield*, Dutch ship *John Van Horn*, Danish bark *Caroline Amelia*, English bark *Vicar of Bray*, English ship *William Sprague*, American ship *Acbar*, American ship *Hamilton*, English ship *London*, Norwegian bark *Frea*, Danish ship

Creola, American bark *Mydas*, American bark *John Franklin*, Portuguese bark *Novo Paquet*, American ship *Roger Sherman*, English bark *Eudora*, ship *Emily*, Hamburg brig *Norma*, and American schooner *Petrel*.

67. NARG 24, *Warren* Logbook, January 20, 1850.
68. NARG 24, *Warren* Logbook, March 13, 1850.
69. Windeler, *Gold Rush Diary*, pp. 44–45.
70. NARG 24, *Warren* Logbook, June 17 and 29, 1850.
71. Thomas Ap Catesby Jones to Charles S. McCauley, USS *Falmouth*, underweigh, July 2, 1850, NARG 45, M625, roll 286.
72. *Dictionary of American Fighting Ships*, vol. 8, p. 106.
73. Joseph Warren Revere, *Naval Duty in California*, reprint (Oakland, Calif.: Biobooks, 1947), p. 223.
74. Ibid., pp. 223–224.
75. By executive order Millard Fillmore exempted from sale and reserved for "public purposes" most of the lands recommended by the joint board. Fillmore's order, and subsequent government correspondence pertaining to it, can be found in John W. Dwinelle, *The Colonial History of the City of San Francisco; Being a Narrative Argument in the Circuit Court of the United States for the State of California, for Four Square Leagues of Land, Claimed by that City under the Laws of Spain, and Confirmed to it by that Court, and by the Supreme Court of the United States* (San Francisco: Towne and Bacon, 1867), pp. 221–223.
76. See Johnson, *Thence Round Cape Horn*, p. 104; and Arnold S. Lott, *A Long Line of Ships: Mare Island's Century of Naval Activity in California* (Annapolis: United States Naval Institute, 1954), pp. 7–8 for an account of the establishment of Mare Island Navy Yard.
77. Ibid., p. 8.
78. Ibid. pp. 9–10.
79. San Francisco *Daily Alta California*, September 20, 1854.
80. Lott, *Long Line of Ships*, pp. 56–58.
81. Pierre Charles Saint-Amant, *Voyages en Californie et dans L'Oregon* (Paris: n.p., 1854), p. 107.
82. W. H. Ranlett to Secretary of the Treasury, San Francisco, December 15, 1852, NARG 26, Records of the United States Coast Guard, "Records of the Lighthouse Board," Engineers and Inspectors Letters, 12th district.
83. See Erwin N. Thompson, *The Rock: A History of Alcatraz Island, 1847–1972; Historic Resource Study, Golden Gate National Recreation Area, San Francisco* (Denver: National Park Service, 1979), pp. 455–456. Also see Ralph C. Shanks, Jr., and Janetta Thompson Shanks, *Lighthouses of San Francisco Bay* (San Anselmo, Calif.: Costano Books, 1976), pp. 15–16.
84. Shanks and Shanks, *Lighthouses*, pp. 7, 33–34, 49–50.
85. Thomas Oliver Larkin to William Rufus Langley, Monterey, December 16, 1848, in Hammond, *Larkin Papers*, vol. 8, p. 66.
86. William Henry Aspinwall to Alfred Robinson, New York, May 25, 1849, Aspinwall Letterbook, Huntington Manuscript FAC 308, Henry E. Huntington Library, San Marino, California. (Hereafter cited as Aspinwall Letterbook.)
87. Ibid., October 5, 1849.
88. Minutes of the Common Council, City of Benicia, May 11, May 18,

1850, in "Minute Book, May 7, 1850–May 8, 1854," Manuscript in City Clerk's Office, City of Benicia.

89. William Henry Aspinwall to Robinson, Bissell, and Company, New York, August 13, 1850, Aspinwall Letterbook.

90. Ibid.

91. William Steuart to Thomas Oliver Larkin, August 5, 1850, in Hammond, *Larkin Papers*, vol. 8, p. 331.

92. Samuel Comstock to Robinson, Bissell, and Company, New York, January 2, 1850, Aspinwall Letterbook.

93. Diary, Edward Ely, entry for September 18, 1851. Collections of the G. W. Blunt White Library, Mystic Seaport Museum, Mystic, Connecticut.

94. Ely Diary, entry for September 27, 1851.

95. San Francisco *Daily Alta California*, November 30, 1852.

96. Kemble, *Panama Route*, p. 135. Other major industrial enterprises did not commence until 1854, when the first major lumber sawmills were constructed on the coast north of San Francisco, and a mint was constructed in San Francisco. The first woolen mill in California was erected in San Francisco in 1858 in the lee of Black Point. Mineral and agricultural wealth, and an active maritime trade negatively influenced California industrial development. A number of small iron and brass foundries were established but as of 1852 had yet to achieve significance.

97. San Francisco *Daily Alta California*, November 30, 1852.

98. Ibid., May 8, 1858.

99. Ibid., November 30, 1852; and Kemble, *Panama Route*, p. 135.

100. United States Census, Special schedule G, "Products of Industry," 8th U.S. Census, (Washington, D.C.: National Archives, 1860), Benicia Township, lists forty-eight men as the "average number of hands employed." The population schedule of the same census lists forty-eight men in Benicia employed at the depot and ironworks. The only surviving early census for Benicia, the State of California's 1852 census, lists fifty-three men employed at the depot and ironworks. Eight of these men persisted in their residence and occupation and are listed in the 1860 census.

101. San Francisco *Daily Alta California*, October 31, 1857.

102. Ibid., June 3, 1856.

103. William Henry Aspinwall, *First Annual Report of the Pacific Mail Steamship Company, May, 1855* (New York: George F. Nesbitt, 1855), pp. 13–14.

104. United States Census, Special schedule G, 8th U.S. Census, (Washington, D.C.: National Archives, 1860), Benicia Township.

105. "Minute Book," Benicia Common Council Minutes, June 20 and July 18, 1853.

106. Dale L. Morgan and James R. Scobie, eds., *Three Years in California: William Perkins' Journal of Life at Sonora 1849–1852* (Berkeley and Los Angeles: University of California Press, 1964), pp. 317–318.

107. Francis P. Farquhar, ed., *Up and Down California in 1860–1864: The Journal of William H. Brewer* (Berkeley and Los Angeles: University of California Press, 1974), pp. 291–292.

108. "Minute Book," Benicia Common Council Minutes, September 13, 1852.

109. "Minute Book," Benicia Common Council Minutes, March 19, 1851; May 14, October 4, December 13, 1852; April 12, May 3, November 21, 1853; April 3, April 24, 1854; October 16, 1855; January 26, February 1, 1864. See also "The People of the State of California vs. The Pacific Mail Steamship Co.," Case nos. 987, 1207, 1208, and 1211, Solano County Clerk's Office, Fairfield, California.
110. Abijah Mann, et al., *Reports from Two Committees of Stockholders, Appointed at the Annual Meeting, May 1855, of Pacific Mail Steamship Co.'s Stockholders, and Made to an Adjourned Meeting, Held 20th June, 1855* (New York: Baker, Godwin and Co., 1855), p. 13.
111. Financial Journals F, G, H, and I, [1858–1866], entries for May 24, 1862, December 28, 1863, and April 13, 1864, Pacific Mail Steamship Company, Unprocessed manuscript collection, Henry E. Huntington Library, San Marino, California. The journals are not paginated.
112. Aspinwall, *First Annual Report*, p. 10.
113. Mann, *Reports from Stockholders*, pp. 13–14.
114. Abijah Mann, ed., *Statement of 28th June, 1855, from Mr. William H. Aspinwall, President of the Pacific Mail Steamship Company, In Answer to the Reports of Two Committees Appointed by Stockholders, 24th May, 1855, With Replies to the Attacks on Committee's Reports, by Hon. Abijah Mann, Jr., Chairman of First Committee, and Theodore Dehon, Chairman of Second Committee* (New York: Hall, Clayton and Co., 1855), pp. 6–7.
115. Ibid., p. 7.
116. San Francisco *Daily Alta California*, June 3, 1856.
117. J. P. Munro-Fraser, *History of Solano County . . .* (San Francisco: Wood, Alley and Co., 1879), p. 164.
118. Ibid.
119. Kemble, *Panama Route*, p. 136.
120. Hittell, *History of San Francisco*, vol. 1, p. 157.
121. "Certificate of Measurement &c of Steamer *Boston*, March 17, 1851," Miscellaneous manuscripts, National Maritime Museum, San Francisco.
122. San Francisco *Daily Alta California*, July 23, 1851.
123. Kimball, *San Francisco Directory*, passim, and Parker, *San Francisco Directory*, passim.

CHAPTER 5

1. C. H. Ellis, "Journal of a Voyage from Boston to San Francisco in the Brig *North Bend* . . ." as cited in John E. Pomfret, ed., *California Gold Rush Voyages, 1848–1849: Three Original Narratives* (San Marino, Calif.: Huntington Library, 1954), p. 40. See also the New York *Daily Tribune*, February 10, 1849.
2. As cited in Alfred Lansing, *Endurance: Shackleton's Incredible Voyage* (New York: Carroll and Graf, 1987), pp. 225–226.
3. Delgado, *Log of Apollo*, pp. 55, 62, 64.
4. Lamson, *Round Cape Horn*, pp. 73–74.
5. Frederick J. Teggart, ed. *Diary of Nelson Kingsley, A California Argonaut of 1849* (Berkeley: University of California Press, 1914) p. 285.
6. Benjamin Franklin Bourne, *The Captive in Patagonia; Or, Life Among*

the Giants: A Personal Narrative (Boston: Gould and Lincoln, 1853), pp. 205–206.

7. Ibid., p. 210.
8. Hinton R. Helper, *The Land of Gold: Reality Versus Fiction* (Baltimore: Published for the author, 1855), p. 28.
9. San Francisco *Daily Alta California,* December 1, 1849.
10. Windeler, *Gold Rush Diary,* p. 35.
11. San Francisco *Daily Alta California,* August 5, 1851.
12. San Francisco *Daily Alta California,* August 8, 1851.
13. Log of the United States Revenue Cutter *Frolic,* NARG 26, Records of the United States Coast Guard, "Records of the Revenue Cutter Service, 1790–1915," Washington, D.C., entries for January 7–9, 1852. (Hereafter cited as NARG 26, *Frolic* Log, with date of log entry.)
14. Albion, *Square-Riggers on Schedule,* pp. 209, 276–277, and 299.
15. San Francisco *Daily Alta California,* July 14, 1852.
16. Ibid., July 17, 1852.
17. NARG 26, *Frolic* Log, July 18, 1852.
18. Ibid., July 20, 1852.
19. San Francisco *Daily Alta California,* July 24, 1852.
20. Ibid., July 25, 1852.
21. Octavius T. Howe and Frederick C. Matthews, *American Clipper Ships, 1833–1858* (Salem, Mass.: Marine Research Society, 1927), vol. 2, pp. 542–543.
22. New York *Daily Tribune,* March 13, 1854.
23. Ibid.
24. Ibid.
25. Howe and Matthews, *American Clipper Ships,* vol. 1, p. 231; and San Francisco *Daily Alta California,* January 5, 1853.
26. Howe and Matthews, *American Clipper Ships,* p. 232.
27. San Francisco *Daily Alta California,* April 23, 1854.
28. Ibid., April 24, 1854.
29. Ibid., April 25, 1854.
30. Ibid., April 27 and April 30, 1854.
31. Ibid., May 2 and May 3, 1854.
32. Ibid., May 7, 1854.
33. Ibid., March 20, 1850.
34. Ibid., December 19, 1850.
35. Basil Lubbock, *The Opium Clippers* (Glasgow: Brown, Son and Ferguson, 1933), p. 287.
36. Hong Kong *China Mail,* May 30, June 7, and 13, 1850.
37. George Gibbs, "Journal of the Expedition of Colonel Redick McKee, United States Indian Agent, Through Northwestern California," in Henry R. Schoolcraft, ed., *Historical and Statistical Information Respecting the History, Condition, and Prospects of the Indian Tribes of the United States* (Philadelphia: n.p., 1853), vol. 3, p. 113. The wreck of *Frolic* lies near Caspar, California, in less than eight feet of water. The only known Gold Rush wreck with a China trade cargo, *Frolic* is the subject of a detailed archaeological and archival study by Dr. Thomas N. Layton of the Department of Anthropology, San Jose State University. Dr. Layton first encountered *Frolic* cargo while excavating an historic

Pomo Indian village on Three Chop Ridge, Mendocino County, California. The Pomo were evidently among the Indians who salvaged *Frolic*. Most of the historical information on *Frolic* described herein is from chapter 4 of Layton's manuscript: Western Pomo Prehistory; Excavations at Albion Head, Nightbirds' Retreat, and Three Chop Village, Mendocino County, California. University of California, Los Angeles, Institute of Archaeology Monograph 32 (in press 1989). Dr. Layton's research ultimately has led him, with the assistance of local sport divers, to the wreck itself. Dr. Layton is now completing a major study of *Frolic*, her cargo, and her place in the cultural context of mid-nineteenth century commerce.

38. Reminiscence by James Chester Ford, in Dorothy Bear and Beth Stebbins, *Mendocino: Book Two* (Mendocino, Calif.: Gull Press, 1977), pp. 9–11.
39. San Francisco *Daily Alta California*, October 31, 1850.
40. Ibid., April 13, 1853.
41. Marysville *Herald*, February 14, 1851.
42. Sacramento *Union*, August 18, 1851.
43. Marysville *Herald*, June 28, 1851.
44. Ibid., February 6 and 7, 1856.
45. New York *Herald*, December 27, 1850.
46. San Francisco *Daily Alta California*, July 17, 1852.
47. San Francisco *Daily Alta California*, April 2, 1853.
48. Jason Collins, "Loss of the Steamship *Independence*," *The American Neptune* 14, no. 3 (July 1954), pp. 194–195.
49. San Francisco *Daily Alta California*, April 2, 1853.
50. John Greenbank, "The Story of a Gold Miner," *California Historical Society Quarterly* 6, no. 4 (December 1926), p. 358.
51. Collins, "Loss of the Steamship *Independence*," p. 196.
52. San Francisco *Daily Alta California*, April 2, 1853.
53. Ibid.
54. Franklin Langworthy, *Scenery of the Plains, Mountains, and Mines*, ed. Paul C. Phillips, reprint (Princeton: Princeton University Press, 1938), pp. 210–211.
55. Collins, "Loss of the Steamship *Independence*," p. 197.
56. San Francisco *Daily Alta California*, April 1, 1853.
57. Ibid., April 2, 1853.
58. Ibid.
59. San Francisco *Morning Call*, April 3, 1891. This article was a passenger's reminiscence of the wreck.
60. Ibid.
61. Fred W. Stocking, "How We Gave a Name to Tennessee Cove," *The Overland Monthly* 17 (April 1891), p. 353.
62. Ibid.
63. San Francisco *Daily Alta California*, March 8, 1853; and Stocking, "How We Gave a Name to Tennessee Cove," p. 354.
64. Johann Hein, "Reminiscence," (1902) Typescript, Collection of Lois Gilchrist, Penngrove, California.
65. San Francisco *Morning Call*, April 3, 1891.
66. San Francisco *Golden Era*, March 13, 1853.
67. Stocking, "How We Gave a Name to Tennessee Cove," p. 353.

68. Robert Howe, "Reminiscence," n.d., J. Porter Shaw Library, National Maritime Museum, San Francisco.
69. San Francisco *Daily Alta California*, March 7, 1853.
70. NARG 24, *Warren* Logbook, March 6, 1853.
71. San Francisco *Daily Alta California*, March 8, 1853.
72. Ibid., March 7, 1853.
73. NARG 24, *Warren* Logbook, March 7, 1853.
74. San Francisco *Daily Alta California*, March 7, 1853.
75. Ibid., and Stocking, "How We Gave a Name to Tennessee Cove," p. 356.
76. San Francisco *Daily Alta California*, March 9, 1853.
77. Ibid.
78. Stocking, "How We Gave a Name to Tennessee Cove," p. 355.
79. San Francisco *Daily Alta California*, March 11, 1853.
80. London *Illustrated News*, April 23, 1853.
81. San Francisco *Daily Alta California*, March 9, 1853.
82. Alfred DeWitt to "Dear Brother," San Francisco, April 28, 1853, DeWitt Family Papers, Bancroft Library, University of California, Berkeley.
83. William J. Eames to Thomas Oliver Larkin, San Francisco, March 15, 1853, vol. 9, pp. 239–240.
84. Sacramento *Union*, March 22, 1853.
85. William Tecumseh Sherman, *Memoirs of General William T. Sherman* (New York: D. Appleton and Co., 1875) vol. 1, p. 95.
86. Ibid., p. 96.
87. Ibid.
88. San Francisco *Daily Alta California*, April 10, 1853.
89. Ibid., April 11, 1853.
90. Ibid., April 10, 1853.
91. Diary, Asa Cyrus Call, (1849–1854), California Historical Society, San Francisco, entry for December 5, 1853.
92. Edward Bosqui, *Memoirs of Edward Bosqui*, reprint (Oakland, Calif.: Holmes Book Company, 1953), p. 61.
93. Call Diary, December 7, 1853.
94. Charles Enoch Huse, *The Huse Journal: Santa Barbara in the 1850s*, ed. Edith Bond Conkley (Santa Barbara: Santa Barbara Historical Society, 1977), p. 46; and San Francisco *Daily Alta California*, December 8, 1853.
95. Recollections of Charles C. P. Holden, a *Winfield Scott* passenger, in the San Francisco *Morning Call*, July 22, 1883.
96. San Francisco *Daily Alta California*, December 13 and 15, 1853.
97. San Francisco *Daily California Chronicle*, December 16, 24, and 31, 1853.
98. Ibid.
99. San Francisco *Daily Alta California*, December 8, 1853.
100. Ibid., January 30, 1854.
101. Folkman, *Nicaragua Route*, p. 55.
102. San Francisco *Daily Alta California*, May 9, 1854.
103. Kemble, *Panama Route*, p. 68.
104. Ibid., p. 70.
105. San Francisco *Daily Alta California*, October 10, 1854.
106. San Francisco *Daily Herald*, October 10, 1854.
107. Sacramento *Union*, October 14, 1854.
108. San Francisco *Daily Alta California*, October 16, 1854.

109. The history of *Central America,* ex-*George Law,* is related in Cedric Ridgely-Nevitt, "The United States Mail Steamer *George Law,*" *The American Neptune* 4, no. 3 (October 1944), pp. 305–307.
110. San Francisco *Daily Evening Bulletin,* September 23, 1857.
111. See James P. Delgado, "Murder Most Foul: San Francisco Reacts to the Loss of the S.S. *Central America,*" *The Log of Mystic Seaport* 25, no. 4 (Spring 1983), pp. 3–15. See also James P. Delgado, "Their Bones Should Be Left in the Ocean to Rot: Notes on an Unusual Shipwreck Song," *Book Club of California Quarterly News-Letter* 49, no. 2 (Spring 1984), pp. 31–43.
112. San Francisco *Daily Evening Bulletin,* November 2, 1857.
113. John A. Stone, *Put's Golden Songster* (San Francisco: D. Appleton and Co., 1858)
114. Richard A. Dwyer and Richard E. Lingenfelter, eds., *The Songs of the Gold Rush* (Berkeley and Los Angeles: University of California Press, 1964), p. 2.
115. Cornel Lengyel, ed., *Music of the Gold Rush Era,* W.P.A. History of Music Project, vol. 2 (San Francisco: Works Progress Administration, Northern California, 1939), pp. 70–71.
116. Ibid.

CONCLUSION

1. "What Becomes of the Old Ships?" Boston *Daily Transcript,* ca. 1857, J. Porter Shaw Library, National Maritime Museum, San Francisco. Unfortunately many fine clippings of considerable interest were collected by the former San Francisco Maritime Museum without noting the source of the clip or the date.
2. San Francisco *Daily Alta California,* September 4, 1852. Hare testified about his immigration and business in various "Alabama Claims" court cases in the 1860s, which are included in the Charles Hare Papers, California Historical Society, San Francisco. See also James P. Delgado, "What Becomes of the Old Ships?: Dismantling the Gold Rush Fleet of San Francisco," *Pacific Historian* 25 (Winter 1981).
3. L. Eve Armentrout-Ma, "Chinese and GGNRA: Guests of Choice, Guests of Necessity," Manuscript, J. Porter Shaw Library, National Maritime Museum, San Francisco, (1980), p. 48.
4. Prentice Mulford, *Prentice Mulford's Story; Or, Life by Land and Sea* (New York: F. J. Needham, 1889), p. 46.
5. San Francisco *Daily Alta California,* May 22, 1882.
6. San Francisco *Daily Evening Bulletin,* February 11, 1857.
7. Ruth Teiser, ed., *This Sudden Empire California: The Story of the Society of California Pioneers, 1850 to 1950* (San Francisco: The Society of California Pioneers, 1950).
8. Several articles were published in the Society of California Pioneers *Quarterly* through the years, including John Morland Cushing's reminiscences of a voyage on the ship *Niantic.* By far the most pertinent issue of the *Quarterly,* however, is volume 1, number 4, published in December 1924, which included thirty-four pages of introductory narrative on "The Rush of '49," and ten pages of original harbormaster's records of "Boats arriving in San Francisco Bay from March 26, 1849 to December 30,

1849," listing the date of arrival, name, type and registry of vessel, port of departure, and the number of days' passage.

9. Richardson, "Gold Seekers," pp. 119–121.

10. For a helpful bibliographic essay, see Dale L. Morgan, "Through the Haze of Time: The California Gold Rush in Retrospect," in Gardiner, *In Pursuit of the Golden Dream*, pp. vii–xlii. See also John Windle and Ronald R. Randall, *Rare Books VIII: The Race for Gold* (San Francisco: Randall House, 1979). Robert Becker is at this time compiling a bibliography of Cape Horn voyage journals and accounts.

BIBLIOGRAPHY

BOOKS

Aspinwall, William Henry. *First Annual Report of the Pacific Mail Steamship Company, May 1855*. New York: George F. Nesbitt, 1855.

Auger, Edouard. *Voyage en Californie. . . .* Paris: Librairie de L. Hachette et Cie., 1854.

Barry, T. A. and B. A. Patten. *Men and Memories of San Francisco, In the Spring of '50*. San Francisco: A. L. Bancroft and Co., 1873.

Beechey, William Frederick. *Narrative of a Voyage to the Pacific and Beerings's Strait, to Cooperate with the Polar Expeditions, Performed in His Majesty's Ship Blossom, under the Command of Capt. F. W. Beechey, R.N., F.R.S., etc., in the Years 1825 . . . 1828*. 2 vols. London: Colburn and Bentley, 1831.

Beilharz, Edwin A., and Carlos U. Lopez. *We Were '49ers! Chilean Accounts of the California Gold Rush*. Pasadena, Calif.: Ward Ritchie Press, 1976.

Borthwick, J. D. *Three Years in California*. Reprint. Oakland, Calif.: Biobooks, 1948.

Bosqui, Edward. *Memoirs of Edward Bosqui*. Reprint. Oakland, Calif.: Holmes Book Co., 1953.

Bourne, Benjamin Franklin. *The Captive in Patagonia; Or, Life Among the Giants: A Personal Narrative*. Boston: Gould and Lincoln, 1853.

Brock, Jethro C., comp. *A List of Persons from Nantucket Now in California, Or On Their Way Thither; Including the Names of the Vessels in Which They Sailed, the Time of Sailing, and of Their Arrival There; Also, Persons Returned, &c*. Nantucket: Jethro C. Brock, 1850.

Brown, D. Mackenzie, ed. *China Trade Days in California: Selected Letters from the Thompson Collection, 1832–1863*. Berkeley and Los Angeles: University of California Press, 1947.

Brown, John Henry. *Early Days of San Francisco*. Reprint. Oakland, Calif.: Biobooks, 1949.

Bruff, J. Goldsborough. *Gold Rush: The Journals, Drawings, and Other Papers of J. Goldsborough Bruff, Captain, Washington City and California Mining Association. . . .* Edited by Georgia Willis Read and Ruth Gaines. New York: Columbia University Press, 1944.

Buffum, E. Gould. *Six Months in the Gold Mines: From a Journal of Three Years'*

Residence in Upper and Lower California 1847–8–9. . . . Edited by John W. Caughey. Los Angeles: Ward Ritchie Press, 1959.

Caughey, John Walton, ed. *Seeing the Elephant: Letters of R. R. Taylor, Forty-Niner.* Pasadena, Calif.: Ward Ritchie Press, 1951.

Charter of the Pacific Mail Steamship Company, With Its Amendments Inclusive of May 1st, 1867. New York: Pacific Mail Steamship Co., 1867.

Christman, Enos. *One Man's Gold: The Letters and Journal of a Forty-niner.* . . . Edited by Florence Morrow Christman. New York: Whittlesey House, 1930.

Coffin, George. *A Pioneer Voyage to California and Round the World, 1849 to 1852.* Chicago: Privately published, 1908.

Dana, Richard Henry. *Two Years Before the Mast.* New York: Modern Library, 1936.

Davis, William Heath. *Seventy-five Years in California.* Reprint. San Francisco: John Howell Books, 1967.

Delavan, James. *Notes on California and the Placers: How to Get There, and What to Do Afterwards.* Reprint. Oakland, Calif.: Biobooks, 1956.

Delgado, James P. *The Log of Apollo: Joseph Perkins Beach's Journal of the Voyage of the Ship Apollo from New York to San Francisco, 1849.* San Francisco: Book Club of California, 1986.

Dougal, William H. *Off for California: The Letters, Log and Sketches of William H. Dougal, Gold Rush Artist.* Edited by Frank M. Stanger. Oakland, Calif.: Biobooks, 1949.

Downey, Joseph T. *The Cruise of the Portsmouth: A Sailor's View of the Naval Conquest of California.* Edited by Howard R. Lamar. New Haven and London: Yale University Press, 1963.

Dunbar, Edward E. *The Romance of the Age; Or, The Discovery of Gold in California.* New York: D. Appleton, and Co., 1867.

Dwinelle, John W. *The Colonial History of San Francisco; Being a Narrative Argument in the Circuit Court of the United States for the State of California, for Four Square Leagues of Land, Claimed by that City under the Laws of Spain, and Confirmed by That Court, and by the Supreme Court of the United States.* San Francisco: Towne and Bacon, 1867.

Farquhar, Francis P., ed. *Up and Down California in 1860–1864: The Journal of William H. Brewer.* Berkeley and Los Angeles: University of California Press, 1974.

Fawkes, Ulla Staley, ed. *The Journal of Walter Griffiths Pigman.* Mexico, Mo.: Walter G. Staley, 1942.

First Steamship Pioneers, Edited by a Committee of the Association. San Francisco: H. S. Crocker, 1874.

Forbes, Robert Bennett. *Personal Reminiscences.* Reprint. London: McDonald and Janes, 1974.

Gardiner, Howard C. *In Pursuit of the Golden Dream: Reminiscences of the Northern and Southern Mines and San Francisco, 1849–1857.* Edited by Dale L. Morgan. Stoughton, Mass.: Western Hemisphere, 1970.

Garner, William Robert. *Letters from California: 1846–1847.* Edited by Donald Munro Craig. Berkeley and Los Angeles: University of California Press, 1970.

Gerstaker, Friedrick. *Scenes of Life in California.* Reprint. Oakland, Calif.: Biobooks, 1949.

Gleason, Duncan, and Dorothy Gleason, comp. *Beloved Sister: The Letters of James Henry Gleason, 1841 to 1859 from Alta California and the Sandwich Islands*. Glendale, Calif.: Arthur H. Clark Company, 1978.

Goodman, John B. III, ed. *The Gold Rush Voyage of the Ship Loo Choo Around the Horn in 1849*. Mount Pleasant, Mich.: Cumming Press, 1977.

Gregory, Joseph W. *Gregory's Guide for California Travellers Via the Isthmus of Panama . . . Containing All the Requisite Information Needed by Persons Taking This Route*. Reprint. San Francisco: Book Club of California, 1949.

Hammond, George P., ed. *The Larkin Papers: Personal, Business, and Official Correspondence of Thomas Oliver Larkin, Merchant and United States Consul in California*. Vol. 9. Berkeley and Los Angeles: University of California Press, 1963.

————. *Digging for Gold Without a Shovel: The Letters of Daniel Wadsworth Coit from Mexico City to San Francisco, 1848–1851*. n.p.: Old West Publishing Co., 1967.

Haskins, C. W. *The Argonauts of California: Being the Reminiscences of Scenes and Incidents that Occurred in California in Early Mining Days, By a Pioneer*. New York: Fords, Howard and Hulbert, 1890.

Helper, Hinton R. *The Land of Gold: Reality Versus Fiction*. New York: Published for the author, 1855.

Hitchings, A. Frank, comp. *Ship Registers of the District of Salem and Beverly, Massachusetts*. Salem: Essex Institute, 1906.

Holdcamper, Forrest R., comp. *List of American-Flag Merchant Vessels That Received Certificates of Enrollment or Registry at the Port of New York, 1789–1867*. 2 vols. Washington, D.C.: National Archives, 1968.

Hotchkiss, Charles F. *On the Ebb: A Few Log-Lines from an Old Salt*. New Haven: Tuttle, Moorehouse and Taylor, 1878.

Huse, Charles Enoch. *The Huse Journal: Santa Barbara in the 1850s*. Edited by Edith Bond Conkley. Santa Barbara: Santa Barbara Historical Society, 1977.

Jenkins, F. H. *Journal of a Voyage to San Francisco, 1849*. Northridge: California State University, 1975.

Johnson, Theodore T. *Sights in the Gold Region, and Scenes by the Way*. New York: Baker and Scribner, 1849.

Kelly, William. *A Stroll through the Diggings of California*. Reprint. Oakland, Calif.: Biobooks, 1950.

Kemble, John Haskell, ed. *To California and the South Seas: The Diary of Albert G. Osbun, 1849–1851*. San Marino, Calif.: Huntington Library, 1966.

Kendall, Joseph. *A Landsman's Voyage to California*. Edited by Wilbur Hall. San Francisco: Privately published, 1935.

Kimball, Charles P. *The San Francisco City Directory*. San Francisco: Journal of Commerce Press, 1850.

Kingsley, Nelson. *Diary of Nelson Kingsley, a California Argonaut of 1849*. Edited by Frederic J. Teggart. Berkeley and Los Angeles: University of California, 1914.

Lamson, J. *Round Cape Horn: Voyage of the Passenger-Ship James W. Paige, from Maine to California in the Year 1852*. Bangor, Maine: O. F. and W. H. Knowles, 1878.

Langworthy, Franklin. *Scenery of the Plains, Mountains, and Mines.* Edited by Paul C. Phillips. Reprint. Princeton: Princeton University Press, 1938.

Letts, J. M. *California Illustrated; Including a Description of the Panama and Nicaragua Routes by a Returned Californian.* New York: William Holdredge, 1852.

Low, Garrett W. *Gold Rush by Sea: From the Journal of. . . .* Edited by Kenneth Haney. Philadelphia: University of Pennsylvania, 1941.

Lyman, Albert. *Journal of a Voyage to California, and Life in the Gold Diggings. . . .* Hartford, Conn.: E. T. Pease, 1852.

M'Collum, William. *California As I Saw It: Pencillings by the Way of its Gold and Gold Diggers! And Incidents of Travel by Land and Water, by . . . a Returned Adventurer, With Five Letters from the Isthmus by W. H. Hecox.* Edited by Dale L. Morgan. Los Gatos, Calif.: Talisman Press, 1960.

Mann, Abijah, ed. *Statement of 28th June, 1855, from Mr. William H. Aspinwall, President of the Pacific Mail Steamship Company, In Answer to the Reports of Two Committees Appointed by Stockholders, 24 May, 1855, With Replies to the Attacks on the Committee's Reports, by Hon. Abijah Mann, Jr., Chairman of First Committee, and Theodore Dehon, Chairman of Second Committee.* New York: Clayton and Co., 1855.

Mann, Abijah et al. *Reports from Two Committees of Stockholders, Appointed at the Annual Meeting, May 1855, of Pacific Mail Steamship Co.'s Stockholders, and Made to an Adjourned Meeting, Held 20th June, 1855.* New York: Baker, Godwin and Co., 1855.

Marryat, Frank. *Mountains and Molehills; Or, Recollections of a Burnt Journal.* London: Green, Longmans, Green, 1855.

Megquier, Mary Jane. *Apron Full of Gold: The Letters of Mary Jane Megquier from San Francisco, 1849–1856.* San Marino, Calif.: Huntington Library, 1949.

Morgan, A. W. and Company. *San Francisco City Directory.* San Francisco: A. W. Morgan and Company, 1852.

Morgan, Dale L., and James R. Scobie, eds. *Three Years in California: William Perkins' Journal of Life at Sonora, 1849–1852.* Berkeley and Los Angeles: University of California Press, 1964.

Mulford, Prentice. *Prentice Mulford's Story; Or, Life by Land and Sea: A Personal Narrative.* London: William Rider and Son, 1913.

Nunis, Doyce B., Jr. *Josiah Belden, 1841 California Overland Pioneer: His Memoir and Early Letters.* Georgetown, Calif.: Talisman Press, 1962.

Parker, James M. *The San Francisco Directory for the Year 1852–53. . . .* San Francisco: James M. Parker, 1852.

Phoenix, John [Lt. George H. Derby]. *Phoenixiana; Or, Sketches and Burlesques.* New York: D. Appleton and Co., 1856.

Pomfret, John, ed. *California Gold Rush Voyages, 1848–1849: Three Original Narratives.* San Marino, Calif.: Huntington Library, 1954.

Reading, June Allen, ed. *Consignments to El Dorado: A Record of the Voyage of the Sutton by Thomas Whaley.* New York: Exposition Press, 1972.

Re-Union of the Pioneer Panama Passengers, on the Fourth of June, 1874, Being the Twenty-fifth Anniversary of the Arrival of the Steamship Panama at San Francisco. San Francisco: Stock Report Office, 1874.

Revere, Joseph Warren. *Naval Duty in California.* Reprint. Oakland, Calif.: Biobooks, 1947.

Ringgold, Cadawallader. *Series of Charts, With Sailing Directions.* . . . Washington, D.C.: U.S. Coast and Geodetic Survey, 1850.

Russ, Carolyn Hale, ed. *The Log of a Forty-Niner: Journal of a Voyage from Newbury-port to San Francisco in the Brig Genl. Worth Commanded by Capt. Samuel Walton, Kept by Richard L. Hale, Newbury, Mass.* Boston: B. J. Brimmer, 1923.

Saint-Amant, Pierre Charles. *Voyages en Californie et dans L'Oregon.* Paris, 1854.

Schaeffer, L. M. *Sketches of Travels in South America, Mexico and California.* New York: James Egbert, 1860.

Shaw, William. *Golden Dreams and Waking Realities; Being the Adventures of a Gold-Seeker in California and the Pacific Islands.* London: Smith, Elder and Co., 1851.

Sherman, William Tecumseh. *Memoirs of General William T. Sherman.* 2 vols. New York: D. Appleton and Co., 1875.

Stillman, Jacob D. B. *Seeking the Golden Fleece: A Record of Pioneer Life in California, to Which is Annexed Footprints of Early Navigators, Other than Spanish, in California, With an Account of the Voyage of the Schooner Dolphin.* San Francisco: A. Roman and Co., 1877.

———. *Around the Horn to California in 1849.* Palo Alto: Lewis Osborne, 1967.

Stone, John A. *Put's Original California Songster, Giving in a Few Words What Would Occupy Volumes, Detailing the Hopes, Trials and Joys of a Miner's Life.* San Francisco: John A. Stone, 1856.

———. *Put's Golden Songster: Containing the Largest and Most Popular California Songs Ever Published.* San Francisco: D. E. Appleton and Co., 1858.

Taylor, Bayard. *Eldorado: Or, Adventures in the Path of Empire.* Reprint. New York: Alfred A. Knopf, 1949.

Taylor, William. *Seven Years' Street Preaching in San Francisco.* . . . New York: Published for the author, 1856.

Teggart, Frederick, ed. *Diary of Nelson Kingsley, A California Argonaut of 1849.* Berkeley: University of California Press, 1914.

Thomes, William G. *On Land and Sea, Or California in the Years 1843, '44, and '45.* Boston: deWolfe, Fiske and Co., 1884.

Upham, Samuel C. *Notes of a Voyage to California Via Cape Horn, Together with Scenes in El Dorado, in the Years 1849–50.* . . . Philadelphia: Published by the author, 1878.

Weber, Shirley H., ed. *Schliemann's First Visit to America, 1850–1851.* Cambridge: Harvard University Press, 1942.

Webster, George G., and Linville J. Hall, *The Journal of a Trip Around the Horn.* Ashland, Oreg.: Lewis Osborne, 1970.

Weinpahl, Robert W, ed. *A Gold Rush Voyage on the Bark Orion: From Boston Around Cape Horn to San Francisco, 1849–1850.* Glendale, Calif.: Arthur H. Clark Co., 1978.

Wilkes, Charles. *Narrative of the United States Exploring Expedition, during the Years 1838, 1839, 1840, 1841, 1842.* 5 vols. Philadelphia: Lea and Blanchard, 1845.

Windeler, Adolphus. *The California Gold Rush Diary of a German Sailor.* Edited by W. Turrentine Jackson. Berkeley: Howell-North Books, 1969.

Works Project Administration. *Ship Registers of the District of Boston, Massachusetts, 1831–1840.* Boston: National Archives Project, 1939.
———. *Ship Registers of the District of Plymouth, Massachusetts, 1789–1908.* Boston: National Archives Project, 1939.

BOOKS, SECONDARY SOURCES

Albion, Robert Greenhalgh. *Square-Riggers in Schedule: The New York Sailing Packets to England, France, and the Cotton Ports.* Princeton: Princeton University Press, 1938.
———. *The Rise of New York Port, 1815–1860.* Reprint. Boston: Northeastern University Press, 1984.
Albion, Robert Greenhalgh, William Avery Baker, and Benjamin W. Labaree. *New England and the Sea.* Mystic, Conn.: Mystic Seaport Museum, 1972.
Baker, William Avery. *A Maritime History of Bath, Maine and the Kennebec River Region.* 2 vols. Bath: Marine Research Society of Bath, 1973.
Bancroft, Hubert Howe. *The History of California.* . . . 7 vols. San Francisco: History Company, 1888.
Bari, Valeska. *The Course of Empire: First Hand Accounts of California in the Days of the Gold Rush of '49.* New York: Coward-McCann, 1931.
Barry, Thomas Senior. *Early California: Gold, Prices, Trade.* Richmond, Va.: Bostwick Press, 1984.
Bateson, Charles. *Gold Fleet for California: Forty-niners from Australia and New Zealand.* East Lansing: Michigan State University Press, 1963.
Bauer, K. Jack. *Surfboats and Horse Marines: U.S. Naval Operations in the Mexican War, 1846–48.* Annapolis: United States Naval Institute, 1969.
Bear, Dorothy and Beth Stebbins, *Mendocino: Book Two.* Mendocino, Calif.: Gull Press, 1977.
Berthold, Victor M. *The Pioneer Steamer California, 1848–1849.* Boston: Houghton-Mifflin, 1932.
Biggs, Donald C. *Conquer and Colonize: Stevenson's Regiment in California.* San Rafael: Presidio Press, 1977.
Bolton, Herbert Eugene. *Outpost of Empire: The Story of the Founding of San Francisco.* New York: Alfred A. Knopf, 1939.
Callaghan, Edward W., ed. *List of Officers of the Navy of the United States and of the Marine Corps from 1775 to 1900: Comprising a Complete Register of all Present and Former Commissioned, Warranted, and Appointed Officers of the United States Navy, and of the Marine Corps, Regular and Volunteer.* Reprint. New York: Haskell House, 1901.
Camp, William Martin. *San Francisco: Port of Gold.* New York: Doubleday and Co., 1947.
Capron, E. S. *History of California, From Its Discovery to the Present Time.* . . . Boston: John P. Jewett and Co., 1854.
Caughey, John Walton. *Rushing for Gold.* Berkeley and Los Angeles: University of California Press, 1949.
Chapelle, Howard I. *American Small Sailing Craft: Their Design, Development, and Construction.* New York: W. W. Norton and Co., 1951.
Chinard, Gilbert. *When the French Came to California.* . . . San Francisco: California Historical Society, 1944.
Cowell, Josephine W. *History of Benicia Arsenal.* Berkeley: Howell-North Books, 1965.

Cutler, Carl. *Queens of the Western Ocean: The Story of America's Mail and Passenger Lines.* Annapolis: United States Naval Institute, 1961.

Delgado, James P. *The Maritime Connotations of the California Gold Rush: National Register of Historic Places Thematic Group Nomination.* Washington, D.C.: National Park Service, 1987.

Dillon, Richard H. *Shanghaiing Days.* New York: Coward-McCann, 1961.

Dwyer, Richard A., and Richard E. Lingenfelter, eds. *The Songs of the Gold Rush.* Berkeley and Los Angeles: University of California Press, 1964.

Easby-Smith, Wilhelmine. *Personal Recollections of Early Washington and a Sketch of the Life of Captain William Easby.* Washington, D.C.: Association of the Oldest Inhabitants of the District of Columbia, 1913.

Eldredge, Zoeth S. *The Beginnings of San Francisco.* 2 vols. New York: John C. Rankine Co., 1925.

Evans, Stephen H. *The United States Coast Guard, 1790–1915.* Anapolis: The United States Naval Institute, 1949.

Fletcher, Robert Samuel. *Eureka: From Cleveland by Ship to California, 1849–1850.* Durham: Duke University Press, 1959.

Folkman, David I., Jr. *The Nicaragua Route.* Salt Lake City: University of Utah Press, 1972.

Foreman, Grant. *The Adventures of James Collier, First Collector of the Port of San Francisco.* Chicago: Black Cat Press, 1937.

Gould, Richard A., ed. *Shipwreck Anthropology.* Albuquerque: School of American Research and University of New Mexico Press, 1983.

Harlow, Neal. *California Conquered: War and Peace on the Pacific, 1846–1850.* Berkeley and Los Angeles: University of California Press, 1982.

Haygood, John A., ed. *First and Last Consul: Thomas Oliver Larkin and the Americanization of California.* Palo Alto, Calif.: Pacific Books, 1970.

Helper, Hinton R. *The Land of Gold: Reality Versus Fiction.* Baltimore: Published for the author, 1855.

History of Solano County, California. . . . San Francisco: Wood, Alley and Co., 1879.

Hittell, John S. *A History of San Francisco and Incidentally of the State of California.* San Francisco: A. L. Bancroft and Co., 1878.

Holliday, J. S. *The World Rushed In: The California Gold Rush Experience.* New York: Simon and Schuster, 1981.

Howe, Octavius Thorndike. *Argonauts of '49: History and Adventures of the Emigrant Companies from Massachusetts, 1849–1850.* Cambridge: Harvard University Press, 1923.

Howe, Octavius Thorndike, and Frederick C. Matthews. *American Clipper Ships, 1833–1858.* 2 vols. Salem, Mass.: Marine Research Society, 1927.

Huff, Boyd Francis. *El Puerto de los Balleneros: Annals of the Sausalito Whaling Anchorage.* Los Angeles: Dawson's Book Shop, 1972.

Hutchins, John G. B. *The American Maritime Industry and Public Policy, 1789–1914.* Cambridge: Harvard University Press, 1941.

Johnson, Robert Erwin. *Thence Round Cape Horn: The Story of United States Naval Forces on Pacific Station, 1818–1923.* Annapolis: United States Naval Institute, 1963.

Kemble, John Haskell. *The Panama Route: 1848–1869.* Berkeley and Los Angeles: University of California Press, 1943.

———. *Gold Rush Steamers.* San Francisco: Book Club of California, 1958.

Lansing, Alfred. *Endurance: Shackleton's Incredible Voyage.* New York: Carroll and Grat, 1987.

Layton, Thomas N. *Western Pomo Prehistory: Excavations at Albion Head, Nightbird's Retreat, and Three Chop Village, Mendocino County, California.* Los Angeles: University of California Institute of Archaeology Monograph 32. In press, 1989.

Lengyel, Cornel, ed. *Music of the Gold Rush Era.* W. P. A. History of Music Project, vol. 2. San Francisco: Works Progress Administration, Northern California, 1939.

Lewis, Oscar. *Sea Routes to the Gold Fields.* New York: Alfred A. Knopf, 1949.

———. *San Francisco: Mission to Metropolis.* Berkeley: Howell-North Books, 1966.

Lotchin, Roger. *San Francisco, 1846–1856: From Hamlet to City.* New York: Oxford University Press, 1974.

Lott, Arnold S. *A Long Line of Ships: Mare Island's Century of Naval Activity in California.* Annapolis: United States Naval Institute, 1954.

Lubbock, Basil. *The Opium Clippers.* Glasgow: Brown, Son and Ferguson, 1933.

MacGregor, David R. *Clipper Ships.* Watford, Herts, England: Argus Books, 1979.

Mack, Gerstle. *The Land Divided: A History of the Panama Canal and Other Isthmian Canal Projects.* New York: Alfred A. Knopf, 1944.

MacMullen, Jerry. *Paddlewheel Days in California.* Stanford: Stanford University Press, 1944.

Monaghan, Jay. *Australians and the Gold Rush: California and Down Under, 1849–1854.* Berkeley and Los Angeles: University of California Press, 1966.

———. *Chile, Peru and the California Gold Rush of 1849.* Berkeley and Los Angeles: University of California Press, 1973.

Moore, C. G., ed. *William Taylor of California, Bishop of Africa: An Autobiography.* London: Hodder and Stoughton, 1897.

Morris, James M. *Our Maritime Heritage: Maritime Developments and Their Impact on American Life.* Washington, D.C.: University Press of America, 1979.

Morrison, Samuel Eliot. *The Maritime History of Massachusetts, 1783–1847.* Boston: Houghton-Mifflin, 1961.

Munro-Fraser, J. P. *History of Solano County, California.* . . . San Francisco: Wood, Alley and Co., 1879.

———. *History of Marin County, California.* . . . San Francisco: Alley, Bowen and Co., 1880.

Newell, Gordon. *Paddlewheel Pirate: The Life and Adventures of Captain Ned Wakeman.* New York: E. P. Dutton & Co., 1959.

O'Brien, Robert. *The Beginnings of the Marine Exchange.* San Francisco: Marine Exchange, 1959.

Ogden, Adele. *The California Sea Otter Trade, 1784–1848.* Berkeley and Los Angeles: University of California Press, 1941.

———, ed. *Greater America: Essays in Honor of Herbert Eugene Bolton.* Berkeley and Los Angeles: University of California Press, 1945.

Olmsted, Roger, Nancy Olmsted, and Allen G. Pastron. *San Francisco Water-*

front: Report on Historical Cultural Resources. San Francisco: Wastewater Management Program, 1979.

Otis, Fessenden Nott. *Illustrated History of the Panama Railroad, Together with a Traveler's Guide and Business Man's Handbook for the Panama Railroad and Its Connections*. New York: Harper and Brothers, 1861.

Perez-Venero, Alejandro. *Before the Five Frontiers: Panama from 1821–1903*. New York: AMS Press, 1978.

Randier, Jean. *Men and Ships Around Cape Horn, 1616–1939*. New York: David McKay Co., 1969.

Rasmussen, Louis J., comp. *San Francisco Ship Passenger Lists*. 4 vols. Colma, Calif.: San Francisco Historic Records, 1966–1970.

Ridgely-Nevitt, Cedric. *American Steamships on the Atlantic*. Newark: University of Delaware Press, 1981.

Ryder, David Warren. *Men of Rope; Being the History of the Tubbs Cordage Company*. . . . San Francisco: Historical Publications, 1954.

Scherer, James A. B. *The Lion of the Vigilantes: William T. Coleman and the Life of Old San Francisco*. Indianapolis and New York: Bobbs-Merrill Co., 1939.

Schoolcraft, Henry, ed. *Historical and Statistical Information Respecting the History, Condition, and Prospects of the Indian Tribes of the United States*. Philadelphia, n.p., 1853.

Shanks, Ralph C., and Janetta Thompson Shanks. *Lighthouses of San Francisco Bay*. San Anselmo, Calif.: Costano Books, 1976.

Simon, John Y., ed. *The Papers of Ulysses S. Grant, Volume I: 1837–1861*. Carbondale and Edwardsville: Southern Illinois Press, 1967.

Somerville, Col. Duncan S. *The Aspinwall Empire*. Mystic, Conn.: Mystic Seaport Museum, 1983.

Soule, Frank, John H. Gihon, and James Nisbet. *The Annals of San Francisco . . . Containing . . . A Complete History of all Important Events Connected with Its Great City*. . . . New York: D. Appleton and Co., 1855.

Spratt, H. Philip. *Transatlantic Paddle Steamers*. Glasgow: Brown, Son, and Ferguson.

Starbuck, Alexander. *History of the Whale Fishery from Its Earliest Inception to the Year 1876*. 2 vols. Washington, D.C.: Government Printing Office, 1878.

Stuart, Charles B. *The Naval and Mail Steamers of the United States*. New York: Charles B. Morton, 1853.

Teiser, Ruth, ed. *This Sudden Empire California: The Story of the Society of California Pioneers, 1850 to 1950*. San Francisco: Society of California Pioneers, 1950.

Thompson, Erwin N. *The Rock: A History of Alcatraz Island, 1847–1972; Historic Resource Study, Golden Gate National Recreation Area, San Francisco*. Denver: National Park Service, 1979.

Treutlein, Theodore E. *San Francisco Bay: Discovery and Colonization, 1769–1776*. San Francisco: California Historical Society, 1968.

Wheeler, Alfred. *Land Titles in San Francisco, and the Laws Affecting the Same, with a Synopsis of All Grants and Sales of Land Within the Limits Claimed by the City*. San Francisco: Alta California Steam Printing Establishment, 1852.

Whipple, A. B. C. *The Challenge*. New York: William Morrow and Co., 1987.

Wiltsee, Ernest A. *Gold Rush Steamers of the Pacific*. San Francisco: Grabhorn Press, 1938.

Windle, John and Ronald R. Randall. *Rare Books VIII: The Race for Gold*. San Francisco: Randall House, 1979.

ARTICLES

"Boats Arriving in San Francisco Bay from March 26, 1849 to December 30, 1849." *Quarterly of the Society of California Pioneers* 1, no. 4 (December 1924).

Camp, Charles L., ed. "An Irishman in the Gold Rush: The Journal of Thomas Kerr." *California Historical Society Quarterly* 7, no. 3 (September 1928).

Chase, Philip P., ed. "On the Panama Route to California During the Gold Rush to California." *Transactions of the Colonial Society of Massachusetts* 27, no. 3 (1932).

Chavanne, Andre. "The Burning of the *Golden Gate* in July 1862." Translated and edited by Desire Fricot. *California Historical Society Quarterly* 19, no. 1 (March 1940).

Clyman, James. "Diaries and Reminiscences." Edited by Charles L. Camp. *California Historical Society Quarterly* 4, no. 2 (June 1926).

Collins, Jason. "Loss of the Steamship *Independence*." *The American Neptune* 14, no. 3 (July 1954).

Creighton, Richard E. "The Wreck of *San Francisco*." *The American Neptune* 45, no. 1 (Winter 1985).

Cushing, John Morland. "From New York to San Francisco in 1849 Via the Isthmus of Panama, Including the Voyage from Panama to San Francisco on the Ship *Niantic*." *Quarterly of the Society of California Pioneers* 6, no. 3 (October 1929).

Delgado, James P. "Water Soaked and Covered with Barnacles: The Wreck of the S.S. *Winfield Scott*." *Pacific Historian* 27, no. 2 (Summer 1983).

———. "Murder Most Foul: San Francisco Reacts to the Loss of the S.S. *Central America*." *The Log of Mystic Seaport* 25, no. 4 (Spring 1983).

———. "Their Bones Should Be Left in the Ocean to Rot: Notes on an Unusual Shipwreck Song." *Book Club of California Quarterly News-Letter* 49, no. 2 (Spring 1984).

deMassey, Ernest. "A Frenchman in the Gold Rush." Edited by Marguerite Wilbur. *California Historical Society Quarterly* 5, no. 1 (March 1926).

Doughty, Robin W. "The Farallones and the Boston Men." *California Historical Society Quarterly* 53, no. 4 (Winter 1974).

Farwell, Willard B. "Cape Horn and Cooperative Mining." *The Century Magazine* 42, no. 75 (1896).

Fritz, Christian G. "Judicial Style in California's First Admiralty Court: Ogden Hoffman and the First Ten Years, 1851–1861." *Southern California Quarterly* 64, no. 3 (Fall 1982).

Gordon, Robert. "Journal of a Voyage from Baltimore to San Francisco via Cape Horn." Edited by Reginald R. and Grace D. Stuart. *The Pacific Historian* 6, no. 3 (August 1962).

Goss, Helen Rocca. "An Ill-Starred Voyage: The S.S. *Golden Gate*, January 1854." *California Historical Society Quarterly* 32, no. 4 (December 1953).

Greenbank, John. "The Story of a Gold Miner." *California Historical Society Quarterly* 6, no. 4 (December 1926).

Gudde, Erwin G. "Mutiny on the *Ewing.*" *California Historical Society Quarterly* 30, no. 1 (March 1951).

Guice, C. Norman, ed. "The 'Contentious Commodore' and San Francisco: Two 1850 Letters from Thomas Ap Catesby Jones." *Pacific Historical Review* 34, no. 3 (August 1965).

Jones, James P., and William Warren Rogers. "Across the Isthmus in 1850: The Journal of Daniel A. Horn." *Hispanic American Historical Review* 41, no. 4 (November 1961).

"A Journey from New York to San Francisco in 1850." *American Historical Review* 9 (October 1903).

Kemble, John Haskell. "The Genesis of the Pacific Mail Steamship Company." *California Historical Society Quarterly* 13, nos. 3–4 (September–December 1934).

"List of Passenger Ships Arriving From March to December, 1849." *Quarterly of the Society of California Pioneers* 1, no. 4 (December, 1924).

Lyman, John. "The Intercoastal Trade before 1850." *Log Chips* 4, no. 4 (August 1957).

Menges, Charles F. H. "The *Gold Hunter* and the U.S. Custom House, San Francisco." *Nautical Research Guild Secretary's Monthly Letter* 2, no. 11 (November 1949).

Murphy, Elizabeth. "From High Seas to Mudflats." *Benicia Sentinel* (October 1977).

Morse, Edwin Franklin. "The Story of a Gold Miner: Reminiscences of Edwin Franklin Morse." *California Historical Society Quarterly* 6, no. 3 (September 1927).

Palmer, John W. "Pioneer Days in San Francisco." *The Century Magazine* 32 (1882).

Pangborn, David Knapp. "A Journey from New York to San Francisco in 1850." *American Historical Review* 9 (October 1903).

Read, Georgia Willis, ed. "The Chagres River Route to California in 1851." *California Historical Society Quarterly* 8, no. 1 (March 1929).

Richardson, Katherine Wood. "The Gold Seekers: The Story of the *LaGrange* and the California Pioneers of New England." *Essex Institute Historical Collections* 115, no. 2 (April 1979).

Ridgely-Nevitt, Cedric. "The United States Mail Steamer *George Law.*" *The American Neptune* 4, no. 3 (October 1944).

Roske, Ralph J. "The World Impact of the California Gold Rush." *Arizona and the West* 5, (Autumn 1963).

Schultz, Charles R. "A Forty-Niner Fourth of July." *The Log of Mystic Seaport* 38, no. 1 (Spring 1986).

"Steamers Building in Philadelphia, August 1, 1851." *Journal of the Franklin Institute*, 3d ser., vol. 22, no. 3 (September 1851).

Stocking, Fred W. "How We Gave a Name to Tennessee Cove." *The Overland Monthly* 17 (April 1893).

Tays, George, ed. "Commodore Edmund B. Kennedy, U.S.N., vs. Governor Nicolas Gutierrez—An Incident of 1836." *California Historical Society Quarterly* 12, no. 2 (June 1933).

Tomes, Robert. "A Trip on the Panama Railroad." *Harper's New Monthly Magazine* 11, no. 65 (October 1855).
"A Trip Around Cape Horn by the Steamer *Tennessee*." *Journal of the Franklin Institute*, 3d ser., vol. 19 (June 1850).
Vail, Marie Rogers, ed. "Gold Rush Letters of the Reverend James Rogers." *The New-York Historical Society Quarterly* 44 (July 1960).

THESES AND DISSERTATIONS
Delgado, James P. "Great Leviathan of the Pacific: The Saga of the Gold Rush Steamship *Tennessee*." Master's thesis, East Carolina University, Greenville, 1985.
Dow, Gerald Robert. "Bay Fill in San Francisco: A History of Change." Master's thesis, San Francisco State University, 1973.

MANUSCRIPTS
The Baker Library, Harvard School of Business, Boston.
———. R. B. Forbes and P. S. Forbes Papers, Forbes Collection.
Bancroft Library, University of California, Berkeley.
———. Beck, Robert. Diary, 1850.
———. DeWitt Family Papers. (Aspinwall)
———. Pacific Mail Steamship Co. Letterbook, 1848–1850.
———. San Francisco Customhouse Papers.
California Historical Society, San Francisco.
———. Brown, Anne. Papers.
———. Call, Asa Cyrus. Diary, 1849–1854.
———. Cosad, Daniel. Letters.
———. Dodge, Henry L. Papers.
———. Hotchkiss, Edward. Letters.
———. Keeler, James P. "Journal of a Voyage from New Haven to San Francisco in the Bark *Anna Reynolds* . . . 1849."
———. *Panama.* Logbook, 1849.
———. Winslow, Charles F. Papers.
City of Benicia, California.
———. Journal of the City Council, 1854–1857.
———. "Minute Book, May 7, 1850,–May 8, 1854."
Essex Institute, Salem, Massachusetts.
———. Ferrell, Robert N. Journal of a Trip to California in the Ship *Arkansas*, 1849.
Federal Archives and Records Center, San Bruno, California.
———. RG 21. Records of the United States District Court, Northern District of California. Admiralty cases.
Lois Gilchrist, Penngrove, California.
———. Hein, Johann, Reminiscence, 1902.
Henry E. Huntington Library, San Marino, California.
———. Aspinwall, William Henry. Letterbook, 1848–1850.
———. Butler, Ralph. Account book with a list of passengers, officers, and seamen in the bark *James A. Thompson,* sailing from Augusta, Maine, to San Francisco, August 8, 1849, to July 17, 1851.
———. Crackbon, Joseph. "Narrative of a Voyage from New York to California, via Chagres, Gorgona, & Panama; Journey Across the Isthmus &c.," 1849.

———. DeCosta, William H. Journal of a voyage to San Francisco on the ship *Duxbury*, February 9, 1849, to August 24, 1849.

———. Ellis, Charles H. Journal of a voyage from Boston to San Francisco on the brig *North Bend*, January 1849 to July 1849.

———. Goodman, John B. III. *The California Gold Rush Encyclopedia*. 11 vols., 1950–1987.

———. Kent, George F. Journal of a gold-hunting expedition voyage from Boston to San Francisco aboard the ship *Rudolph*, 1849.

———. List of persons on board brig *North End*, bound to San Francisco, January 1849.

———. Nourse, George. Papers.

———. Osbun, Albert Gallatin. Diary of a voyage to California and return from San Francisco to Acapulco on the *Eureka*, 1849–1851.

———. Pacific Mail Steamship Company Collection, 1851–1935.

———. Parker, Robert. "Notes by the Way," 1852.

———. Stone, John N. Brief notes of a Cape Horn voyage in *Robert Bowne*, February 6, 1849, to August 28, 1849.

———. Story, Charles Robinson. Journal of a Voyage from Salem, Massachusetts, to San Francisco via Cape Horn in the Bark *LaGrange*, March 17, 1849, to September 17, 1849.

Library of Congress, Manuscripts Division.

———. Meredith, Jonathan. Papers.

———. Ripley, Augustus Burbank. Diary, 1851.

The Mariner's Museum, Newport News, Virginia.

———. Elwin Eldredge Collection.

Mystic Seaport Museum, Mystic, Connecticut.

———. Bill for ship *Charles Crooker*, 1850.

———. Ely, Edward. Diary, 1849–1852.

National Archives, Washington, D.C.

———. RG 24. Records of the Bureau of Naval Personnel, "Logs, 1801–1946." Log, U.S.S. *Warren*, 1849–1854.

———. RG 26. Records of the United States Coast Guard. "Records of the Revenue Cutter Service, 1790–1915." Logbook, U.S. Revenue Cutter *Cornelius W. Lawrence*, 1848–1851.

———. RG 26. Records of the United States Coast Guard. "Records of the Revenue Cutter Service, 1790–1915," Logbook, U.S. Revenue Cutter *Frolic*, 1851–1853.

———. RG 26. Records of the United States Coast Guard. "Records of the United States Revenue Marine." Financial Correspondence, 1848–1851.

———. RG 26. Records of the United States Coast Guard. "Records of the United States Revenue Marine." Correspondence from Revenue Marine Officers to the Secretary of the Treasury, 1848–1852.

———. RG 26. Records of the United States Coast Guard. "Records of the United States Revenue Marine." Correspondence from Collectors of the Port to the Secretary of the Treasury, 1849–1853.

———. RG 26. Records of the United States Coast Guard. "Records of the Lighthouse Board." Correspondence.

———. RG 36 & 41. Records of the Bureau of Marine Inspection and Navigation, "Records Relating to Merchant Vessel Documentation, 1775–1958."

———. RG 45. Naval Records Collection of the Office of Naval Records and Library. Record Group 45.

———. RG 45. Squadron Letters.

———. RG 125. Records of the office of the Judge Advocate General (Navy). "Records of Courts-Martial and Courts of Inquiry" M 273, case no. 1187.

———. United States Census, 8th United States Census, 1860, Special schedule G.

National Maritime Museum, San Francisco.

———. "A Tribute to Those Life-Lasting Feelings of Disgust, Contempt, and Scorn Unanimously Entertain'd, By the Passengers, Officers, and Crews of the Bark JOHN G. COLLEY; For Captn. William Smith," 1849.

———. *Apollo.* Log, 1849.

———. Armentrout-Ma, L. Eve. "Chinese and GGNRA: Guests of Choice, Guests of Necessity," 1980.

———. Ayer, Edwin. Reminiscence, 1877.

———. Catalog, Folger and Tubbs, Ship Chandlers. Circa 1851. Unoccasioned document.

———. "Certificate of Measurement &c of Steamer *Boston,* March 17, 1851." Miscellaneous manuscript.

———. *Falcon.* Log, 1848–1849.

———. Howe, Robert. Reminiscence.

———. McFarlan, Alexander. "Log Book from Boston to San Francisco via Cape Horn, 1849, Ship California Packet," 1849–1850.

———. *Niantic.* Logbook, 1848–1849.

———. Pease, Cyrus. Letters, 1849.

———. Smalley, Brian H. "Some Aspects of the Maine to San Francisco Trade, 1849–1852," 1967.

National Register of Historic Places, Washington, D.C.

———. Delgado, James P., "Inventory Form, National Register of Historic Places: Point Lobos Marine Lookout Stations," 1980.

Naval Historical Center, Washington Navy Yard, Washington, D.C.

———. "Z" Files.

New York Public Library, Special Collections.

———. Peters, Henry H. Diary, 1849–1850.

San Francisco Public Library. San Francisco

———. Financial Record Book, 1849–1850.

Society of California Pioneers, San Francisco.

———. Cushing, John M. Memoirs, 1925.

Solano County Clerk's Office, Fairfield.

———. The People of California vs. The Pacific Mail Steamship Co. Case nos. 987, 1207, 1208 and 1211.

Webb Institute of Naval Architecture, Glen Cove, New York.

———. Webb, William H. Certificate Books.

GOVERNMENT DOCUMENTS

Act of Incorporation and Ordinances of the City of San Francisco San Francisco: *Daily Evening Picayune,* 1850.

An Act Providing for the Building and Equipment of Four Naval Steamships, 28th Cong. 2d sess., 1847.

Boundary, United States and Mexico; Message from the President of the United

States, Transmitting the Information Required by a Resolution of the House. . . . Supt. of Docs. 311–42.

Compiled Laws of California. . . .

Laws of the State of California, Passed at the First Session of the Legislature. . . .

Mail Contracts by Steamships Between New York and California; Letter from the Postmaster General Transmitting Information in Relation to Contracts for Transportation of the Mails Between New York and California. 32nd Cong. 1st sess., 1852, H. Exec. Doc. 124.

Message from the President of the United States to the Two Houses of Congress. . . . December 5, 1848. 30th Cong. 2d sess., 1848, H. Exec. Doc. 1.

Message from the President of the United States, Transmitting Information in Answer to a Resolution of the House of the 31 of December, 1849, on the Subject of California and New Mexico. 31st Cong. 1st sess., 1850, 31st Cong.

Minutes of the Legislative Assembly of the District of San Francisco . . . And a Record of the Proceedings of the Ayuntamiento or Town Council of San Francisco, From August 6, 1849 until May 3, 1850. . . . San Francisco: Towne and Bacon, 1860.

Ordinances and Joint Resolutions of the City of San Francisco. . . . San Francisco: Munson and Valentine, 1851.

Report of the Secretary of the Treasury, Communicating, in Compliance with a Resolution of the Senate, the Report of Gilbert Rodman, esq. Upon the Subject of the Custom-House at San Francisco, Cal. Special sess., 1853, S. Exec. Doc. 5.

Report of the Secretary of the Treasury on the State of the Finances for the Year Ending June 30, 1862. 37th Cong. 3d sess., 1863, S. Exec. Doc. 1.

NEWSPAPERS

Boston *Gleason's Pictorial Drawing Room Companion*
Boston *Daily Transcript*
Hong Kong *China Mail*
London *Artizan*
London *Illustrated News*
Marysville *Herald*
Monterey *Californian*
New Bedford *Mercury*
New Bedford *Whaleman's Shipping List*
New London [Conn.] *Daily Chronicle*
New York *Daily Tribune*
New York *Herald*
New York *Sun*
Panama *Echo*
Philadelphia *North American*
Sacramento *Placer Times*
Sacramento *Transcript*
Sacramento *Union*
Saint Malo *La Verite*
Salem [Mass.] *Gazette*
San Francisco *California Star*
San Francisco *Californian*

San Francisco *Chronicle*
San Francisco *Daily Alta California*
San Francisco *Daily California Chronicle*
San Francisco *Daily Herald*
San Francisco *Daily Evening Picayune*
San Francisco *Evening Bulletin*
San Francisco *Golden Era*
San Francisco *Morning Call*
San Jose [Calif.] *Pioneer*
Wilmington [N.C.] *Weekly Commercial*

Index